# PERSONAL CO
## FOR
## DISTANCE EDU

The authors all work in the Institute of Educational Technology (IET) at the Open University. For the past five years they have been core members of the team which has been evaluating the Open University's home computing policy.

*Ann Jones*
Ann Jones is interested in the applications of computers in education, and has been involved in course development and evaluation in this area for several years. Her doctorate was on novices learning programming. She has co-edited (with E. Scanlon and T. O'Shea) *The Computer Revolution: New Technologies for Distance Teaching*, Harvester Press, 1987, and *Educational Computing 5–13* with P. Scrimshaw, Open University Press, 1988.

*Gill Kirkup*
Gill Kirkup is a senior lecturer in IET. She works on course evaluation, especially in technology and information technology courses, and in women's studies. She co-authored (with R. Carter) *Women in Engineering: A Good Place to Be?*, Macmillan, 1990, and is the editor (with L. Smith Keller) of *Inventing Women: Women in Science and Technology*, Polity Press with the Open University, 1992.

*Adrian Kirkwood*
Adrian Kirkwood has been involved in the development and evaluation of undergraduate and continuing education courses since 1981. He is currently undertaking research and evaluation studies on a number of topics related to access and applications of media and information technologies in distance education, with publications in a range of academic journals.

# PERSONAL COMPUTERS
## FOR
# DISTANCE EDUCATION

*The Study of an Educational Innovation*

Ann Jones, Gill Kirkup and
Adrian Kirkwood

P·C·P
Paul Chapman
Publishing Ltd

Copyright © Jones, Kirkup and Kirkwood, 1992

Paul Chapman Publishing Ltd
144 Liverpool Road
London
N1 1LA

British Library Cataloguing in Publication Data

Jones, Ann
  Personal Computers for Distance Education
  I. Title
  371.334

ISBN 1-85396-187-6

Typeset by Hewer Text Composition Services, Edinburgh
Printed and bound by Athenaeum Press Ltd., Newcastle-upon-Tyne

A B C D E F G H   9 8 7 6 5 4 3 2

# Contents

# *Acknowledgements*

This book grew out of the evaluation of the Open University's Home Computing Policy which was implemented in 1988. The authors have been core members of the Home Computing Evaluation Group, which has conducted a wide range of quantitative and qualitative studies since the introduction of home-based computing at the OU. Many people contributed to the work of the Evaluation Group and we would like to acknowledge the contributions of our colleagues – Robin Mason, Alison Ashby, Clive Lawless, Alistair Morgan, Mary Thorpe, Diana Laurillard, Eileen Dale, Janice Dale, Chris Saxton, Ronnie Singer, Jim Morrison and Tony Kaye. Members of the Survey Processing Office in the Institute of Educational Technology have undertaken much of the survey administration and the subsequent data analysis. We would also like to thank colleagues from other departments who have given permission to quote from their published and unpublished papers and also John Naughton and Jake Chapman who shared their memories of events with us. Finally, but not least, we thank the many students and tutors of the OU who participated in the studies conducted by the Evaluation Group. Responsibility for the interpretation of events and for the views expressed in the book rests, of course, with the authors. The work of the Evaluation Group has contributed to the development of subsequent phases of the Home Computing Policy. However, the authors do not claim credit for the formulation of the OU's Home Computing Policy or for the design of the practical computing components of the courses that require students to use a personal computer in their studies. The formulation and implementation of the policy resulted from the creative energy of members of OU course teams, staff in the University's Academic Computing Service and far-seeing administrators, too numerous to acknowledge individually.

# *Preface*

This book grew out of a research project which evaluated the Open University's Home Computing Policy. We set out to investigate the effects of requiring students on particular courses, which are included in the policy, to make their own arrangements for acquiring a microcomputer. This was a radical policy change: Open University (OU) students had been using computers for their OU work for twenty years but they had not been using personal computers (PCs) in their own homes in large numbers, nor had access to a PC been a course requirement.

There are three main reasons why we have written up this case study as a book. The first is the nature and size of the innovation. To date, about 17,000 OU students are using PCs to study at home as part of this policy. To our knowledge there is no other similar, PC-based innovation on this scale. The sheer numbers give us a comfortable base from which to generalise. The scale also means that there are 17,000 households which have access to a powerful commercial PC. The second reason is the importance of the issues we originally set out to investigate: for example, the impact of the policy on different groups of students such as women and those with disabilities; the use of communications networks; the types of problems students experienced and their need for support, and whether the use of PCs and software spread to the students' immediate families. Other issues arose as the evaluation progressed – for example, the question of how best to design instruction for use with computers at a distance, and the potential of student-based computers to change radically the nature of distance education. Finally, because there has been a growth in the applications of new technology to education and to open-learning techniques, along with an increase in the availability of PCs suitable for use in academic work, and a decrease in their price, it is a particularly appropriate time to publish this case study. This book looks at how these developments interact with each other by focussing on a case study of a particular innovation: the introduction of the use of PCs in students' homes in one distance-learning institution.

The first three chapters provide the context for the study, and set up the main issues. The first chapter deals with the global context by examining the recent history of the use of computers in education and specifically in higher education. It also examines the way in which economic and technological developments have shaped the most frequent types of use of computers in education. The various uses of information technology in distance learning are underpinned by a number of different models about the nature of learning itself and, in particular, of the way in which adults learn. This becomes the focus of Chapter 2. The third chapter introduces the specific context of the study by looking at the Open University itself. It introduces the evaluation study and the issues that will be examined in depth in the rest of the book.

Chapter 4 examines in detail the social and physical context in which OU students study and carry out their practical computing work. It discusses how part-time study (which includes the use of computers) relates to household activities and leisure time and the extent to which the PC is used by OU students and their immediate families as part of a general household resource. The following chapter, Chapter 5, is concerned with equal opportunities and access. The Open University has an equal opportunities policy and one of the issues which the evaluation set out to investigate was whether the introduction of a home computing policy conflicted with the University's commitment to equal opportunities. There are two stages of access for students to negotiate. The first is access to the machine itself, and the second is the process of developing sufficient competence with the system to use it efficiently and effectively. Having looked at the issue of access to the machines themselves, Chapter 6 looks at the difficulties that students have in learning to use computers in a variety of contexts, and possible ways of making it easier. This chapter draws on ideas and research concerning students' understanding of the system they are dealing with and the implications of this for designing associated teaching material.

Chapter 7 considers ways in which distance learners using a home-based PC can be offered institutional support. In implementing the policy, the University was aware of the potential problems of students working in isolation, and set up ways of monitoring problems and of providing help and advice. This chapter examines the kinds of problems that students encountered, the support they were offered and the extent to which it was helpful. Chapter 8 reflects on the process of innovation as it occurred in the OU. It discusses the optimal conditions for educational innovations and in particular the importance of individual roles in the process of change.

The concluding chapter summarises the important issues arising from the Open University case study which may be useful for others involved in similar developments. It then goes on to consider the educational potential of technological developments which are currently in an experimental stage and the models of distance education which can best incorporate them. This reflects a theme that runs throughout the book: that the evolution of educational models is tied in with the evolution of the technologies on which they depend. However, new technologies such as personal computers bring new problems as well as new solutions. At the OU the use of student-based PCs is opening up new teaching possibilities, while at the same time highlighting long-standing educational issues such as the nature of educational disadvantage and how to 'individualise' learning in a mass-education system. All these are key educational debates for the twenty-first century.

Ann Jones, Gill Kirkup
and Adrian Kirkwood
Milton Keynes, 1992

# List of Abbreviations

(*Note:* *Denotes a trademark.)

| | |
|---|---|
| ACS | Academic Computing Service |
| AI | Artificial intelligence |
| BBC | British Broadcasting Corporation |
| CAD | Computer-aided design |
| CAI | Computer-assisted instruction |
| CAL | Computer-assisted learning |
| CBL | Computer-based learning |
| CBURC | Computer Board for Universities and Research Councils |
| CD-ROM | Compact disc, read-only memory |
| CMA | Computer-marked assignment |
| CMC | Computer-mediated communication |
| CTI | Computers in Teaching Initiative |
| DE | Distance education |
| DES | Department of Education and Science |
| DTI | Department of Trade and Industry |
| EC | European Community |
| ESG | Educational Software Group |
| GCE | General Certificate of Education (at two levels: 'O' = ordinary and 'A' = advanced) |
| GEM* | Graphics Environment Manager |
| HC | Home computing |
| HEK | Home experiment kit |
| HNC/D | Higher National Certificate/Diploma |
| IBM | International Business Machines Ltd |
| IBM* PC | Microcomputer developed by IBM |
| IFIP | International Federation for Information Processing |
| IT | Information technology |
| ITOL | Information technology-based open learning |
| LAN | Local area network |
| MIT | Massachusetts Institute of Technology |
| MS-DOS* | MicroSoft Disk Operating System |
| NUS | National Union of Students |
| ONC/D | Ordinary National Certificate/Diploma |
| OSI | Open systems interconnection |
| OU | Open University |
| PC | Personal computer |
| SPSS* | Statistical Package for the Social Sciences |
| TMA | Tutor-marked assignment |

| UCCA | Universities Central Council for Admissions |
| UCSD | University of California, San Diego |
| UFC | Universities Funding Council |
| UGC | Universities Grants Committee |
| VCR | Video-cassette recorder |
| VDU | Visual display unit |
| WIMP | Window, icon, mouse, pointer |
| WITS | Women into Technology Scheme |

# 1

# *The Potential, History and Development of Computers as Educational Tools*

This book reviews and discusses the potential uses of the personal computer (PC) as an educational tool in higher education. This first chapter considers the question of why there is so much concern about the use of computers in education. What can they offer? The chapter reviews the claims made for the potential use of computers in education and looks at their history and the differing ways in which computers can be used in education. It goes on to describe experiments to provide widespread computer access in various parts of the world and, in particular, the notion of the electronic campus. These examples of computer use set the scene and provide a context within which to place the Open University (OU) experience. Most of the examples drawn on in the chapter are from higher education, where the greatest developments in the use of personal computing in education have been.

## Uses of Computers in Education

Computers have been used in a variety of ways in education since the 1960s, although the types of use have expanded and the number of students using them has grown. It is useful to look at these different uses and to classify them as we have done below. Our classification is not based on any theoretical model but on what we have seen as the main discrete areas of use through a decade of working with higher education students.

These categories are broad and can be sub-divided. In some cases the subject matter itself concerns computers, e.g. in courses in programming or microcomputers, but our main focus is on the use of computers as a medium for learning *about* other subject areas. In the UK, such use is usually referred to as computer-assisted learning (CAL). Often this term is confined to the use of particular educational programs, which are developed to help the student learn a particular subject area or topic. Where the package used is not specifically an educational package (for example, the use of applications derived from business or commercial use), the computer can be thought of as a tool. Although it is used for educational purposes, it could equally well be used for other purposes. The more general term computer-based learning (CBL) encompasses both of these uses.

### *The Computer as a Vehicle for Learning to Program*

Computer science only became part of the higher education curriculum relatively recently, and since the rapid growth of information technology (IT) in the 1980s, other courses have developed which are concerned with the appropriate use of IT, awareness of how IT is used in our society, and the development of skills in using IT, rather than programming itself. In these courses PCs now replace the mainframe computers which were used in the past.

## Computer-Assisted Learning (CAL): The Use of Computers to Assist Learning in a Variety of Ways

CAL is clearly going to account for much of the use of computers in education. CAL is itself usually categorised by the different types of program being used, such as tutorial CAL, drill and practice, simulation, microworlds, hypermedia and tutoring systems. Such categories are a helpful way of organising the use of computers in education, and will be used later in the chapter when CAL is discussed in further detail.

## The Computer as a Study Tool

The use of the computer as a tool dates back to the 1960s, but initially such use was confined to particular subject areas, usually science, mathematics and technology, where computers have been used for modelling, computer-aided design in engineering, for statistical analysis and for data-processing and information handling. We can distinguish between tools which are specific to some disciplines, e.g. computer-aided design (CAD) for design, or modelling in mathematics, and more general study tools. The use of more general study tools has increased dramatically over the past fifteen years, and is now commonplace in schools, whereas previously it was confined to further and higher education. The most common examples include the following: *wordprocessing packages*, the most sophisticated of which have desktop publishing facilities, and writers' tools such as planning facilities, access to dictionaries, thesauruses and quotations, as well as commonplace facilities for easy editing and manipulation of text; *spreadsheet programs* for modelling and simulation; *databases* and information handling packages which facilitate data manipulation and provide a structure for entering and organising information (for example, survey or census data); and *calculation* tools which include data-analysis packages.

CAL and the use of computers as a study tool can and often do overlap. For example, in schools the use of wordprocessing has been particularly beneficial to children who have difficulties writing and who have resisted putting pen to paper because of the effort concerned. Schools also include the use of databases in work on information handling, which can be part of projects where the children may be learning about science or local history. The categories have been kept separate here, though, to reflect the fact that computers can be used as study tools in *non*-educational contexts, e.g. databases for developing mailing lists, wordprocessing for commercial use, etc.

General study tools all have their origins in commercial applications and so in a sense their use for educational purposes is a side-effect of their development for other purposes.

## The Computer as an Assessment Tool

Using computers for assessment often means running a program of multiple-choice questions in which a question and several alternative answers are presented to the student who is then asked to select the correct answer. In fact the OU uses such a method for its computer-marked assignments (CMAs) and these are discussed further in Chapter 3. However, sophisticated assessment programs can provide a range of testing devices to assess a variety of skills as well as providing feedback on performance to students.

## The Computer as a Communication Device

The two main forms of computer-based communication are electronic mail and computer conferencing. Both provide the user with a means of communicating with one or more other user(s) across both space and time, but computer conferencing gives additional facilities for organising the communications into topics. Electronic mail messages, in the form of a discrete piece of text (or sometimes graphics, etc., as well) can be sent to one or more named recipients. The messages are sent by the system to a particular section of the host computer which is reserved for the addressee; they then wait there until the recipient next uses the computer. Computer conferencing systems have all of these facilities, but they also support group and many-to-many communication facilities. Individuals 'join' conferences on specific topics, and each conference consists of the messages put there by the various conference members. Like electronic mail it is asynchronous in that the members do not need to make their contributions at the same time.

Kaye (1989) cites two important features of computer-mediated communication (CMC) for educational purposes. Firstly, although it is used for written messages, it has some of the spontaneity and flexibility of spoken discourse and, secondly, it can be a powerful device for group communication and for co-operative learning.

## As a Tool for Special Needs

Vincent (1991) points out that for many people with disabilities and special educational needs, a standard computer is not accessible. The design of output devices (such as a screen) is based on assumptions about visual ability, keyboards assume manual dexterity, and so on. However, there have been a number of developments to overcome these barriers that have resulted in new or adapted devices and systems as well as developments in software for special needs. For example, Braille keyboards and displays, Braille/text transcription software, enlarged text and speech output can all be used with computers to help access for those with visual disabilities, while alternatives to keyboard inputs have been developed for those with physical disabilities.

This broad classification will be used throughout the book, but first we look at how different aspects of the uses of computers in education have developed since the 1960s.

## Early Uses of Computers in Education

Before considering the claimed benefits for computers in education it is useful to give a historical perspective. In what ways have computers been used in education in the last twenty years? And what claims were made for them?

This particular account of the history of computers in education starts at the end of the 1970s, when two major conferences on the use of computers in education were held in the UK. Both were concerned with CAL. The first, CAL '79, was held in April and the forum was to become a biennial event; the second was an IFIP (International Federation for Information Processing) working conference, held in September. These two events provide a good indicator of what was happening in the UK at the time. At the first conference, sessions included ones on algorithmic and heuristic approaches to CAL, the impact and implication of microelectronics, the educational basis of CAL, the user interface, business, industrial and military training, and the place of CAL in the educational spectrum. Case studies concentrated on specific subject areas, but all were concerned with the computer as an aid to learning rather than, for example, teaching programming: subject areas included electrical circuits, engineering, mathematics for chemistry students, ship design and systems analysis and control.

There was already interest in what we would now call computer networking and computer conferencing – then billed as ways of transmitting software over teletext and viewdata. It reflected the new use of microcomputers but acknowledged the complete lack of software. Already one institution was offering a course on computers in education as part of an MSc (but note in mathematical education!). A particular problem for this course, however, was the scarcity of CAL material in mathematics (Edwards, 1979). Interestingly, evaluation of CAL was also already featured. The general picture is of a new field, with examples of fragmented case studies and descriptive accounts of practice: in other words, papers that stand alone rather than reflecting the work of a research community in which participants are commenting on each others' work and current issues. However, it is worth noting that the notion of using computers to support and assist learning, i.e. the use of CAL, although not widespread, was already well established and some of the papers were even then reflecting on the prior ten to fifteen years of CAL development.

Let's now look at the other conference held in 1979, sponsored by IFIP. Here one of the papers reported on an institution-wide project on the use of minicomputers: Dartmouth College in New Hampshire, USA, had started a three-year project to introduce laboratory science students to the use of small computers for their real-time data acquisition, analysis, and control of experiments in biology, chemistry, engineering, physics and psychology. In another paper, Lewis and Want (1980) reviewed ten years' work at Chelsea College, and Bork (1980) described work at the Educational Technology

Center at the University of California. The emphasis in both of these reviews was on the use of simulations, and in Bork's paper also on laboratory work with computers. An interesting aspect of Bork's work is the documenting of funding: over a period of twelve years, a million and a half dollars had been granted by the USA's National Science Foundation.

Both of these conferences came at the end of a major UK funding initiative. NDPCAL (the National Development Programme in Computer Assisted Learning) had ended in 1977, and so it is not surprising that so much CAL was reported. The audience at such conferences is self-selecting: speakers were those with experience of CAL, and other participants, if they did not have experience, had a particular interest in the area. Whilst CAL may not have been widespread, it was not uncommon, and neither was it new: as we have seen, some papers were reporting on ten or fifteen years' experience. What is not available, from examining the programmes of such conferences, is any comprehensive picture of other uses of computers in education, such as the use of the computer as a tool in laboratories, for data-processing, etc., and for programming. Such use was not seen as special enough to warrant reporting on. Finally, very little use of any kind was taking place in schools: for example, just 6 papers out of 62 in CAL '79 concerned the use of computers in schools. This is probably a reflection of the available hardware (still mainframe computers) and the price. The situation regarding both these factors was starting to change and continued to change very rapidly but, given the constraints of the period, we need to consider why computers were being used in education at all.

## Benefits of Using Computers in Education

Prior to the 1980s, most arguments for the use of computers in education centred around five main kinds of uses. The first three of these were different types of CAL programs, while the fourth and fifth were examples of using the computer as a study tool.

The first argument concerned the potential for 'individualised' learning through programs that offer *drill and practice.* Such programs do not themselves attempt to teach: indeed they assume that the teaching has already been carried out, and so they provide repeated practice in learning a procedure or gaining a skill or knowledge. Such programs are often used in such subjects as mathematics or learning a new language. For example, Figure 1.1 shows an example of part of a drill-and-practice program for teaching French personal pronouns. The English word is displayed at random in the box. If the learner clicks on the correct French word, part of a tune plays and the score is incremented. If they get it wrong, a low buzzer sounds, the score is decremented and the correct answer is highlighted for a few seconds before the next English word is displayed. Words not mastered are tested again within three attempts and untested words are only introduced as others are mastered.

Although drill-and-practice programs are still in frequent use in UK schools, their use in higher education is much more common in the USA than in the UK, a fact which reflects more on the nature of assessment in

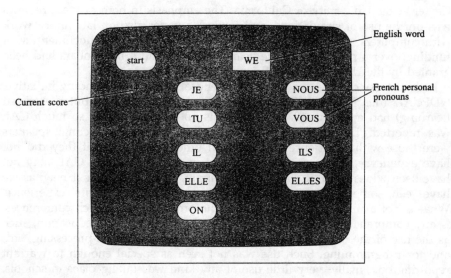

Figure 1.1   An extract from a drill-and-practice program for French pronouns (Source: Marullo and Laurillard, 1990)

the US system than on any different availability of equipment and software.

A second argument was that there was great further potential for individualised learning through *tutorial CAL*. Unlike drill-and-practice programs which do not try to teach, in tutorial CAL a topic is presented through text, diagrams, animation and so on, with practice in the form of questions answered by the learner, who usually types in words, letters or numbers. The program then tells the learner whether they are right or wrong, gives further explanation of the topic, and may give a comment or exercise.

A third argument was that *simulation programs* can offer the student experience they may not otherwise get at all: for example in cases such as nuclear reactions, which by their nature are not amenable to real-life experimentation! Simulation programs are built around a mathematical model of a real-world event or process. It might be a nuclear or a chemical reaction, or the changing ecology of a pond and its inhabitants. It allows the user to change the values of variables in the model and displays the resulting behaviour of the system, e.g. the frog population declines if frogs are removed from the pond. Students are expected to gain insight into the process they see being modelled. Usually the student is more than a spectator; he or she will be invited to take on the role of experimenter or scientist – investigating the result of making changes to particular variables.

These first three arguments, then, are for the use of CAL; the fourth example is rather different and concerns the use of the computer as a study tool in order to carry out laboratory work and analysis, and data manipulation. As we have seen, this has been a common use of the computer in education, right from the start. The argument is that having a computer available to carry out more complex calculations and manipulations in laboratory work can free the student (and teacher) to concentrate on the purpose of the laboratory exercise, and to use their laboratory time efficiently, rather than spending large proportions of the laboratory classes carrying out calculations and statistical analyses.

Finally, the computer can be used to learn programming. Before the 1980s students who learnt programming were typically either learning specialist languages (such as Fortran, Pascal, Cobol, etc.) or BASIC, which was more accessible to beginners and non-computer scientists. However, in more recent years, there has been considerable interest in programming as a form of problem-solving: a way of making one's ideas explicit. The best-known proponent of this philosophy is Papert, who wrote in his book, *Mindstorms*, in 1980: 'children can learn to use computers in a masterful way, and . . . learning to use computers can change the way they learn everything else' (p. 8).

Papert's book was quite controversial. Much of the previous emphasis of computers in education, especially in American schools, had concentrated on computers helping children to learn what they were already learning. Papert, however, was suggesting that, used in certain ways, computers could radically alter the nature of education itself. In developing these views, he was greatly influenced by his work with the Genevan psychologist, Piaget. It is not appropriate to discuss Piaget's ideas here, nor is there space, but like Piaget, Papert views children as 'builders of their own intellectual structures'. Piaget emphasised the way in which knowledge is structured and organised and the way in which these knowledge structures are changed in order for information to be added to them, and he argued that children's perceptions of their experiences are themselves modified to fit into these structures.

Papert lays out his philosophy of learning in *Mindstorms*. Essentially, he aims to provide a culture which helps to make abstract mathematical concepts simple and concrete so that children can relate them to their existing knowledge, i.e. fit them into their knowledge structures. The vehicle he used was the programming language LOGO, which he contrasted (unkindly) with languages like BASIC. Through using a drawing device called the turtle, which is part of the LOGO language, children can explore mathematical shapes and ideas, which will help in the development of certain aspects of mathematics.

These, then, were the main ways in which it was expected that computers could be used in education. The potential seemed enormous, but until there was widespread access to computers there could not be widespread use. During the 1980s, however, this changed. One obvious change was the decreasing price of hardware, which will be discussed later, but another was in the expected use. By the end of the 1980s there were still plenty of drill-and-practice programs in use. DES figures from 1989 (quoted in Chapman, 1990, p. 11) show that 'practice exercises and puzzles' make up 56 per cent of the software packages used by 5-year-olds and 22 per cent of those used by 11-year-olds in UK primary schools. In secondary schools they make up 23 per cent of the software used by 13-year-olds, a percentage which diminishes to 10 per cent by the time pupils are 17 years old or older. (Of course it's not clear what proportion is drill-and-practice programs and what proportion is 'puzzles', which presumably are often games.) However, although they can be useful, drill-and-practice programs are limited in their scope and applicability. It is assumed that instruction and information have already been supplied, and that what is needed is massed practice – perhaps to help a skill become automatic. Such programs are therefore often found in such areas as arithmetic and foreign language learning. As Laurillard (1991a, p. 43) points out,

> The assumption is always that drill-and-practice programs work alongside other forms of teaching. They do not give the basic information, and they do not assist directly in transferring the skills to novel situations, or in integrating them with other skills or knowledge. Their value lies in consolidating the basics so that the learner can concentrate on other things.

Such a high use, therefore, suggests an emphasis on basic skills rather than the application of skills, or integration of skills into different areas. It also implies a particular theoretical approach to learning and teaching: drill-and-practice programs are essentially based on behavioural theories of learning, which are discussed further in Chapter 2. This was a view of learning that became much less popular in UK schools and teacher training during the 1960s, when child-centred learning was much more in the forefront and the ideas of Piaget were influential. Instead of the emphasis being on teaching, with the child viewed as a more or less passive recipient who responds to reinforcement, the emphasis moved to the child, seen as an active construer of his or her knowledge. According to this philosophy, educational software such as LOGO was much more sound than the behaviourist drill-and-practice programs.

The argument for tutorial CAL, the next type of use, is also based on the promise of individual tuition. However, it has become clear that to address particular students' needs is very hard. As Laurillard (1991a, p. 41) comments, 'Dealing with the learner's answer is also complex. Whichever learner response format is used, the tutorial program knows how the learner has responded. . . . The sophistication of tutorial programs varies according to how well they identify the learner's difficulty.'

The problem is that it's very hard to program in ways that really identify particular student problems. To do this successfully, a program would have to encapsulate some of the techniques used by human teachers, e.g. looking at a number of answers and trying to identify a pattern. This kind of process turns out to be surprisingly complex and difficult to program into a computer and, because of this, some researchers believe that artificial intelligence (which we can define briefly by saying that it is behaviour that would be intelligent if performed by humans) might be of help: 'The designers of computer systems to be used in education should take account of the subject of artificial intelligence and the users of such systems may expect them soon to provide facilities considerably more sophisticated than those available today' (O'Shea and Self, 1983, p. 6).

However, as yet, developments in artificial intelligence are not available as mass-produced software and there is no expectation that this will change dramatically in the foreseeable future. In fact, the not unreasonable expectation that educational software should be cheap causes another problem for CAL programs. They are clearly expensive to write (tutorial programs in particular) and, though very hard to cost, estimates have been given at various times, for example 'it takes about two to four professional person months to produce a one hour CAL exercise capable of engaging a range of students of differing abilities' (Scanlon et al., 1982, p. 60).

In fact it had been clear by the beginning of the 1980s that there were not sufficient good examples of all types of educational software to fill the demand. There were lamentations about the quality of software both from those who believed that the whole approach was misguided, such as Self (1985) (who as we saw above was arguing for the application of artificial intelligence to the design of educational software), and from those who wanted to see good-quality traditional CAL. The predictions of widespread extensive use were not being borne out. In the following two sections two areas will be considered: school education and higher education, to explore what was happening at this time.

## Schools

In the late 1980s, Foster (1988) reported that in spite of a large initiative by the British government, the majority of school teachers were not using computers. Among other factors, Foster blamed poor programs that were difficult to use, trivial in content and not meeting perceived needs. In an article looking at the provision of educational computing in the 1980s, Boyd-Barrett discussed the problems of the lack of good educational software. Reporting on a computer supplement to a quality newspaper in 1988, he says: 'several contributors seriously questioned the viability of the UK [educational software] market. There were 300 educational software publishers averaging only modest turnover, yet the development of good quality software was costed at between £10,000 to £100,000 over periods ranging from one to five years for development and marketing' (Boyd-Barrett, 1990, p. 19).

This lack of software was a major stumbling block for widespread take-up of educational computing: certainly for institutions who could only afford modest outlay on software. It affected all levels of education. However, during the 1980s two new uses of computers emerged which had not previously been seriously considered. These were the use of generic content-free software and the use of computers for communication purposes. Both largely avoided the problem of lack of software. Quality generic software packages such as wordprocessors, spreadsheets and databases were developed for the commercial market, which (unlike the educational market) could afford to pay for the development. Educators could thus benefit from quality software without paying the full price of its development costs. Such software as data analysis and statistical packages, which could potentially be applied to a number of areas, had previously only been used in specialised subjects like science and mathematics, and had not been as accessible or flexible as the new packages developed for microcomputers. These applications also became more popular for general educational use.

With the use of commercial software offering a partial solution to the software problem, the possibilities of using computers in education were greater. At the same time, hardware was falling in price. It finally seemed possible, therefore, that the concept of personal computing could become a reality. As with many developments in this area, moves towards the 'electronic campus' or towards widespread access began first of all in the USA and in higher education.

## Higher Education in the UK

For higher education in the UK, one important point in the 1980s was the publication of the Nelson Report (Computer Board for Universities and Research Councils (CBURC), 1983), which highlighted the inadequate provision of student workstations in UK universities. The report argued that the well-equipped campus in the early 1990s should have one workstation for every five undergraduates. Subsequently, the Computers in Teaching Initiative (CTI) was set up with funding for five pilot projects from the CBURC, who had commissioned the report. Further funding followed from the University Grants Committee (UGC) in 1985. The primary aims of the CTI were to encourage the development of computer-mediated training and learning in UK universities, to evaluate the educational potential of IT within the context of university teaching and to promote an enhanced awareness of the potential of IT among academics and students in all disciplines. Secondary aims concerned assessment of hardware and software requirements, consideration of organisational issues and development and evaluation of educational software. To do this, 139 separate projects were selectively funded, for which the total resources, as reported by Gardner (1988), amounted to over £9.5 million. This was increased by support to projects by host universities.

What has been achieved by this initiative? Almost all UK universities received at least one new major microcomputer network from CTI resources and 179 new posts were created, usually short term. Initially, little was demanded from grant holders. The primary goal for almost all projects was the introduction of some element of computer-mediated training or learning into undergraduate provision. There was also much effort invested in software production (though, where appropriate, projects were encouraged to adapt or use existing software).

The strategy for implementing the initiative was through selective funding of individual projects. Many of these were concerned with developments in a particular department or faculty, but a few were concerned with exploring the potential of campus-wide access to computers. The projects that took place at Aston and Swansea will be discussed next, followed by other projects that have been undertaken.

### Aston

Gardner (1989, p. 344) cites Aston as being 'probably the best example in the UK of a university seeking to secure and maintain competitive advantage through positive use of information technology'. Between 1983 and 1988, Aston was able to provide PCs for over 85 per cent of all staff. Project Accent was started in 1989, providing a broadband open systems interconnection (OSI) local area network (LAN), connecting every room on campus, and giving both data and video to over 2,500 service points. Brindley (1989b) reported that Aston was well advanced in its objective of providing access to information and information processing to users at their desks. She reports that 'for users IT offers greater personal choice for independent learning and discovery'. Project Accent is supported by both the government's Department of Trade and Industry (DTI) and the UGC, and seen as a demonstrator centre for British industry. The LAN serves as a launch pad for future IT initiatives based on a more distributed approach to IT and computing provision. So how has this extensive network been used? There are three major initial service applications: first, library and information services; second, electronic mail; and, third, graphics software. At the point of reporting (early 1989) serious consideration was being given to support a scheme for students to buy PCs using a loan arrangement through the National Union of Students (NUS). The suggestion is that purchase is not compulsory, but that *those who want to can easily and cheaply own one*. This notion of easy, cheap access to IT is often encountered and is one we shall be challenging in chapters to come.

## Swansea

At University College, Swansea, an experiment was carried out to provide clusters of terminals in student halls of residence (Startup and Brady, 1989). The aims of the two year project were to examine the managerial and operational problems of installing terminals in student residences and to find out what educational advantages the students gained. University College, Swansea, has three types of student residence: on-campus halls, off-campus halls and a student village with over 1,000 residents. Each type of residence presented different operational and managerial problems for installing a computer network. While the halls are closely managed by wardens or tutors, no such system exists in the village. The residences involved in the experiment were one on-campus hall, two off-campus halls (which are managed together as a single unit) and the student village. In the halls, reading rooms were used as terminal rooms, but in the village, where accommodation pressure was acute, it was decided to house the new facilities in a temporary building. The project was successful, after initial problems were overcome, and long term advantages for the students were reported. These were greater flexibility in organising working schedules, more economical and widespread use of computing facilities and a better working relationship between users and staff of the Computer Centre. The Computer Centre itself had also benefited from the project.

## Dublin

Another project, this time a European one, assessing the impact of having PCs is Project Macintosh at Trinity College, Dublin (Unwin, Harding and Buckley, 1990). The project sought to redress the balance of computing provision by providing students rather than staff with micros and investigating the impact. One hundred students were involved in the study, comprising two distinct groups: all the students on the management science degree and all the first-year mathematics students. The management science students were chosen because they were potentially heavy users, and the mathematics students were selected as a first-year group which could be compared with students in other countries. Financial support was sought from computer manufacturers, as a result of which Apple provided a Macintosh for each student. The first-year students were not given access to the Macs straightaway, as it was felt that there were enough demands on entry and, for the same reasons, there was little formal training, just some introductory presentations. In addition to their PCs, two computing rooms were set up to give computing time during the day and to make printing facilities available: experienced postgraduates were available to offer help and demonstrations, and tutorials were arranged for individual pieces of software. Halfway through the project its successes and achievements were reported to be mixed. Seventy-three per cent of the students reported some achievements, but these were closely linked to previous experience, skill and familiarity. Less than half of the students reported specific difficulties or problems. Those reported were mainly operational difficulties arising from inexperience. About a third of the students reported negative experiences: these included difficulties with the hardware, the system folder and manuals. An interesting aspect of the study was the exploration of home use of the computer. The students included those living with parents, those sharing a house or living with relatives and those in student hostels or at college. The parents, siblings and flatmates of students were surveyed to investigate whether use had spread beyond the students themselves and to investigate the attitudes of these groups towards the computer. In general, there was a very positive attitude towards the Macintosh.

## *Salford*

Some institutions, such as the Information Technology Institute at Salford, do now require every student and member of staff to have a computer and they are connected to the local mainframe and to remote services. Such computing provision relies heavily on a network of industrial partners. Turnbull (1987) reports on funding to the undergraduate programme at Salford, received from the government's Technology and Engineering Programme ('Switch'), of £1.4 million over three years, matched by similar industrial funding. It is not clear how many students are being catered for: the first intake was 45, and the new building will take 150. The aim is to meet skill shortages in IT at graduate level. The course leads to a BSc in IT. The IT content of the course is necessarily broad, as are the entry requirements, and in the first intake the majority of entrants did not have mathematics or science A-levels. One workstation is allocated per student, linked to the university's system and to electronic mail facilities. Turnbull's article reported on the situation halfway through the first intake of students: there is optimism that this is a viable approach, and there is continuing support and encouragement from industry.

Behind the growth of the institute is a major research programme of monitoring and evaluation.

Although individual projects, such as those described here, may sound impressive, there has been no formal evaluation of the CTI and so it is hard to assess what overall impact it has had, and what impact the projects' work continues to have on the host institutions once the funding has ended. Unfortunately, with many of the new technology projects it was relatively easy to find information about the projects being set up, and interim reports of their success, but very little is reported about the final outcome or their continued existence. Supporting the continuation of new-technology endeavours over a period of time does seem to be problematic: it is an area that requires continual updating and substantial maintenance. Whilst grants for limited projects will provide pump-priming money, they cannot contribute to the long-term maintenance of such endeavours. For long-term success, widespread access to and use of new technology must become a fundamental part of the institution's policy and compete for resources like every other aspect.

## Developments in Higher Education in the USA

The vision of the 'electronic campus' was one where all the different areas and departments of the physical campus were linked electronically. Gardner's review (1989) of developments in the USA and the UK divides the growth of the 'electronic campus' into three phases. These progress from a period in which there is pervasive provision of cheap microcomputers, to a more developed and sophisticated appraisal of the potential of IT, leading to a demand for a more co-ordinated approach and in many cases the appointment at a very senior level of what Gardner refers to as IT 'Czars'. During the first phase of large-scale provision of microcomputers, the ownership of such equipment by all or a substantial majority of students was a mandatory requirement of several universities in the USA, but this did not generally require any outlay of institutional resources or restructuring of the curriculum on their part. During the next stage, developments were more principled and institutions planned and organised their programs so as to make the best use of electronic networking. Tucker (1984) describes the developments in three universities: Carnegie-Mellon, Brown and MIT, which he refers to as the 'Star Wars' Universities. As Tucker explains in his introduction (*ibid.* p. 1), the written information about the development of IT in universities is not to be found in the conventional places:

Committees are formed on campuses to decide what should be done. Sometimes they have written charges; sometimes they issue written reports. Proposals are written to firms that might be willing to underwrite equipment purchases or to public and private agencies that might be willing to fund applications to particular courses of study. Faculty and alumni are kept up-to-date on developments with occasional progress reports.

Tucker drew on sections of such documents and commented on them and as he explains, the result is a collection of working papers which he intended would give the reader 'an opportunity to "visit" for a while with others struggling with similar problems in a variety of contexts' (*ibid*.).

The first of these 'Star Wars' universities is Carnegie-Mellon University (CMU). A task force was created by the president of CMU in 1981 to formulate a view of what computing at CMU should be like in the mid- to late 1980s. The first critical issue was seen to be access. Good access was viewed as essential if computing was to expand. The view taken by the task force was that access needed to be made easy and pleasant and should include a high-quality local network. The computer itself was seen as a tool which could be used in a wide variety of ways:

> The uses of modern computation range from the management of education
> . . . to information display in the classroom (dynamic situations), to text-
> processing for writing (both generally and in composition courses), to
> problem solving in data-rich (social science) and computational rich
> (engineering) areas, to tutorials in drill and practice domains (e.g., solfege
> in music), to simulations (engineering), to exercise checkers (proofs in
> logic), to design tools (engineering) and much more.
> (Preliminary Report of the Task Force, February, 1982, quoted in Tucker,
> 1984, p. 5)

It was, however, accepted that use of computers would be diverse and very uneven. For its introduction to be successful, it was essential that the facility was robust and reliable. Students had reported bad initial experiences, which had put them off. Such experiences are, unfortunately, not uncommon (see, for example, Jones and O'Shea, 1982). The decision was made, therefore, that sufficient resources must be provided both to build and maintain a high-quality infrastructure. Computer literacy was defined as an important educational goal and was seen as encompassing the intelligent use of computer tools: understanding the fundamental nature of the computer and hence its potential uses and competence in the local computational facilities. There was also an emphasis on the importance of a social dimension to the extent that it was recommended that computers should be used in a social context. It was recognised that this might mean that resources would have to be diverted from computers themselves to support modifications to student residences or provision of auxiliary working places.

The widespread introduction and use of IT was seen as an area in which CMU could become a centre of excellence and a leader in the field. The report avoided specific recommendations on hardware: the decision was to go forward with the design and installation of a state-of-the-art system based on powerful workstations, connected to a network, such that every student and member of staff, whether on or off campus, would be able to communicate electronically with all the campus's computing facilities. There still remained, however, the question of finding the necessary finance to cover the costs of the workstations themselves, of the system as a whole, of software, and of maintenance. CMU reduced the cost it had to bear, and sought to increase the broader impact of the project in two ways. Firstly the students themselves were required to buy their own workstations and pay for them in instalments over four years. Secondly, a commercial partner was sought who would share the costs of development, installation and maintenance. This partner was IBM.

Tucker's second case study is Brown University, which was also considering its future in terms of IT at around the same time. Soon after the CMU/IBM announcement, Brown realised that the 'window' for doing a similar deal with IBM would be very small. As a leading liberal arts institution, it was ideal for showing that computers could be used to advantage in such an environment. It already had the most extensive and up-to-date campus telecommunications network in American higher education and, like CMU, Brown was faced with a rapidly increasing demand for computer services. It was felt that advanced IT could greatly enhance scholarly activity in every domain.

A ten-year programme began with the installation of 10,000 workstations in Brown's campus communications systems that, when complete, would provide enough workstations to serve all students. At that time it had not been decided whether to make student purchase of computers compulsory. To assist with the project, two equipment grants were obtained ($600,000 from Apollo Computers and $500,000 from Apple Computers), but the main financial support was again provided by IBM to the value of roughly $15 million over three years. One reason for starting the project was that the demand for computing facilities on campus was high and growing very quickly. Academics could see the advantages of the widespread availability of computers: van Dam, chairman of the computer science department and one of the proponents of the proposal, described the scholar's workstation as 'a teaching tool of unrivalled dimensions. It's like having the best of television, transparency projectors, and chalkboards: but it's much more malleable than any of those, and the student can control it' (van Dam, cited in Tucker, 1984, p. 13).

Van Dam cites examples of the use of the computer in a poetry project which made use of hypertext, drawing attention to the way in which groups of people collaborated in working together and commented on each other's work. Other interests included the use of the computer in a journalistic writing class and in music. Tucker (*ibid.* p. 14) quotes Mary Lewis, an associate professor of music:

> One thing we'd like to see in my field is the development of a music editor, which could edit music the way you do text. It seems to me easy to integrate graphics and text. Once we can run music [through a computer] the way you do words, the next step would be the development of a music laboratory where you could use the workstation to develop music skills - composition skills, harmony, music reading; all the fundamental skills of musical literacy that go beyond theory.

The Institute for Research in Information and Scholarship (IRIS) at Brown was set up with support from IBM, which Brown's President described as the cornerstone of Brown's entire project . . . From IRIS will stem the technical and creative impulses that will drive and focus a broad range of experiments. Information developed by IRIS will show us how the next generation of computing can best serve faculty and students in the humanities as well as in the sciences, preserving our strong liberal arts tradition.

(Swearer, cited in Tucker, ibid. p. 16)

MIT is the third university discussed by Tucker. Its IT project, project Athena, is described by Lerman (1984, p. 5) as an educational project whose mission is to 'explore the value of advanced networked graphics workstations . . . throughout MIT's curricula'. In order to achieve this goal, Athena took advantage of generous grants from Digital Equipment Corporation (DEC) and IBM, which included maintenance as well as hardware and software. With the aid of such grants, a campus-wide network was developed comprising 2,000 PC workstations. The system was networked so that users could not only communicate electronically but also exchange all kinds of software including graphics and pictures. At the time of planning, the specification of the workstation was sophisticated: one that would still be suitable after five years. A single campus-wide network was developed, within which LANs could be used. Having this 'twin' system allowed for the main campus network and local area technology (for the LANs) to be updated independently. The system was to support a range of uses across the curriculum including databases, computer laboratories, and administrative organisation and management, such as the choice of course options.

## IT in Distance and Open Learning

There has been a growing interest, both in the UK and internationally, in the possibilities that new technology offers for open and distance learning. We discuss what is meant by distance and open learning in Chapter 3, and so here we will confine ourselves to just two examples of its use, to complete our selective view of models of IT use in higher education.

### Computer Conferencing at Jutland Open University

The interest at Jutland Open University in Denmark is in the possibilities and potentials of electronic communication and how the flexibility provided by this medium can be exploited to match the needs of students who are not working within a classroom or campus. Jutland Open University has a particular philosophy and approach to open learning which embraces the following: an educational equality principle; education viewed as a social learning process which includes active student involvement made possible through two-way communication; social interaction and student involvement in decision making (Lorensten, 1989).

Such ideas and commitment have been characterised as the *third generation teaching concept*. Jutland Open University has analysed the difficulties of studying part time, at a distance, and is concerned about the following problems: keeping up motivation; combining work-related, family-related and study-related requirements; tackling the difference in students' backgrounds and students' qualifications; and study-related insecurity. Jutland's emphasis on student involvement and the social nature of the learning process have made CMC an obvious potential solution. Jutland therefore contracted with Denmark IBM for three years between 1987 and 1989, the assumption being that 'computer conferencing systems can help support a realisation of Jutland Open University's pedagogical concept'.

Lorensten (*ibid.*) reports on an evaluation of the project in 1988, when three different groups of students took part. One of these first-year groups had access to a PC at home, while the other group used the computer at various study centres, from which they were a maximum of 30 kilometres away.

As with so many computer innovations in education, the data from this small study (which is still continuing) does not provide conclusive evidence of the success or otherwise of the introduction of computer conferencing. Preliminary results from the study show a significant variation in the use of the system by the different groups as well as within groups. However, it appears that the main differences between groups can be largely accounted for by factors other than the conferencing system itself, e.g. for one group of students, the facilities available were not those most in demand and as they were experienced students who knew each other, the aims of strengthening communication and social interaction were not as salient. Also, along with one of the other groups, they did not have access to a PC at home and, not surprisingly, this appears to be a significant factor. For the other two groups the position was different: no discrepancy was apparent between their perceived needs and what could be provided by a computer conferencing system, and they made more use of the system.

For Jutland, the issue of integration of computer conferencing into their courses has presented something of a dilemma. On the archaeology course, where the conferencing system was low-key and not an integrated part of the course, the use was minimal (though other factors contributed to this, as mentioned above). On the other two courses, where computer conferencing was an integral part of the courses, it was felt to have taken up too much time, and seemingly to have reduced other forms of communication. Both lack of integration and full integration are therefore perceived as problematic. These issues about what role new technology plays within the course of which it is part, the extent to which it is integrated and the consequences, are very pertinent to the successful introduction of personal computing and are issues we will be returning to in the context of the OU case study.

## Electronic Distance Learning of Business Studies

The second example is of the use of a combination of electronic communication and hypertext as a vehicle for teaching business studies at a distance. This project was due to start in Italy in the autumn of 1991. The courses offered are run jointly by SEGES, an Italian educational foundation, and Liverpool Polytechnic and are a 'distance learning' version of courses already well established at Liverpool. The plan was for the courses to be taught on a semester structure of 15 weeks per semester, and eventually to form part of a degree course. Students would have their own PCs and all learning materials would be distributed on floppy disk to start with, and later by CD-ROM. Students were to access the materials using hypertext.

The particular model of open learning adopted by this project is quite different from the OU model discussed in Chapter 3, in that it assumes that learners are experienced and competent in directing and organising their own learning. It is intended that a wide range of support mechanisms should be available for the students, but the fact that all the course materials are to be accessed only by hypertext raises interesting issues about the viability of using computers as the main source of learning material. It also raises questions about the ease of successfully navigating through a system like hypertext to search for relevant information. In fact, although hypermedia clearly have much potential for accessing, using and searching through large amounts of material, there is growing evidence that learners need some help in organising their way through so much information (Zhao, 1991). This kind of distance learning does have advantages of flexibility and fast development, which the largely text-based OU model does not, but, although it offers the potential for a less didactic and more social form of teaching where students can themselves contribute to the material, it assumes a certain competence and sophistication in learning skills, which new students in higher education cannot be assumed to have. This debate, like the others, will continue in the chapters ahead.

This chapter has attempted to set up a context in which to consider the OU case study by looking at both the historical context of the use of computers in education and other developments in setting up widespread access to computers in higher education. The five categories of the ways computers are used in education which have been discussed here will be used again in later chapters. It is interesting to see that claims made for the use of computers in education can be traced back at least as far as the early 1970s and that by the end of that decade the use of CAL was quite widespread. The main developments which have led to higher education institutions seeking to provide widespread access to computers are the development of commercial general-purpose software, which can be used as study tools, and the rapidly decreasing price of hardware. In such a climate, the 1980s was a period of rapid growth in the expansion of access to computing. Nevertheless, once the initial period of setting up such access is complete, the success of such projects is hard to ascertain. For many projects there is little or no information about their continued existence and little or no evaluation, leaving the impression that they may well have failed to become integrated into the institution's infrastructure. In open and distance learning, the chapter has considered two aspects of the use of computers. The first is the idea of an electronic community which provides social as well as academic support for students who would otherwise be working largely alone. Such moves also echo the move from an interest in (and assumption of) individual learning to more socially based learning. This social view of learning is well exemplified by the Jutland project and will be discussed further in Chapter 2. The second aspect is the idea of using electronic communication and IT as a *teaching medium,* as in the business studies example. Like the social view of learning, this is a very different model from that of the OU described in Chapter 3: in fact both the use of computers to create an electronic community and the use of computers as a teaching medium are based on particular models of how adults learn, and how best to teach them. They are discussed further in this context: that of considering how and why adults go about learning.

# 2
# *Adults Learning – Why and How?*

## Introduction

Chapter 1 provided a review of the history and development of computing for educational purposes. This chapter has as its focus the adults who learn 'at a distance' and some of the implications of using a personal computer (PC) in that process. All teaching activities, including the design of educational software, are based upon assumptions about how and why people learn. Usually these assumptions are implicit and may not even have been consciously considered. The interaction of learning theories with pedagogy and the design of teaching materials and learning tools is complicated. The impression in academic texts is usually that theory leads practice; in our experience this is rarely the case in education. Often such pragmatic issues as resources drive the design of practice; learning theory is used to help explain why the practice was successful or not. The problems that arise in practice at any time may then determine why a particular branch of theory becomes popular. The potential and limitations of computers in learning have been influential in the 1980s in developing theories in cognitive psychology .

An appreciation of why adults want to study and how they learn can help teachers and course designers to develop educational materials and support systems that enhance learning. And it is in the context of such models of the adult learner that computers are introduced as educational devices and as a teaching medium. What might their potential be for supporting the adult learner? In distance education, computers can certainly be used for the electronic delivery of educational material, but can they make significant contributions to social and educational aspects of learning and development?

## Why do adults study?

In order to examine this question, three mini-biographies are presented here to provide case studies which give a flavour of the different backgrounds and motivations of adult students who enrol for higher education through distance study. Anne had enrolled for part-time degree studies when her children were quite young. After having worked in a succession of different jobs, she felt ready for a change in direction, although she wasn't very clear about the direction she wanted to take. Anne (like all her classmates) had left secondary school at the earliest opportunity, but she had come to recognise that she wanted to understand more about the world around her, particularly when her children started school. She had enjoyed the literature and history sections of the Open University's (OU's) foundation course in humanities and had subsequently studied more specialised courses in those disciplines. At first she had dreaded essay writing: as a typist she had transformed other people's words and thoughts into written text, but now she had to structure and present her own ideas.

Barry's strongest subject at school had been technical drawing and he had worked his way up through the drawing office of a local engineering company. The company had supported his day-release and evening studies to gain qualifications as a draughtsman. Threatened with redundancy when his employers were hit by the recession of the early 1980s, Barry moved to another company that had recently been acquired by a multinational corporation. Computer-aided design (CAD) as well as computer control of certain production processes had just been introduced. Barry felt that he needed not only to adapt his skills to the new demands of computerisation but also to widen his knowledge about engineering production systems. After completing an OU course in design, he continued his studies in related subjects aiming to get a degree – partly, he admitted, to be able to keep up with the younger graduate entrants in the company.

Carol left school at 18, trained as a social worker and had ten years' experience of working in an urban setting. Several reorganisations in local government resulted in an erosion of her employment security, despite growing demands upon the services provided by the departments in which she worked. She explained beginning a distance-education degree in terms of acquiring job-related academic qualifications that would complement her work experience and enhance future job applications. She also felt that studying for a degree would provide an educational challenge she had missed by not going on to university after leaving school.

Why have these people chosen to undertake formal education by registering for a course of study? Why distance learning rather than conventional face-to-face study? Why have they chosen certain courses rather than others? How do their expectations of outcomes from their studies differ from those of younger students (i.e. school-leavers) and of other students taking the same courses? And how will they respond if a computer becomes a necessary tool for their studies? In an attempt to answer these questions in ways that make sense for the many thousands of adults learning at a distance, a number of theories will be examined to assess the contributions they can make to an overall picture. The range of educational activities is heterogeneous and none of the theories can provide a complete explanation; it is important to consider the limitations of each. Some of these theories concern explanations from the standpoint of a detached external observer (an 'outside' perspective), while others are more concerned with understanding behaviour from the position of the learner (an 'inside' perspective).

## An 'Outside' Perspective on Motivation

One important common link in these three biographies is the *choice* that each person has made to learn: they each want to gain something from the experience and they feel that formal education can help them. They have made decisions about their learning needs and about how they can learn while maintaining their other interests and commitments. When we consider theories that attempt to explain *why* and *how* adults learn, we find that only some assume a role for individual choice and decision-making; a number of the theories that were very influential in the early days of both distance education and computer-assisted learning (CAL) assume that people's behaviour is mechanistically determined by various forces. For example, behaviourist theories are only concerned with the observable environment and suggest that an individual's behaviour is initiated by stimuli and determined by the associations that have been developed (as a result of reinforcements) between those stimuli and various responses. Behaviourists have been primarily concerned with learning as the result of organisms reacting to factors in their environment: motivation has tended to be considered as an unobservable internal factor and, as such, of little importance. At most, behaviourists view motivation in terms of satisfying basic physiological drives.

In contrast to the mechanistic approach of behaviourism, the choices made by people are considered central to cognitive theories of motivation. The theory of intrinsic motivation proposed by Deci (1975, p. 61) suggests that 'a person will feel competent and self-determining when he is able to deal with challenging situations'. Individuals actively seek such situations; they do not just react to circumstances. If they are in a situation that provides insufficient challenge, they will seek opportunities to exhibit their creativity and resourcefulness. If a situation is too challenging, however, they may leave it for another situation which offers a challenge which is more reasonable for them. This is an information processing theory which envisages people making choices about what to do based upon an awareness of potential satisfaction.

There is considerable empirical support (reviewed by Deci) for the primacy of intrinsic motivation and evidence of such motivation being decreased in situations where extrinsic rewards are offered. While our desire to feel competent and self-determining motivates us to undertake learning 'for its own sake', in many educational settings extrinsic rewards are pervasive with the result that learners' intrinsic motivation is depleted or destroyed. The three people whose mini-biographies were presented earlier in this chapter appear to exhibit elements of both intrinsic and extrinsic motivation. Carol and Barry, in particular, wanted to take courses that would be of interest, but they were also aware of economic pressures that led them to pursue vocationally useful qualifications. Currently many employers look for people who can demonstrate a capacity to handle new technology. In response to this, training courses that offer adults the opportunity to gain experience of using computers have become very popular. While some people are keen to learn and develop computing skills on courses of this kind, others do so unwillingly, being primarily motivated by their need for employment and the economic advantages it secures.

## An 'Inside' Perspective on Motivation

It still comes as a surprise to some teachers in post-school education that learners may not be studying solely to develop their understanding of the course content. Although many will have an academic interest in the subject they have chosen to study, it is often not the only interest they have. For some, it may be far less important than other factors.

In its early years, the OU was often referred to as 'the university of the second chance', because it provided an opportunity for degree level studies to adults who had not previously been able to benefit from higher education. Many students reported that they wanted to prove to others or to themselves that they could succeed in their degree studies. Others were and are clearly intent on obtaining a degree for career advancement or a change of job. Of course, in most cases, more than one of these factors is important.

An early study of OU students (Goodyear, 1976) suggested that at the time of submitting their application individuals were seeking either *qualification* or *compensation* (or a combination of both). However, motives changed during the course of their studies. Students felt that study with the OU helped them gain self-confidence, a sense of purpose, a new look on life, a framework for facts and a tangible qualification.

An interview study of adult learners taking the social science foundation course, *Making sense of society* (Gibbs, Morgan and Taylor, 1984, p. 187), identified three distinct 'educational orientations':

> students with an *academic orientation* had goals that were concerned with the academic aspects of their studies, those with a *vocational orientation* were pursuing their studies with a view to job opportunities, while those with a *personal orientation* sought personal development. Each type of orientation had *intrinsic* and *extrinsic* sub-divisions, depending upon whether learners had a direct interest in the content of the course or were studying largely as a means to an end. *Educational orientation* provides a useful construct for understanding a student's personal context for study. It encapsulates the complex nature of a student's aims, attitudes, purposes for studying. . . . It describes the relationship between the individual and both the course of study and the institution – it can change and develop over time.

Students' orientations help us to understand why individuals choose to study particular courses, what they seek to achieve and how they approach their studies. For example, the mini-biography of Anne suggests that she has an orientation combining personal intrinsic and academic intrinsic aspects, while Carol's orientation includes vocational extrinsic and personal aspects. A student's orientation can also help to explain the amount of effort they are willing to expend on facets of the educational experience and the effect that the introduction of new technology (i.e. computers) might have on their motivation. For example, someone whose main concern is vocational might welcome the opportunity to develop computing skills as part of their studies, whereas someone who is keen to follow their intellectual interests (academic intrinsic orientation) might consider the need to use a computer to be a barrier.

## Learning and Development

Earlier in this chapter some of the assumptions underlying behaviourist theories of learning were introduced. These theories underpin many of the attempts to individualise instruction. The teaching machines and programmed learning methods of the 1950s and 1960s have been replaced by drill-and-practice computer programs used in education and training today, although the principles remain essentially the same.

The basis of behaviourism is that learning depends upon associations that are formed between stimuli and responses. Laboratory experiments conducted principally with animals had demonstrated that behaviour can be shaped by providing a reward (for example, food, praise, knowledge of results) as immediate reinforcement of the desired response. Responses that are rewarded tend to be repeated; those that are not rewarded are eventually avoided. Complex sequences of behaviour can be built up by systematic reinforcement and Skinner in particular has argued that behavioural principles of learning can be applied in education and training. He proposed the linear programming of topics, with each small step in a learning sequence being followed by a question which allows the student to check his or her response before progressing to the next step (or returning to review the same part of the sequence if an incorrect response is made):

> Out of the behavioural 'shaping' of pigeons and rats, grew a research industry, and a whole educational technology (programmed learning), which put impressive weight behind the importance of immediate reinforcement (through knowledge of results) and of the presentation of increments of knowledge arranged in small sequential steps. Knowledge could thus be efficiently assembled, like a brick wall, out of its component parts.
>
> (Entwistle, 1984, p. 6)

Researchers and educational policy-makers have questioned the adequacy of this approach for most of the teaching and learning that takes place in school and subsequent educational activities, in that it views learning as largely the acquisition of knowledge. There are also concerns about the ethics of using an essentially manipulative approach to behaviour in education. However, the legacies of programmed learning are not difficult to find in Western education: behaviourist principles continue to exert a considerable influence on the design of open and distance-learning materials and educational software for CAL, for example the widespread use of 'drill-and-practice' computer programs referred to in Chapter 1.

Although the work of Piaget was focussed mainly on intellectual development in children and adolescents, his approach has been applied more widely and is often referred to in discussions of adult learning. Three central assumptions underpin his theories and much subsequent work. Firstly, an individual actively interprets the world by processing information from the environment using cognitive structures that are constructed and modified in the light of experience. Knowledge does not come to us 'intact' from outside. Neither are we born with it: we must construct it. Secondly, it is assumed that development occurs as an interaction between the person as they mature and elements in their environment; both are necessary if growth is to occur. Thirdly, development is assumed to progress along a hierarchical continuum which is divided into a sequence of stages, with each stage representing a qualitatively different way of thinking. In this scheme of cognitive development, the fourth and highest stage, 'formal operations', is distinguished from the third stage, 'concrete operations', by the ability to follow the form of an argument without needing the concrete materials which make up the structure of the argument. This final stage is considered to be the mode of thinking of an intelligent adult, although it is now acknowledged that most adults use different modes of thinking for different domains of knowledge. Also, adults often retain a concrete mode for material they are unfamiliar with.

Piaget's ideas have greatly influenced Seymour Papert, who developed the computer programming language LOGO (see Chapter 1) to provide children with a means of building their own intellectual structures through the exploration of mathematical shapes and ideas.

Bruner (1967) developed a different three-stage model of thinking. The three modes were: the *enactive* mode (including activities such as swimming and walking); the *iconic* mode (including visual or other sensory organisation and summary imagery); and the *symbolic* mode (including language and abstract manipulations). Each of these modes is more powerful than the one before it, and each represents a necessary part of individual intellectual growth, relating approximately to Piaget's stages of development. However, it may be that adults have a predisposition to one or other of Bruner's modes. For example, a predisposition to the iconic mode would be shown in a facility for visual learning – from diagrams, videos, etc. Bruner's theory supports an argument for the importance of using a variety of media and instructional styles – alternatives must be made available to suit many learner styles. The OU's multimedia approach to teaching engenders some aspects of Bruner's model, in that students with different learning styles can derive educational benefit from the mode of presentation and interaction they find most suitable.

Turkle and Papert (1990) have argued, from studies of people learning to use and program computers, that the stages identified by Piaget may not be hierarchical, but merely reflect individual differences and preferences. They suggest (p. 132) that 'epistemological pluralism' is appropriate in learning to use computers, but that abstraction is emphasised and valued in most instruction: 'Although the computer as an expressive medium supports epistemological pluralism, the computer culture often does not. Our data points to discrimination in the computer culture that is determined not by rules that keep people out but by ways of thinking that make them reluctant to join in.'

Although Piaget and his followers have contributed greatly to our understanding of the development of children's thought, not least by stressing the active role of the learner in constructing knowledge, their theories have been criticised for paying insufficient attention to the role of social influences on cognitive development (for example, Donaldson, 1978). It has been argued that it does not make sense to divorce individual cognitive processes from the social processes of which they are part. This 'individualistic' emphasis in Piaget's work becomes problematic when using a Piagetian framework to consider the use of computers in education. For example at primary school level, there is very little individualised work with computers. Light (1990, p. 6) comments that 'in a survey of Hertfordshire Primary Schools, Jackson, Fletcher and Nesser (1986) obtained clear evidence that the predominant pattern was for children to work in pairs or small groups rather than individually at the computer'.

Piaget's theory of learning is very much centred on the individual and this approach is being increasingly challenged by a more social view of learning. Different theoretical frameworks have been proposed for analysing the process of learning with computers:

> The relevance of [Vygotsky's] . . . work here is that it provides the basis for a 'communicative' perspective on the process of teaching-and-learning, a way of observing and analysing that process which contrasts with those more 'individualistic' approaches which have informed many computer-assisted learning developments. . . .
>
> Vygotsky emphasises the social aspects of cognition in two ways. Firstly he points to the vital role that language plays in cognitive development, problem solving and learning. . . .
>
> Secondly, for Vygotsky, the learner is not construed as the 'lone organism' of the behaviourists or Piagetians acting on and adapting to some impersonal 'environment'. Instead 'human learning presupposes a specific social nature and a process by which children grow into the intellectual life of those around them.'
>
> (Vygotsky, 1978, p. 88, cited in Mercer, 1990, p. 61)

*Collaborative* learning has been playing an increasingly prominent role in school education, and the effect of working in a small group with the computer rather than working individually has been investigated in a number of studies (e.g. Fletcher, 1985; Light *et al.*, 1987; Meverech, Silber and Fine, 1987). The evidence from such work suggests that 'conditions need to be set up so that learners engage both with the task and with one another in the course of their learning' (Light, 1990, p. 43).

This area of group or collaborative learning is another example of the complex relationship between educational theory, social practice and research. There has been a considerable increase in interest and research in collaborative learning and social aspects of learning, and theories which reflect this approach have become more popular. However, although the practice in classrooms reflects the currently dominant educational theories, its origins are much more to do with limited resources. After all, it is easier to share out limited numbers of computers when children are working in groups. Nevertheless, theories of learning which can account for the *social* aspects of learning are clearly much more relevant in trying to analyse and understand the computer's role in collaborative learning. Another result of the shift towards a more social view of learning is an excitement about the potential of the computer in enhancing collaborative learning. Computer conferencing in particular has been viewed as a tool for doing this, and this issue will be discussed later in this chapter.

Another criticism of developmental theories proposed by Piaget and others is that they imply that there is no cognitive development in the adult years: 'the adult has been conceptualized within a framework that derives from the study of children and adolescents' (Allman, 1982, p. 42). It has been assumed, both by psychologists and most adults in our society, that, after reaching maturity, physiological decline is accompanied by intellectual decline. However, there is increasing evidence to support the view that for adults the richness and complexity of social, cultural and environmental factors become more important in sustaining intellectual performance than physiological factors. The 'plasticity' model (developed by Labouvie-Vief after Birren) suggests that during adult life, cognitive development can progress and regress.

How do adults develop as learners through involvement in educational processes? How can we account for differences between adults in the way they go about learning, even when they are tackling the same learning task?

## Developing as Learners

The fact that people learn in different ways could reflect the fact that they have different ideas about what constitutes learning. In studies with adults, Säljö (1979) found qualitatively different conceptions of learning among the people he interviewed. At one extreme were those who saw learning as a quantitative increase in knowledge, with facts, etc., being acquired in a reproductive, rote memorising way. At the other extreme, people saw learning as an interpretive process aimed at an understanding of reality. Five conceptions were identified, in which learning was seen as

- a quantitative increase in knowledge,
- memorising,
- the acquisition of facts, procedures, etc., which can be retained and/or utilised in practice,
- the abstraction of meaning, and
- an interpretive process aimed at understanding reality.

While the first three conceptions are concerned with the passive accumulation and reproduction of knowledge, the fourth and fifth conceptions involve the active construction of meaning which is related to reality and experience. Unfortunately it has always been easier to write teaching materials, and now computer-based learning materials, which encourage memorisation rather than interpretation. However, as we shall see in Chapter 6, studies of adults learning to use computer applications showed that these adults are not willing to be cast into too passive a role. Rather, their approach to learning is encapsulated in the fifth conception mentioned above: they are concerned with interpreting the consequences of their actions at the computer. This has important consequences for designing instructional material for use with computers, which is discussed in Chapter 6.

Perry (1970) looked at the moral and intellectual development of students and noted that their perceptions of a learning task (whether it be a lecture or video programme, reading a textbook or using a PC application, etc.) may be limited by their intellectual development. Individuals seem to progress from a belief that all questions have answers that are either right or wrong (dualistic thinking), to a gradual recognition that few problems, particularly in real life situations, have simple solutions (relativistic thinking). In the final stage of the scheme, students made a commitment to a personal interpretation derived from relevant evidence (commitment in relativism). However, Perry's scheme does not assume that all students will develop through all the stages, nor even that forward progress can be taken for granted. Students can revert to earlier stages in their intellectual development for security in highly challenging situations when their ideas are most under threat. The educational environment has a significant influence on learners' conceptions of knowledge and learning and on shaping or changing those conceptions. Development can be fostered through raising learners' awareness of the intellectual demands of their study tasks. Support can come through a range of formal and informal contacts with teachers and fellow students. However, in distance education such contacts are usually minimal, so it is all the more important to make explicit the nature and purposes of the learning that students are expected to undertake *within* the teaching of courses.

## Approaches to Learning

Marton and his associates at the University of Göteborg in Sweden were concerned with how everyday academic work was undertaken by university students. They observed and asked students to explain how they went about learning passages of prose. The descriptions and accounts revealed qualitative variations in the aspects of the learning material to which students attended. Two levels of processing were identified: *surface-level processing*, in which learners focussed on the discourse itself (the sign); and *deep-level processing*, in which attention was directed towards comprehending what the discourse was about (what is signified) –

The first way of setting about the learning task was characterized by a blind, spasmodic effort to memorize the text; these learners seemed, metaphorically speaking, to see themselves as empty vessels, more or less, to be filled with the words on the pages. In the second case, the students tried to understand the message by looking for relations within the text or by looking for relations between the text and phenomena of the real world, or by looking for relations between the text and its underlying structure. These learners seemed to have seen themselves as creators of knowledge who have to use their capabilities to make critical judgements, logical conclusions and come up with their own ideas.

(Marton and Säljö, 1984, p. 40)

Differences in approach were identified not only in studies by the Göteborg group but also in research with higher education students in the UK (e.g. Laurillard, 1979; Ramsden, 1979; Morgan, Taylor and Gibbs, 1982, etc.) and elsewhere (e.g. Watkins, 1983). Although individual students tended to be consistent in their approach to learning, many were found to be capable of using 'deep' or 'surface' approaches: 'Students adopt an approach determined by their expectations of what is required of them' (Marton and Säljö, 1976, p. 125). Similarly, Laurillard (1979, p. 400–1) found that over a series of tasks, individual learners were capable of different kinds of approach to their work: 'The adoption of . . . two strategies by the same student means that we can see surface-level processing not merely as the approach of a lazy or immature student, but as a chosen, rational, expedient strategy, commensurate with the conditions of the task.'

The conclusion is that students' learning strategies are *context-dependent*, leading to concern being expressed about the perceived demands of assessment systems which foster a surface-level approach by requiring mainly the recall of factual information to the detriment of a deeper level of understanding. This is an issue which is very important in the context of learning to use a computer: if students are taught by giving step-by-step instructions, which may help to make them feel secure, we need to ensure that this is not at the expense of helping them to understand the system they are dealing with. Otherwise such an approach can encourage a surface-level approach to the material. This is discussed in detail in Chapter 6.

Experiments have attempted to improve the quality of learning outcome by influencing students' approaches to learning tasks: for example, questions have been inserted within texts with the intention of orienting learners towards particular content (Marton and Säljö, 1976). Although such devices, which are often now used in computer-based learning packages, had an effect upon which things were attended to, they did not achieve the desired effect in terms of the *quality* of attention, i.e. the level of approach. This raises doubts about the usefulness of in-text questions and other 'mathemagenic' devices aimed at improving learners' understandings by encouraging a more active approach, but which may have the unintended effect of inducing surface-level processing. The way to help students to become more effective learners, it is suggested, is to develop their awareness of what learning is and what it involves – in other words, their conception of learning. Developing students' ideas of what it takes to learn will make a difference to their perceptions of learning tasks.

## The Context of Adult Learning

Distance teaching has enabled many people to gain access to formal education despite personal, domestic, occupational, geographic or other factors that might otherwise make study impossible. Most wish to study while remaining in paid employment and/or retaining responsibility for dependent children or adults. Study is largely undertaken at home, although many learners will use any opportunities they have for some time to themselves – travelling to work, during break times, when other members of the family are out or asleep. Fitting study time around other commitments often means that the circumstances for learning are not optimal. Students may not have all the necessary study materials with them while commuting to work: they may risk being interrupted while studying during their lunch break; some may have to compete with children for access to the television set and video-recorder; they may be tired and lack concentration at the end of a long day. Some students may be reluctant to let other people, particularly those with whom they work, know that they are studying part time. However, the level of support and encouragement received from family, friends and colleagues can have a significant effect upon the learner's morale, motivation and, ultimately, their ability to complete their studies successfully.

Many of the adults who enrol to study at a distance may have had little or no experience of education since leaving school. The OU demands no entrance qualifications and in recent years about 40 per cent of OU undergraduate students have not possessed the normal entrance qualifications for tertiary study in the UK.

Although some may lack the qualifications that are normally expected for entry, they have all made a deliberate decision to study and they already possess attitudes, skills and conceptions about the subject they are studying and the world in which they live. Adults' lived experience and self-motivation are two of the factors emphasised by Knowles (1970) when drawing attention to differences between adult learning and that undertaken by children. He suggests (p. 39) that an appropriate process of adult education (andragogy) must be based upon the underlying assumption that

> as a person matures, (1) his self-concept moves from one of being a dependent personality toward one of being a self-directing human being; (2) he accumulates a growing reservoir of experience that becomes an increasing resource for learning; (3) his readiness to learn becomes oriented increasingly to the developmental tasks of his social roles; and (4) his time perspective changes from one of postponed application of knowledge to immediacy of application, and accordingly his orientation toward learning shifts from one of subject-centeredness to one of problem-centeredness.

Andragogy requires the recognition of adults' learning needs and aspirations and a redefinition of the process of education that has implications for the planning and design of learning situations: 'it is no longer functional to define education as a process of transmitting what is known; it must now be defined as a lifelong process of discovering what is not known' (*ibid*. p. 38).

Despite the qualities and predispositions that they may bring to an educational situation, learning at a distance may reveal tensions between students' own needs and the constraints of the institution with which they have enrolled. Computer-based educational technology appears to have the potential to collapse that distance in a variety of ways, and so make distance education much less constrained. Distance learners usually work by themselves with only infrequent contact with a tutor or other students. In this situation, many informal learning opportunities may not be available – for example, discussing the course with their tutor and peers, or browsing the shelves of an academic library or even a good bookshop. But distance can be educational and psychological as well as geographical. Teaching at a distance involves the separation, both geographically and temporally, of learners and those who prepare the teaching materials or learning opportunities. Distance education is made possible by mediating most of the teaching and communication through written or recorded materials, and the form of the media (print, audio, video, computer, etc.) and the way in which it is used can influence the nature of learners' interactions with the concepts, ideas and relationships that are the essence of the educational experience. The nature and degree of separation of learner and teacher in an educational process has been described by Moore (1983, p. 157) as *transactional distance*, which is 'a function of two variables called "dialogue" and "structure". Dialogue describes the extent to which, in any educational programme, learner and educator are able to respond to each other . . . Structure is a measure of an educational programme's responsiveness to learners' individual needs.'

A greater degree of dialogue can be achieved by some media than by others. For example, educational programmes broadcast on radio involve communication in only one direction, while an audio teleconference makes it possible for dialogue to occur. Similarly, a textbook offers little opportunity for dialogue, while correspondence makes two-way communication possible, although correspondence by 'traditional' mail causes this to be slow and sometimes only one way while 'electronic' mail has the potential to collapse the time between message and response. Materials that are highly structured are teacher centred because they allow little or no flexibility in terms of the educational objectives and methods, and disregard the differing needs of individual learners. The linear structure of a transmitted television programme permits very little flexibility for learners, whereas interactive computer programs offer greater potential for learners to control the pace and depth of their studies by determining a route through the material that is appropriate to their own needs. An educational situation in which little structure has been imposed by the teacher and dialogue can easily be achieved permits very personal learning and teaching to occur, but if there is too little structure then the unsophisticated learner can struggle and sometimes fail. Since different individuals thrive on different amounts of support and independence, it is difficult to design a mass system which provides optimal amounts of both for everyone.

The limited extent to which dialogue has been encouraged in distance education has led to expressions of concern. Evans and Nation (1989, p. 42) argue for more extensive use of dialogue in distance education and, while acknowledging the limitations imposed by certain media, suggest that 'It is the status of the messages within the media which are of crucial importance, not the media themselves.' It can be argued that very many OU students experience great transactional distance, in that the teaching and assessment for the majority of courses are highly structured and that opportunities for dialogue are restricted. In particular, Harris (1987) is critical of many of the University's procedures and materials, which, he suggests, encourage passivity and 'conceptual closure' among students.

What potential, then, do computers offer for reducing transactional distance in distance education? The 'structure' of materials can be made more flexible by allowing learners not only to study at their own pace but also to a depth appropriate to their prior knowledge and understanding and to their desired outcomes. By providing learners with the opportunity to select their own routes through teaching materials, they are able to exert a level of control that is greater than that offered by more linear media. Although most CAL programs have tended to be largely didactic in design, the use of simulations and 'intelligent tutorials' can give learners considerable control over content manipulation and their learning strategies (Laurillard, 1987a). However, it is far from clear that such structures can be of benefit to all learners and in all types of learning, and matching individualised learning with standardised mass-assessment structures is problematic.

Recent advances in computer hardware and software have made it possible to design learning materials in the form of non-linear text or *hypertext* and some distance-education courses have been produced in this format (see Chapter 1). Whereas text material (in printed or electronic form) is normally presented in a linear, sequential manner, hypertext creates multiple pathways (structures, branches or alternatives) for readers with different interests, permitting them to determine their own individual presentation sequence based on their preferred styles of reading or their information needs (Jonassen, 1986). However, structures of this kind may not be appropriate for all learning processes nor for all learners. Text may be broken down into segments that may make it difficult for the learner to perceive the intended argument structure. There is also evidence to suggest that when learners are given control of their learning strategies they do not necessarily select an effective sequence to achieve their desired learning outcomes. This is taken up further in Chapter 9.

Computers can make available resources that have not been specifically prepared for educational use, e.g. databases that can be searched and accessed as the learner desires. Although it is claimed that very many computer programs provide a great deal of interaction, it is very often teacher centred and offers only predetermined interactions between the learner and the program. True 'dialogue' becomes possible when communication links are established amongst many users via computers.

The term computer-mediated communications (CMC) embraces a number of systems that allow the users of linked computers, or terminals connected to a mainframe, to communicate with other users. Electronic mail (e-mail) systems allow for the transmission of information, usually from one sender to one or more person(s) who are able to receive the message. For those using a computer in their home this requires use of a modem and the public telephone network. Electronic mail enables communication that is similar to traditional correspondence to take place. Computer conferencing systems allow users to go further by enabling and supporting sophisticated group and many-to-many communications; dispersed learners and teachers can communicate in ways that are more open-ended and less didactic than is usual in other forms of distance education.

CMC is seen as having the potential to overcome distance learners' feelings of isolation, by providing a means of sharing study problems and suggestions about how to overcome them from both course tutors and fellow students. It also reflects a theoretical framework which encompasses the social aspects of learning, as we saw earlier. The facility to communicate with others can reduce feelings of isolation among students who, for one reason or another, are remote from their tutor and fellow students. For example, in a small-scale Australian project involving the use of PCs in distance-education courses (Latham *et al.*, 1990, p. 13–14) over 95 per cent of the participating students stated quite strongly that using electronic mail to contact lecturers and other students was their greatest benefit: 'This contact with the College and having almost immediate response made the students feel "as if we are part of the student body".' Computer conferencing can give rise to similar feelings of community and social interaction (Kaye, Mason and Harasim, 1989).

It is also possible for CMC to reduce the transactional distance in a course by allowing individual learners to develop an awareness of a range of views and perspectives on issues and topics related to their studies, possibly interacting with others by engaging in dialogue. A qualitative analysis of contributions to some conference topics for the OU course *An introduction to information technology* suggests that CMC can enable students to learn from the experiences and expertise of their peers as well as giving them the opportunity to contribute their own views and experiences:

> By offering ideas and describing personal experience relevant to course issues, students are given the opportunity of integrating new material with their existing concepts. By following inputs from their peers, students are exposed to models about how others think and talk about course issues, and how they draw conclusions from existing evidence. With computer conferencing, the number of students who can benefit from this exposure is much larger than those who attend good face-to-face tutorials, and the time frame for discussions is considerably longer.
>
> (Mason, 1991, p. 172)

Although computer conferencing is not undertaken enthusiastically by all the students eligible to do so, the evidence suggests that it provides for many learners a stimulating social environment in which valuable educational interactions can be achieved. The use of computer conferencing, at the OU in particular, is described in Chapter 3. Its use has been extensively evaluated (for example, Mason, 1989 and 1991).

These kinds of new applications for computers to distance education were not developed by their designers to address the theoretical problems raised by those learning theories we have discussed here. In fact they were not designed specifically for educational purposes at all, but for commercial and industrial purposes. However, their potential in distance education for improving learning was very soon apparent. Their actual impact on learning has yet to be determined but it has caused people to re-assess the whole range of learning theories in order to see which might help inform decisions about future developments, and predict some of the impact computer use might have on individual learners and on the social aspects of learning.

# 3
# Student Computing at the Open University

## The Open University

Despite the fact that very few of its students ever visit the central campus of the Open University at Milton Keynes in Buckinghamshire, the Open University (OU) is a household name in the UK. In 1992 a Gallup survey of people aged 16 and over in England, Scotland and Wales indicated that 86 per cent had heard of the OU. Seventy-one per cent knew that studying with the OU meant studying at home and in your own time, and 44 per cent knew that there were no formal entry requirements (Swift, 1992). This is in large part due to the regular exposure it receives through the BBC broadcasts of the radio and television programmes which are part of its multimedia courses. However, although the University's name may be well known, its educational philosophy and teaching methods are often misunderstood. This chapter begins by clarifying the main educational concepts on which the University is based – distance teaching, open access and open learning – and the nature of the multimedia courses it produces. It describes the development of student computing, from the relatively small but nationally distributed terminal network that was established in 1970, to the extensive use of student-owned personal computers (PCs) in the 1990s, concluding with a description of the policy which established 'home computing' in 1986. This is a necessary grounding for the discussions of the effects of that policy in later chapters.

The UK government was the first national government to fund the establishment of a higher education institution dedicated both to distance teaching and to open access. Distance teaching, or what was known before the 1970s as correspondence teaching, had gained respectability throughout the twentieth century, but most providers were either private institutions (such as correspondence colleges) or face-to-face institutions who modified some of what they taught so that it could be delivered in correspondence mode. Since its inception in 1969 (the first courses were offered in 1970) the OU has provided for many other countries a well-funded experiment from which to observe and learn. Since its establishment there has been a tremendous increase in the provision of distance education globally, and many systems and institutions have based themselves on the UK OU model, for example the Open Universiteit in The Netherlands and the Indira Ghandi National Open University in India.

The initial commitment to develop the University came in a government White Paper of 1966 called 'A University of the Air'. The hope that broadcasting would be the main teaching medium was soon seen as unrealistic and, although broadcasting (and more recently video) is an important component of the teaching system, the body of the teaching material in all courses has always been hardcopy text, delivered to students through the regular mail service.

## What is Distance Education?

In the 1980s distance education began to be seen to offer unrivalled flexibility for people in employment who wanted updating and further training. The image of the low-status 'correspondence college' has been replaced by one of accredited institutions producing high-quality self-study materials using a variety of media, and the OU can claim much of the credit for making distance education 'respectable'. For anyone unfamiliar with the term 'distance education' the following is a quite traditional definition, and the exclusive teacher/pupil model is questionable and, it can be argued, describes a particular form of 'teaching' rather than education. Later in this book we discuss some of the new ways in which computer-based communication can 'open up' this educational process even more:

> For education to occur, there must be someone who needs educating and someone to do the educating. This implies that there is both a learner and a teacher, and some form of two-way communication . . . In the context of education, distance means that the learner and the teacher are not face-to-face. Thus two-way communication must take place despite the fact that they are not in the same room together. Two-way communication can be established using any medium that is available.
>
> (Perry and Rumble, 1987, p. 1)

Distance education can be seen in terms of location: students are separated not only from their tutor but also often from each other. It can also be seen in terms of time: teaching material is used many years after it has been produced. Course writers cannot get immediate feedback from their students as can teachers in face-to-face situations, since the production process for high-standard media means that course authors hand their material over to an editor many months before students receive it. Distance feedback and evaluation systems must also be developed to inform course designers of any problems with their materials. OU courses are often presented annually for up to eight years with little change to the basic materials.

For most OU students their main teacher is their course material, but they also have allocated to them a local 'live' tutor who assesses their work and provides optional group tutorials and, where needed, individual tutorials to support their study. The tutor also marks assignments and comments on students' work. While recognising the value of face-to-face teaching support the University has also always known that valuable education occurs when students interact with each other and it has tried to provide opportunities for students to learn from one another, with and without a tutor, by organising tutorials and residential schools as well as encouraging self-help study groups. More recent developments in computer-mediated communication (CMC – discussed in Chapter 2) have opened other avenues for this interaction, while some computer-assisted learning (CAL) developments have taken a different direction in working on an educational model of students learning through free exploration and interaction with a computer-modelled situation or environment.

## What is Open Learning?

Open learning became a popular concept in the 1980s especially in the fields of professional updating and training:

> Open Learning arrangements enable people to learn at the time, place and pace which satisfy their circumstances and requirements. The emphasis is on opening up opportunities by overcoming barriers that result from geographical isolation, personal or work commitments or conventional course structures which have often prevented people from gaining access to the training they need.
>
> (Manpower Services Commission, 1984, p. 7)

Open-learning systems are often local and incorporate multimedia components such as CAL and video, which must be studied by students at the company training centre or local college. However, they can be studied at times which are convenient to the student. Often the choice of start date and the pace of study and timing of assessment are also under the control of the individual student. Distance teaching usually incorporates some of the aspects of open learning, but in the OU undergraduate programme courses run to an allotted schedule each year with all students on any course submitting assessments and sitting examinations at the same time. These courses do not fulfil all the criteria for open learning. Because the idea of open learning has been so popular, the University is improving its flexibility especially in the way professional updating courses are studied, with students on some courses being able to choose from a number of start times during the year, and also from alternative assessment and examination dates.

The University's degree and diploma structure is flexible and 'open' in that it is modular, with the successful completion of a course gaining a student 'credit' towards a qualification. Courses are 'worth' different amounts of 'credit' (from one-quarter to a full credit) and a student needs to acquire six credits for an ordinary degree and eight, some at higher level, for an honours degree. After completing an obligatory first-year foundation course, students can choose modules from any faculty in the University and at any level. In 1992 the University offered 134 courses in the undergraduate programme. Where courses within a discipline are hierarchical a student will be advised when it is felt that prerequisite skills or other courses of study are necessary preparation. However, no student is obliged to study any prerequisite courses if he or she is determined to go ahead, and their application for a place on a course will be basically on a first-come, first-served basis, although unfortunately every year some courses are oversubscribed and students cannot be accommodated. In that sense all courses within the University are equally open to all students. This is part of the University's open-access policy.

## What is Open Access?

The 'Open' aspect in the title of the Open University signals not that it is an 'open learning' institution in the 1980s' use of the term, but that it is based on an earlier educational and political philosophy committed to equality of opportunity through *open access*. The policy was first declared in the White Paper of 1966, 'A University of the Air': 'Enrolment as a student of the University should be open to everyone on payment of a registration fee, irrespective of educational qualifications, and no formal entrance requirement should be imposed' (quoted in McIntosh *et al.*, 1976, p. 3).

In the inaugural address of the first Chancellor, Lord Crowther, this commitment was confirmed, and led to the University being spoken of as the University of the 'second chance':

> The first and most urgent task before us is to cater for the many thousands of people, fully capable of a higher education, who, for one reason or another, do not get it, or do not get as much of it as they can turn to advantage, or as they sometimes discover too late, that they need.
>
> (*Ibid.* p. 6)

As far as the undergraduate programme and most of the other programmes are concerned, all adults residing in the UK have been equally eligible for a place on a course, subject to availability, and from 1992 this will apply to European Community (EC) citizens.

In the British and North American education systems in particular, concern to expand access to higher education and improve equality of opportunity grew during the 1980s. What is still the special and peculiar aspect of the OU – an undergraduate programme open to people with no prior educational qualifications – has become something other institutions are working towards with the development of special access initiatives and 'bridging courses'. The University has demonstrated that it is possible to take enthusiastic and hardworking students including those with only basic levels of literacy and, by guiding them through well-designed courses, produce graduates with the levels of skill and knowledge equivalent to graduates from traditional institutions.

Much of this success has been due to the nature of the first-year 'foundation' courses in the five faculties: Arts, Mathematics, Social Science, Science and Technology, one of which must be studied by any student in the first year of their undergraduate programme. These courses are designed to equip students with the necessary literacy, numeracy and study skills needed to succeed at undergraduate level. Computer literacy has become, for the faculties of Technology and Mathematics, one of the skills the foundation course teaches.

## Media Technologies in the OU System

From its inception the University has been a multimedia teaching institution and student computing was a medium which was used, although in a very limited way, in some of the earliest courses produced by the University. In the early 1970s the combination of media which could be a part of any course included the following:

- Text: as bound, specially written course units; as published texts; and as loose-leaf 'supplementary' material.
- Broadcast material in the form of radio and television programmes (although by 1980 audio-cassettes had replaced much broadcast radio).
- Audio material initially on record but soon on audio-cassette tape.
- Visual material as colour reproductions or frames of film.
- 'Home experiment kit' (HEK): a generic term covering a variety of scientific and technical instruments and materials for students to carry out practical work, not necessarily experimental work (in the 1970s and 1980s some courses included small digital computers as HEKs).
- Face-to-face tuition in the form of locally based tutorials and week-long residential summer schools.
- Mainframe computing which the student experienced in two ways: (1) as an assessment device (some courses had a computer-marked assignment (CMA) component where students submitted answers on a special form which was posted to Walton Hall and read on to a computer by an optical reader. They subsequently received their grades by post); and (2) by access through a teletype terminal at a local study centre or a residential school site, via telephone connections, to a mainframe computer dedicated to students' computing use.

The OU has always encouraged experiments with media and since 1970 a number have taken place; however, the two major media innovations which are now used extensively by students are video-cassettes and personal computers. And although great things are claimed for the future use of PCs as delivery systems, in the early 1990s printed text remains the primary delivery medium for University courses.

## Student Computing via a Mainframe/Terminal Network (1970–88)

The OU has always been an innovator in the field of student computing. The decision to require students to use PCs from 1988 onwards was based on almost twenty years' experience of the great potential of student computing as well as the technical and organisational limitations of a national network of linked terminals. This section examines that experience, drawing extensively on two articles written by people who were themselves instrumental in developing the system: 'Using computers in distance education: the first ten years of the British Open University' by Max Bramer

(1980), and 'Educational computing at the Open University: the second decade' by Phil Butcher and Joel Greenberg (1992).

The OU has always involved its students in using computers both to learn about computing and as a teaching medium for other subjects. This began in 1970, with the mathematics foundation course for which students were required to spend roughly five hours during the course, online to the mainframe computer. In 1970 mathematics and computing students in traditional universities were using computers through online, time-share terminal access, but the equipment they used was usually massed in computing 'labs' on campus. Given the constraints of distance education the University wanted to offer its mathematics students an experience similar to that of undergraduates in the rest of higher education. Three Hewlett-Packard minicomputers were set up in three University sites in different cities in Britain. Each site had 32 ports available for dial-up access from terminals at local study centres. Initially there were 110 study centres with usually one, but sometimes more, terminals for student use. This system was dedicated to running BASIC programs, which was the language chosen to introduce students to computing. The system proved to be very successful overall, despite practical problems of access which we will discuss later. In 1972 the first Vice Chancellor, Lord Perry, made the following comment about the success of the system:

> It is estimated that, even in these very early years, we have turned out 2,000 students from the mathematics foundation course who are capable of writing simple but non trivial programs. To acheive this in an environment where tutorial support was readily available would not be easy; therefore to do so within the Open University system is extremely creditable.
>
> (Perry, 1972, quoted in Berry and Burrows, 1990, p. 946)

By 1980 the use of the terminal access system had expanded well beyond mathematics courses and students on 35 courses were using the system for some aspect of their study.

In 1973 the University began offering computer science courses. The requirements of students on these courses for online time were greater, but still very limited. The actual terminal connect time for students on the two initial computer science courses (which were of 32 weeks' duration) was 13 hours and 9.5 hours. A third computing course was presented which explored the operation of digital computers. It did not use the terminal network; instead, students were loaned a small computer as a HEK. This scheme was an interesting forerunner for the future, but the technology of the time meant that the usefulness of the loan machine was restricted by its small internal memory, and for some tasks it was necessary to use it as a terminal linked to the network. Although OU courses are designed for distance learning many are used both formally and informally on traditional face-to-face courses. This was true of the digital computer course, which was produced in collaboration with the University of Essex where it was used as a component of a first degree in electronics. These three computing courses were popular and by 1980 over 9,000 OU students had successfully completed one of them.

Other course designers were interested in using the terminal network, but not for BASIC programming; for example, in 1978 a course in cognitive psychology used a non-numerical programming language based on the programming language LOGO. From 1972 onwards CAL was incorporated into some courses using packages bought in, such as CALCHEM, or packages developed internally in the University by a dynamic and expanding academic computing unit. Two new and original CAL systems, Merlin and Cicero, were developed internally.

The originator of Merlin was Prof. William Dorn of the University of Denver, who was a Fulbright Scholar at the OU in the early 1970s. Merlin made creative use of the technology of a networked terminal system so that telephone contact with a tutor was initiated when a student had problems with the CAL material. Ian Every, one of the developers of the system, described it as follows (1987, pp. 93–4):

The major innovation in the MERLIN project was the way human tutors were totally integrated into the system. On each of 36 or so evenings of the year (which became known as 'supervised nights') a human tutor runs a supervising program known as TUTPAC using a VDU terminal at one of the main computer sites. TUTPAC studies the current student interactions with MERLIN and displays a summary of the progress of students in that session. At the tutor's request, TUTPAC can also analyse in detail the answers of the particular student in a particular section of the tutorial and attempt to show the tutor exactly what conceptual difficulties the student has.

If the assessment built into each tutorial program suggests that a student would benefit from assistance from a human tutor, then TUTPAC will arrange for the MERLIN program to halt itself temporarily. At the appropriate time it will inform the tutor to perform manual switching which will put the student's telephone in voice contact with the tutor's loudspeaking telephone . . . Once the student and tutor are speaking to one another (this usually only takes a few seconds) the tutor can assist the student in what is essentially a 'telephone tutorial'. . . . In addition to contacts initiated by the assessment built into the tutorial, contacts can also be requested by either student or tutor independently.

The tutor was only available at set times, but the student was free to use the computerised tutorials at any time. Bramer (1980) remarks that logistically this kind of CAL is best for courses with relatively low and geographically scattered populations. Cicero was a more conservative system with computer-based tutorials that provided self-assessment feedback for students and, by 1980, it was incorporated into six courses.

By 1979 a total of approximately 47,000 hours of student 'connect time' had been recorded; programming accounted for roughly 60 per cent of this time with computation and modelling a further 30 per cent, CAL tutorial packages 7 per cent and statistics packages 3 per cent. Some courses which had residential summer schools as an obligatory component decided to use terminals during the residential time. This gave students an experience more like that of other higher education students, since terminals were massed in a 'lab' and students had the support of each other and staff while they worked. It was first tried at the residential school for *the mathematics foundation course*, but by 1980 fifteen courses with summer schools were using terminals.

By 1980 the organisational and technical problems of this kind of network for student use were well known within the University, but an affordable technical solution did not exist. Attending a study centre to use a terminal was difficult for some students due to their work and family commitments. Once there, many 'novice' users had problems making connections. Hardware was sometimes faulty and telephone lines noisy, and terminals were sometimes housed in unwelcoming locations or were even locked away in cupboards. Many students avoided using a terminal unless it was an integral or assessed part of their course.

Unlike the group setting of residential school or a traditional computer 'lab', where misunderstandings and errors could be discussed with others, students working at study centres were isolated. The University recognised this and tried to provide extra support through briefing sessions on the equipment at the beginning of a course and the setting up of a telephone help-line. This was staffed by the computer operators at the three mainframe sites. The telephone number of the nearest operator was displayed beside each terminal and students were encouraged to make use of the help-line whenever they found themselves 'stuck'. It was possible for the operator to access the student's file from his or her own terminal and this greatly helped the at-a-distance diagnostic process. Over the years the help-line operators developed extensive skills in helping students with the system. However as more courses with different uses came online it became harder for the operators to be familiar with the range of activities that students were engaged in.

Because of the problems of using study centre terminals, the University offered a back-up postal service. Students could send their programs on coding sheets to the Walton Hall site where they were input into the computer and returned to the student by post. This service had a significant amount of use and Bramer (1980) records that in 1978 4,000 separate jobs were processed. This service was for programming and data-analysis computing activities and did not apply to CAL.

Despite these problems, student computing at a distance was a success and there was pressure to expand. But the costs required to replace teletype terminals with others which would be faster and have a graphics capability, as well as the costs of expanding the telephone network and paying for the cost of the calls, were more than the University could afford. Butcher and Greenberg (1992, p. 201) record the situation at the end of the first decade of the University:

In 1980 the computing facilities that were available to students on Open University undergraduate courses were in transition from three old

Hewlett-Packard 2000F minicomputers to three new DECsystem-20 mainframes, one of each situated at London, Milton Keynes and Newcastle. To give access to these computers approximately 240 terminals situated in remote study centres were provided. These remote terminals were teletypes operating at 10 characters per second which had been in service for almost a decade; they provided limited facilities which meant that all applications were text based, upper-case only. These terminals were linked to the central computers via dial-up access over the public telephone network.

To compound these limited facilities, administrative and cost constraints meant that most terminals could only be used for three and a half hours per day when the study centres were open and telephone costs were at their cheapest. Despite the combination of inadequate facilities with limited availability, demand for computing facilities from University courses was buoyant.

Even with the terminals and mainframe updated, the system was unable to cope with student demand on existing courses, and there was a demand from new courses. Butcher and Greenberg note that, in 1984, 2,675 students were enrolled on the *Fundamentals of computing* course but a further 1,686 applicants were rejected simply because the network could not cope with the load. The situation was worse on the *Digital computer* course, which was limited by the stock of HEK microcomputers: 2,045 students were enrolled and 3,082 applicants rejected. By 1980 Bramer could see that the ideal solution as far as students were concerned would be to have a home-based machine. The technology of the time meant that this option seemed 'pie in the sky'.

Courses began to experiment with using 'standalone' microcomputers of various kinds at residential schools. This allowed them to use the potential of a computer to run graphics applications, and interactive graphics for CAL could be developed for specific courses. By 1982, 31 microcomputers were installed at residential schools but, despite their small number, they were mechanically unreliable and their maintenance was something of a headache.

As part of the UK government's 'Micros into Schools' programme, the University produced some of the first courses in the UK about computers for teachers: *Microcomputers in schools*. The solution for these courses was to expect that students would already have access to a 'school's' machine. (And, although machines have changed, this is the solution still preferred for teachers' courses.) In the early 1980s British schools had bought microcomputers marketed by the BBC Acorn and Research Machines, and software was provided by the University that was compatible with these. At that time, before the IBM PC was produced, there was no effective 'industry standard' for PCs. None of the popular microcomputers had compatible operating systems, and no one controlled the majority share of the market. Although attempts were made by the *Microcomputers in schools* course team to produce versions of software that were compatible with a variety of machines, it was soon discovered that this was not feasible. Converting software to different systems is a difficult and labour-intensive task, and the University simply did not have the resources. It was clear that any course, and ideally all courses, should have software written for one machine, or one operating system.

Other small population (500 students or less) courses adopted different individual solutions. A course on computer-aided design (CAD) found the funds to buy Nimbus computers which were then loaned to students. A physics course developed CAL software that was available on the mainframe and also in a version for a BBC microcomputer. More than three times as many students used the microcomputer version. But these kinds of solutions could not be applied across a wide range of courses, and the viability of computer science as a subject in the undergraduate programme depended on finding a solution which offered significant computing power to thousands of students.

There was by this time also significant pressure from the student body for the University to issue advice about the best microcomputers and software for educational purposes. Computers were marketed as multipurpose educational devices and many students were buying, or considering buying, one for their own and their family's use. A 1984 survey of OU students (Grundin, 1985) indicated that almost 50 per cent had access to some kind of microcomputer (although the lack of specification of machine made the data hard to interpret). Many students wanted to use, or were already using, a computer for their general OU studies – even if the course that they were studying had no software – and they wanted guidance about not only the best machine to invest their money in but also which would be compatible with the University's future policy.

## The Home Computing Policy, 1988

By 1984 the University was looking at the feasibility of defining one particular machine which would primarily serve the computer science courses, but which would have the capacity to handle a variety of software applications. The popular machines of the time that could possibly fulfil requirements were the Sinclair QL, the Acorn Electron and the Oric 6502. The IBM PC was available, but the overall cost of about £2,500 made it not feasible as a student machine. While the University debated the choice of machine, Acorn and Sinclair both went out of business. The safest and most flexible solution was then to define the equipment on the basis of compatible software rather than hardware and by 1986 the University agreed a 'Home Computing Policy' which specified an operating system and acknowledged, but did not solve, the question of cost:

an MS-DOS machine with 512K, disk storage, mouse, . . . and capable of supporting graphics. It was a requirement that the hardware supported amongst others, MS-DOS, UCSD Pascal, Lotus 1-2-3 and Gem. It was accepted that '...the technical strategy does depend on having an MS-DOS capability for under £500 . . .' Computer manufacturers and suppliers were circulated with the University's requirements and asked to comment particularly on price.

(Butcher and Greenberg, 1992, p. 209)

Although the policy was based on specifying software rather than hardware, it was the appearance on the market of a particular piece of hardware, the Amstrad 1512 selling at about £500, that turned the policy into a reality. It is important to discuss at this point the deeper issue of principle that was involved in a decision to require students to own or have access to a microcomputer, no matter how cheap it might be. There had been a general principle in the University that any equipment required for completing a course – other than a calculator – had to be provided by the University, or its use made an optional part of the course. This was understood as being part of the University's open-access policy, that no student should be disadvantaged in their choice of course because they did not or could not afford to own particular items. This was even applied to radio and television broadcasting, despite its importance in general OU courses. Study centres all had video players and tutors could obtain copies of any broadcast material and students could view it or listen to it on study-centre equipment. Even with this facility most courses worked on the principle that broadcasting should be assessed only if alternative non-broadcast-based questions were offered too. No course ever made broadcasting optional; all course teams argued that in order to fulfil all the aims of a course it was necessary for students to see and hear course programmes, *but* that it was possible for students, who for whatever reason did not hear or see the broadcasts, to complete the course and pass. Any other equipment students needed, even simple chemicals for experiments, were mailed to students as part of a HEK.

Many members of the University would have liked the course fees to have been paid for students, ideally by some government body, and in that way to have removed any financial barriers to access. Although no government had ever previously offered such support, the University did what it could by operating schemes to subsidise students whose income fell below a defined level. However, this support was limited to a very small number of students. When the internal debates about a policy for home-based computing in which students would bear the costs were made public many students and staff were very worried about the impact that this would have on 'openness'. Speculative arguments based on very poor data developed about the numbers of students already owning or having access to microcomputers, with some enthusiasts predicting that ownership of microcomputers would match that of ownership of television by the 1990s. Others predicted that there would be a fall in price such that by 1990 IBM-compatible PCs would retail at about £50. By 1992 these predictions have not been fulfilled and what has actually happened is discussed in detail in later chapters of this book.

What is interesting is the way members of the University tended to fall into one of two dramatically opposed camps: the optimists, who predicted that all homes would soon own cheap computers and all OU courses needed to make use of them if the OU was to retain any reputation as an educational innovator; and the pessimists who argued that personal computing was basically a marketing 'hype', that the University should not be taken in by it, and that if it was, students would be discouraged from applying by their thousands, and those who would be discouraged would be those the University was originally established to cater for. Even some of those who were most enthusiastic and creative in their vision of the uses of PCs as students' tools were worried that for a few years at least a requirement to own a computer for access to some courses would skew the social class distribution of students on those courses and produce the phenomenon described as the 'yuppie menace'. (This phrase was coined by John Naughton, at that time the Chair of the foundation course in technology, himself a keen promoter of educational uses for PCs, and one of the initiators and designers of the Home Computing Policy.) The 'yuppie menace' effect has not struck the University and a discussion of the changes that have occurred in the student body will be discussed in later chapters.

The year 1988 was the first in which the policy operated with three courses having all their software on disk for MS-DOS machines. Two of these courses, *The fundamentals of computing* and *Computational mathematics*, had existed in previous versions with terminal access computing. The third course was totally new: *An introduction to information technology*. The network system was upgraded at the same time by replacing the DEC 20s with a Vax cluster machine, since many other courses still used the network. Students studying the course *An introduction to information technology* were loaned a modem so that they could use a computer conferencing system on the Vax as well as accessing remote databases. The University was also very fortunate in obtaining a £2.25 million grant from the Department of Trade and Industry as well as £200,000 from the Department of Education and Science to buy 2,500 MS-DOS machines (plus a later additional 1,500) that were then loaned out to students on payment of a fee – between £150 and £50 depending on the course. For the first three years there was also a fee reduction of £50 for students registering for computing courses, to lessen the impact of the extra expense.

The University has also been very successful in negotiating very advantageous licensing deals so that students can be supplied with sophisticated commercial applications such as Lotus 1-2-3, GEM, PC automator, UCSD Pascal and Framework, without extra cost.

In 1992 the policy is seen within the University as very successful. Courses with an obligatory 'home computing' element are popular with students. The idea of students using PCs is popular with course teams. In 1992 eleven courses (see Table 3.1) require undergraduate students to have access to an MS-DOS machine, another two courses require students to have access to 'schools' machines. Outside the policy, seven courses use PCs at residential and day schools, two loan students PCs as part of a HEK, and a further six have optional components which need access to a computer. The terminal network is now closed down, although PCs have been placed in some study centres, so that courses which need access to a Vax cluster have to do so through a modem connected to a PC. As yet only one course in the

Table 3.1 Courses with a computing component

---

**A. Undergraduate courses**

*1. Where an MS-DOS machine is a requirement to complete course work*
An introduction to information technology
Computers and learning
Fundamentals of computing
Programming and programming languages
Data models and databases
Computational mathematics
Numerical methods for differential equations
A foundation course in technology
Analogue and digital electronics
Microprocessor-based computers
Computer-aided design

*2. Where computing is provided at residential school or day school*
Mathematical models and methods
Physical chemistry: principles of chemical change
Quantum mechanics
Electromagnetism
Biology: brain and behaviour
A foundation course in science (also available to buy on disk)
A foundation course in mathematics

*3. Where access to a BBC machine or a Nimbus is required*
Learning and teaching mathematics
Using mathematical thinking

*4. Where a microprocessor is provided by the University as a loan 'kit'*
Statistical methods (terminal, modem and monitor provided to link to mainframe)
Control engineering (microcomputer supplied as part of an experimental kit)

*5. Where computer use is optional*
Complexity, management and change: applying a systems approach (MS-DOS machine needed by students choosing a particular project option)
Evolution (MS-DOS machine needed by students choosing a particular project option)
Biology: form and function (optional CAL)
Matter in the universe (optional CAL for BBC machine)
Genetics (optional CAL for BBC machine)
Images and information (optional CAL – Merlin – for MS-DOS machine)

**B. Post-graduate diplomas and degrees**

MBA programme – required for certain modules
MSc in computing for commerce and industry – required
MSc in manufacturing: management and technology – required

---

undergraduate programme and a small number of post-graduate courses have a significant component of time spent doing this, although there is great enthusiasm for its expansion, in particular for CMC. The fee-reduction scheme has ended and, as far as most students are concerned, so has the loan pool of machines. The University has been unable to raise any further funding either to replace the original machines or to expand the numbers available to keep pace with the numbers of students on 'home computing' courses; therefore the pool of loan machines exists only for students who fulfil criteria of particular disadvantage.

The effect of this expansion on different course production areas of the University has also been great. Academic course authors have had to come to grips with PCs themselves if they are members of a course which requires students to use them. Computer professionals who make up the Educational Software Group, and the Academic Computing Service, have been very busy adapting software, writing new software and working with non-computing academics to teach them how to use it. The production of software, or the negotiation of large-scale licences, must be taken account of in the course-planning process.

Jim Burrows, the Director of the OU's Academic Computing Service and the main developer of the technical specification for the final Home Computing Policy, summarised the success of the University's software production:

The principal success in the adoption of the MS-DOS standard has been that it has genuinely proved to be hardware manufacturer independent. It has therefore been possible to distribute software which will run on a wide range of manufacturers' systems. Students have been supplied with general purpose, commercially available software and special software produced by the University. There has been a full production system, in operation since 1987, resulting in over 50,000 floppy disks produced in-house and dispatched in 1988. This figure has risen to 200,000 by the end of 1989. The in-house software production system is to BS5750 standards, and the University's Academic Computing Service has set up a quality assurance unit which vets all master disks and samples production runs for quality.

(Berry and Burrows, 1990, p. 947)

## Uses of PCs by Students at the OU

In Chapter 1 we established a set of categories of distinct uses for computers in education. There have been experiments with most of these at the OU. Many were tried out on the mainframe terminal network and have now been developed for PCs. No one course has covered the complete range of uses and most have tended to develop mainly one. In this section we give some examples of OU course material under the various category headings listed in Chapter 1.

### As a Tool to Learn Programming

It seems obvious that any course engaged in teaching computer science should have some practical computing component. However, there are different ways in which this can be done. In 1992 there are three major computer science courses in the OU undergraduate programme. The introductory course, *The fundamentals of computing*, has practical work associated with almost every part of the course, so that students are using their PCs in parallel with their study of other materials. Students learn to write computer programs using what is known as a 'top-down' design technique and are expected to implement programs using the Pascal programming language on their own PCs. They are sent, on disk, a version of Pascal (the UCSD p-system) and five more disks which contain over 200 other files. Some of these are source program templates for students to complete as part of their practical work; others are data files which they also need. Their practical work is assessed through assignments for which they must send their tutor evidence that they have successfully completed various pieces of computer programming.

On a course which follows this, *Programming and programming languages* (the title is self-explanatory), students learn three programming languages: UCSD Pascal, PROLOG and ADA. They have to write more extensive programs in these and are assessed on their ability to do so. The third course, *Data models and databases*, uses both commercially available software (for example, DBQ SQL, a relational database package) and software covering a variety of applications giving realistic examples of databases found in industry. These have been developed by the Educational Software Group in the University (Educational Software Group, 1991). Students receive the commercial software as part of their course material without any extra charge to them, but they have to sign the licensing agreement which the University has arranged to cover the use of the software for all the staff and students involved with the course. This is now the procedure for any commercial software that students are required to use as part of their course material. Because of the numbers involved the University is able to negotiate very good rates for such agreements. The drawback is that the licensing agreement the student signs usually stipulates that they can only use the software themselves.

## As a Tool to Assist Learning, i.e. CAL

Computer-based structured-learning exercises (i.e. CAL) are one teaching component of most courses which now use PCs. Some have adapted material from earlier versions which used the terminal access network, such as the Merlin material discussed above. Others, like those designed for the foundation course in technology, are new and incorporate sophisticated models of learning and error analysis in particular domains of knowledge. A description of the CAL materials produced to aid the development of numeracy skills for students studying this course gives some idea of the way such materials are internally structured and also how they are integrated with other teaching materials.

The subject material of the course is organised around issues called 'blocks' of study, and there are six of these in the course. Different numeracy skills are taught in each block, and CAL materials have so far been produced to cover the numeracy topics of the first three blocks. For the first block these are addition and subtraction of negative numbers, multiplication and division of negative numbers, powers, graphs, formulae, orders of magnitude; for the second block, constructing a graph, gradients and negative numbers; and for the third block, solving equations and manipulating equations. These numeracy topics are also taught in parallel text material so that students can choose both or either of the media. At the beginning of the course students complete a diagnostic mathematics test in the form of a CMA which they post to Walton Hall where it is read into the mainframe computer. The results of the test are returned to each individual student and they include advice about which numeracy topics they need to study to be properly prepared to handle the course material. From this point students can begin using the numeracy teaching materials, accessing either text or CAL for particular topics only, or working through all the material provided. This system of early diagnostic tests has been a component of the foundation course for many years, but before the use of PCs numeracy teaching was provided mainly through text with some use of audio-visual material. However, the design of the numeracy CAL is more flexible than that of the text and the CAL program contains a student profile which is constantly revised as the student works and which gives the student feedback on their progress as well as being used to decide which exercises to present to the student as they progress. Figure 3.1 shows the internal structure of a numeracy topic. Each topic can be taught by several alternative teaching methods with related exercises. The choice of which exercises to do and how many examples is determined by the advice given by the program based on the student profile and the student's own choice.

The following description of how this works is taken from Laurillard (1989, pp. 3–4), one of the designers of the CAL materials:

The teaching material is presented in the form of text, diagrams, animations or simulations, depending on the topic and each one has an exercise associated with it. The instructional strategy advises on (a) how many examples of each type of exercise to do, (b) which exercise to do next, (c) which topic to do next, and (d) when to take the topic test.

The student profile is updated continuously, and holds information about

the presence of error types
teaching material looked at
exercises completed
number of examples completed
scores

Error values are updated on each error type so that the instructional strategy can decide what to offer next. One strategy being adopted to determine the number of examples a learner should do on a particular exercise is as follows:

default error value = 0.4
increase error value to 1 if error diagnosed as present

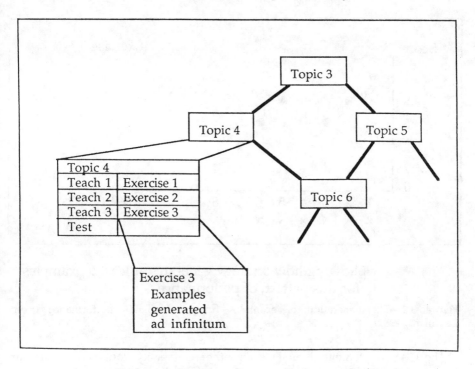

Each topic has several ways of being taught (Teach 1,
Teach 2, etc) each of which has an associated exercise
which generates as many examples as required either
by the student or by the instructional strategy.

Figure 3.1   The internal structure of a numeracy topic (from Laurillard, 1989)

decrease error value by 0.2 if error not diagnosed in relevant example
criterion value (i.e. mastery) = 0

Figure [3.2] shows how this strategy would operate for a given sequence of
learner attempts at an exercise. The particular values used here (0.4, 1, 0.2,
0) are parameters in the system which can be altered if developmental
testing shows that it makes some inappropriate decisions. . . .

However, the error forms do not reveal sufficient information about why
the confusions arise, for us to determine what kind of teaching material
would be effective remediation. For example, do the confusions occur
because the learner has an incorrect model of the number line, or because
they are making inappropriate translations between the verbal and
symbolic forms of an exercise? The pre-test tells us only *that* they make
these particular mistakes, not *why*. The teaching material offers
explanations with associated exercises designed to tackle each type of
learning problem the learner might be expected to have, but there is no
basis for the program to decide between these. The learner can choose
from a menu description, on the basis of what kind of exercise they prefer.
The default option is to go through in a randomly assigned order.

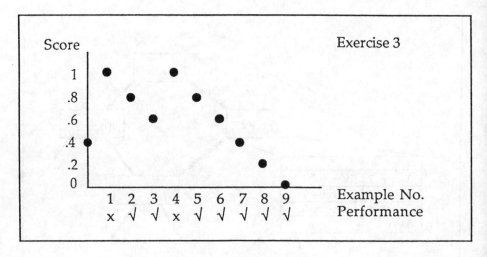

Showing how strategy generates at least 9 examples
for this pattern of performance

Figure 3.2 The generation of examples from a student's performance (from Laurillard, 1989)

The CAL implemented on PCs for other University courses uses similar teaching strategies.

## As a General Study Aid

For many years the fact that tutors have been receiving assignments from students that have obviously been produced on a wordprocessor has indicated that at least a portion of OU students owned or had access to microcomputers which they were able to use as a general purpose tool. It is expected that this will grow in the student population faster than in the general population. However, while the cost of PCs remains significantly high, no course in the University would be allowed to require students to use a computer simply as a general purpose tool, even if they thought it would be a good idea. The University does not even require that students submit assignments in typescript.

The closest any course has come to requiring students to have computers as a general purpose tool is the foundation course in technology. The course team made a strong argument that any course which was part of the education of technologists and engineers must contain elements of practical computing work, with the kind of applications that any technologist would be expected to be familiar with to be considered professionally computer literate. The University obtained a very favourable licensing agreement with the software company Ashton Tate, for a multi-purpose piece of software called 'Framework'. This is industry-standard software containing a wordprocessing and outlining program, a database package and a spreadsheet. Use of all of these facilities is taught in the course and students are required to demonstrate facility with them through their assessments. Use of things like the spreadsheet for manipulating data in repetitive calculations, and the outlining function for planning and writing a report is now integrated into the students' work. And, as we have discussed earlier, there is also a large amount of specially written numeracy CAL on the course for which students also use their PCs.

## As an Assessment Tool

All student assessment should be valid, that is students should be assessed on what they have been taught; it should also be reliable, that is all students should be assessed in the same way against the same set of criteria. The problem of ensuring the first of these is one equally inherent in all forms of assessment, ensuring the second is a problem when the marker is human, since research on assessment shows that even when all assessment is done by one individual there will be discrepancies in the way that work is assessed. When the student population is large and there are many assessors then some standardising process has to be applied across what will inevitably be a great variation in grading. An added problem with distance education is that a delay can develop between work being submitted by students and their receipt of the returned assessed work, and teachers know that the more immediate the feedback then the more learning that takes place. When the University was established a CMA system was set up, which, it was hoped, would overcome the problem of reliability since all students would be assessed on identical criteria, and they would also be provided with very fast feedback. These CMAs usually contributed no more than 20 per cent of the overall assessment marks; the greater part was provided by tutor-marked assignments (TMAs) and a human-marked examination (although computer-marked examination papers were used by some courses).

In the early years of CMAs students answered multiple-choice questions and made marks on specially designed forms which were then posted to the central Walton Hall campus and scanned into a computer by an optical reading device. Students then received feedback showing which answers were correct and a grade for the assignment. By the end of the 1970s this system was developed by some courses so that students were given more elaborate feedback in the form of a personalised letter, which told them which questions they had answered wrongly and attempted to diagnose their error and direct them to the appropriate part of the course so that they could study the material that they had obviously not understood.

CMAs have always been popular with only some disciplines, where it was felt possible to design multiple-choice questions which could discriminate well enough to test undergraduate-level concepts and skills. When students have submitted their CMAs it is possible to assess the individual questions statistically to see which were good discriminators. Questions to which most students got the wrong answer, or there was an inexplicable distribution of students' answers (suggesting that the question was open to misinterpretation) were re-examined and in some cases removed from the assessment. All students' grades could then be adjusted to take account of this. It was only possible to do this with speed with a computer-based system.

However, writing good multiple-choice questions is a skilful task and one which falls on members of the course team. Producing four or six CMAs, each with thirty or forty new questions, every year is an onerous task. Some course teams have assembled 'banks' of good questions which can be re-used, but then there is always concern that students from previous years will pass on the correct answers.

CAL implemented on PCs, as described above, contains assessment and feedback which is given to the student and used to direct the CAL program. However, this is not used as part of formal grading and assessment. The possibility of an interactive CMA system based on students inputting their assessment via their networked PC, and receiving immediate feedback, has been seen as an improvement on the old postal entry system, but it has yet to be implemented at the OU.

## As a Communication Device

The first student use of CMC via a linked PC in students' own homes was on the interdisciplinary course, *An introduction to information technology*, and this used the software application called CoSy which has been developed by the University of Guelph, Ontario.

Kaye, Mason and Harasim (1989, p. 4) list the general facilities of a CMC system as

- electronic mail for one to one communication
- one or more forms of asynchronous group communication (conferences)
- a 'chat' mode for real time exchange of short messages with other users
- a directory of all users, with their resumes and information on when they last accessed the system
- a directory of all listed conferences, with brief details of each one
- an on line editor and a 'scratchpad' for message composition
- facilities for file uploads and downloads.

A metaphor for such a system is the 'writer's desktop' shown in Figure 3.3.

Students on this particular course use CoSy either as a mail system or a conferencing system and they are expected to experiment with both as part of the practical work on their course. Other OU courses are also experimenting with using CoSy for their students, and other conferencing software, such as VaxNotes, is available for University staff use. The use of CoSy has been well documented since over one thousand students have registered for the course every year since 1988, making this the largest-scale experiment with computer conferencing in education. It is also novel that use of the conferencing system is part of a multimedia package and it is *not* optional.

The following describes the way CoSy was used on this course, and has provided a model for further OU developments:

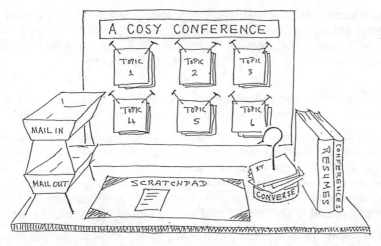

Figure 3.3   The metaphor of the writer's desktop.

one of the aims of introducing the medium was to offer students practical experience in using the technology. In addition, as distance learners, students were provided with half their normal tutorial [i.e. face-to-face] provision on-line. Each of the 65 tutors was given a closed conference in which to hold discussions with 25 assigned students. One conference (the *forum*) which everyone could access was provided for socialising and general discussion of course issues and difficulties . . .

The forum conference consisted of many topics, one for each block of the course, for the practical work, for assignments, for technical difficulties and so on.

                                                                                   (*Ibid.* p. 26)

## As a Tool for Students with Special Needs

The OU has always taken seriously the needs of students with disabilities, and indeed sees itself as the primary UK provider of higher education for people who, because of their disabilities, are unable to attend face-to-face institutions. In 1990 the University had nearly 3,000 students with disabilities (this was just over 4 per cent of the undergraduate population) and the range of disabilities was huge and their severity varied.

Because disabilities are so different, the application of information technology (IT) to attenuate or overcome the effect of these is also very varied. The University has a very active research group in this area who have, over many years, experimented with and developed a variety of hardware and software that students with disabilities have used. However, since the introduction of the Home Computing Policy priority has been given to helping students studying courses which incorporate the use of a PC. There are two main ways in which students can be helped:

a) by a student having specialist equipment (e.g. a computer or terminal that has a braille display and/or keyboard);

b) by adding 'enabling' hardware or software to the hardware used by all students (such as a speech synthesizer).

In both cases, the objective is to give access to 'standard' computing applications without modification to the application software.

(Vincent, 1989, p. 87)

We will examine particular examples of this, in context, later in the book. It is important here to note something else that concerns Vincent (*ibid*. p. 87):

that changes in hardware and software used for courses can have very significant implications for students with disabilities. For example, a change to WIMP [this stands for 'window, icon, mouse, pointer', a system based on commands using visual symbols which are 'pointed at', rather than command names that are keyed in] environments excludes all currently available methods of adding speech output for blind users.

That is, what are design improvements for able-bodied students may make equipment more difficult to use for disabled students.

## Evaluation of the Home Computing Policy

Because of the nature of distance education, feedback from students can take a long time to reach the people who originally designed and produced a course. This is exacerbated in the OU by the long production process, which, although it leads to the production of high-quality materials, further increases the time between the writing of the course by academics and software designers and the receipt of that material by students. The investment both in terms of time and money in the production process also means that it is difficult to make major changes to a course once it is produced. Some aspects of the course components are easier and cheaper to change, for example, radio broadcasts; others are designed to be changed every year, such as assessment materials and what are known as 'stop press' sheets. But all changes have resource implications which must be planned in advance, costed and well justified. Because this has always been recognised in the University, various feedback and evaluation systems and methods are used to get as much reliable feedback as possible, both from students and part-time tutors. Evaluation studies also provide an empirical research base for theoretical work on learning and teaching. Evaluation work in the OU is often used for more than one of these purposes, and this book provides an example of this.

The evaluation of the Home Computing Policy was concerned to provide feedback to a variety of clients. Internally, feedback was to be given to the University course teams and to individual authors of teaching texts and software who wanted comments on what they had produced; to University policy-makers who wanted feedback on the overall success of the policy and data helpful in designing the direction of future policy, as well as indicators of the performance of subcontracted agents such as the company who managed the special purchase and loan schemes. Staff and students wanted general feedback to compare with their own personal experiences, and government

Table 3.2   Returns from evaluation surveys

| Course | Number of student returns for surveys at different points in the year | Staff survey returns |
|---|---|---|
| **1988** | | |
| DT200 | 204 349 | 8 diaries and interviews |
| M205 | 189 320 | 16 interviews, 8 diaries |
| M371 | 142 156 | |
| | Diaries and interviews with 30+ students from 3 courses 268 applicants to the above courses who withdrew very early | |
| **1989** | | |
| DT200 | 140 115 | |
| M205 | 146 108 | |
| M371 | 101 99 | |
| T102 | 164 202 620 | 219 |
| M353 | 206 | |
| M205 | | Interviews with 9 staff tutors and 8 tutors |
| **1990** | | |
| T202 | 175 765 | |
| M205, M353, DT200, T102, M371   626 (tot) 226 students from non-computing courses | | |

*Course titles*: DT200 An introduction to information technology; M205 The fundamentals of computing; M371 Computational mathematics; T102 A foundation course in technology; M353 Programming and programming languages; T202 Analogue and digital computers.

departments wanted feedback on the use of their funding. There is also an interest in the world of distance education and people working in computers in education to know what the outcome of new initiatives and experiments is. We presume that is why you are reading this book right now.

All new courses are surveyed by the Institute of Educational Technology in the first year of presentation to the students. However, unless the course is particularly innovatory or expected to be problematic, only very limited data are collected to give some overall indication of the way students value the various components of the course. It was obvious that this would be insufficient for courses in the Home Computing Policy as other aspects of the policy's operation required investigation. Therefore an extensive and multi-dimensional evaluation project was set up involving a number of linked projects examining the experiences and reactions not only of students but also of the academics who developed the course materials, computing support staff, local tutors and other staff. The data-collecting tools of the evaluation were large-scale student surveys, student journals and interviews with staff and students. The scale of student surveys is demonstrated by Table 3.2 which shows the many hundreds of students who have returned questionnaires for analysis.

The survey questionnaires contained multiple-choice questions which were analysed using SPSS software on a Sperry Univac mainframe computer. They also contained open-ended questions which were analysed directly by the researchers. The numerical data were an excellent source for understanding patterns of student use between courses and the open-ended responses were most useful in identifying the detailed nature of particular course issues and problems. A much smaller number of telephone and face-to-face interviews were carried out, fewer than the evaluation team would have ideally liked, but the time consuming nature of interviewing a nationally distributed population meant that the team were able to carry out very few. Journals, although in theory very attractive since they could provide a longitudinal study of student experience at low cost to the evaluator, proved in practice to have a low completion rate by students. However, those students who did return them provided another source of useful information and opinion which was incorporated with the other evaluation data.

From Chapter 4 onwards we examine the issues that were highlighted by the evaluation. Some uses of PCs on courses have been more successful than others, and PC use is also influenced by student characteristics such as gender and age. Interesting differences emerged between 'novice' users and those who had previous experience of using a computer. All these factors and variables give us a sophisticated picture of how PCs can be used optimally by students in distance education and what problems still exist. It is this that we elaborate on in the rest of the book. Most of the data on which our discussions are based was obtained as part of the integrated evaluation strategy described above. However, such a widely distributed educational innovation has stimulated many individuals and groups from different parts of the University to write about their own experiences and those of their students. This work has enriched the central evaluation and we draw on much of it in later chapters.

# 4
# *The Students' Social and Physical Context*

## Introduction

Open University (OU) students do much of their studying at home and usually have to find time for their academic work when their other commitments allow. Many students are in paid employment; many have domestic arrangements that are of higher priority than studying. The wide range of students' ages and circumstances means that there is no 'ideal' pattern for studying; each student will have a unique set of demands upon their time. While studying their course materials, students need to be free of distractions and unnecessary noise. If their studies demand more than reading, thinking and writing (for example, when audio-visual media or practical activities are required), it may be necessary for them to ensure that they can use facilities (television, video, etc.) when others in the household do not require their use. New students are offered advice about how to organise their time in order to establish a suitable schedule for OU work. For example, *The Good Study Guide* is a set book for the foundation course in social sciences which was specially prepared to provide adult students with advice about studying part time in higher education (Northedge, 1990). Eventually, most students develop a pattern of working that is appropriate to their situation: it will also reflect their overall orientation to studying, as discussed in Chapter 2. The pattern of working might involve periods of intensive study in the evenings or during school hours, possibly while commuting to and from work or when everyone else in the house is asleep. Fitting in between 8 and 20 hours' study per week usually involves spending less time on some other activities like hobbies, entertaining, etc., and is accepted by students themselves who have to re-arrange their lives:

> It's a discipline I've imposed on myself – not much TV or light reading in the week. I count on doing two hours' study most evenings. But I try to keep one day at the weekend clear for entertaining and relaxation.
>
> I get up at 6 am and do an hour or so before the rest of the family appears.
>
> Sunday is my main study day. I need a long stretch of time when I'm writing an assignment. The family know not to disturb me.
>
> (Quoted in Open University, 1991b, pp. 12–13)

However, not all students manage to develop or maintain their ideal pattern for studying. Sometimes changes in students' circumstances disrupt established patterns (for example, a change of job, the birth of a child, etc.); sometimes the particular demands of a course require a major adjustment to ways of working (for example, the need to undertake practical computing activities); and some students just muddle through, never organising a regular study pattern.

This chapter examines the context of studying in distance education in terms of the physical location of study, the social environment in which it takes place and the impact of introducing home computing into these.

## Studying at Home

Usually distance education requires little in the way of special facilities in the home: scientific experiments can be designed to be undertaken in the kitchen, works of art (visual and musical) can be studied in the living room and the dwelling itself can be the subject of studies in design or energy consumption. The course materials sent to students include most of the resources needed. In addition, some materials are distributed to students by other means: the OU has always used television and radio broadcasts for teaching purposes but, while almost all students have had suitable reception equipment in their homes, audio-visual material has rarely formed an essential, compulsory course component. Increasingly over recent years, audio- and video-cassettes have been sent to students as part of multimedia teaching packages, but concern about students' access to such materials has remained an issue. Broadcasting may be almost universally available throughout the UK, but the OU now faces the problem of making television material available to students spread across Europe.

Getting course materials into the homes of students is an important consideration in distance education, but trying to ensure that the materials are used effectively can present even more problems. For example, a student's need to use the television set or video-recorder may be in competition with others in the house; an experiment may need to be undertaken over an extended period of time, possibly creating considerable inconvenience for the users of shared space and facilities. In addition, the use of media for educational purposes requires a more active approach by students than they would normally adopt when using those same media for recreation and entertainment. For example, there is evidence that the familiar style of TV documentaries and case studies can give rise to expectations that inhibit OU students' analysis and evaluation of 'real life' source material presented on television in terms of explanatory theories or frameworks discussed elsewhere in a course (Bates, 1983). This may necessitate the deployment of explicit teaching strategies that encourage students to engage actively with media materials in order to derive the desired educational outcomes.

There are some OU students for whom 'home' is not a permanent dwelling. Distance education makes it possible for people to study in less conventional settings, for example on board a ship, on a North Sea oil rig or in a long-stay prison. Distance education also provides learners with a great deal of flexibility in terms of where they study: individuals can move from place to place, taking their course work with them from one location to another. Although this flexibility of location is made possible by the use of printed teaching materials and audio-cassettes, other teaching media are less 'mobile' and can introduce problems. One example already mentioned is the difficulty of making television material available across international boundaries, given differences in the technical systems and standards that exist between countries. At a more parochial level, students taking courses which require the use of a video or a PC are constrained by equipment requirements that currently make it impossible to study in many locations, for example while commuting to work by train. In the longer term, the development of more portable technologies might ameliorate the situation.

Although studying with the OU primarily involves individual learners working at home, almost all courses offer opportunities for groups of students to meet together with one or more tutors. On a number of occasions throughout the study year tutorial sessions are arranged, usually at a local study centre in the evenings or at weekends. In addition, all students taking a foundation level course (and some other courses at higher levels) must attend a week-long residential school; these are normally held on the campuses of 'conventional' universities during the summer months. However, not all students choose to attend the sessions run by their tutor. For some the 'local' study centre may be a very long way from their home and transport may not be easy to arrange. Some find that the timing of sessions does not fit in with their work or domestic commitments. Others are put off by the physical surroundings of the study centre (usually located in colleges, schools, libraries or community centres), while some simply prefer to study alone without meeting other students.

In contrast, the study centres of some other distance-teaching universities fulfil different functions and are perceived rather differently by students. For example, in the Dutch Open Universiteit students can visit their nearest study centre at any time to seek advice about course choices, to use computing facilities, interactive videos, etc., as well as to attend group sessions with a tutor.

In Chapter 3 there was a description of ways in which OU students have gained practical experience of computing at study centres or at residential schools and a discussion of some of the problems involved in undertaking computing activities in such settings. The development of 'home computing' was seen as a means of overcoming some of these problems. We shall assess the extent to which home computing provided solutions and created new problems after examining more closely the nature of 'leisure' or 'spare' time activities in the domestic context and, indeed, the nature of that context.

## Household Activities and 'Leisure' Time

In recent decades Western societies have increasingly spent leisure time in the home rather than in the public sphere. The widespread access to television has probably been the single most important factor in this transformation of leisure, as regular visits to the cinema, sports venues and 'theatrical' locations have drastically declined. The trend towards increasing domestic leisure has been augmented by the more recent availability of home video-cassette recorders and home computers:

> This process, in which leisure time has increasingly been located in the home, as opposed to within the public sphere – on the street, or in the pub, or cinema – is one in which broadcasting itself has played a key role, by increasing the attractiveness of the home as a site for leisure.
>
> (Morley and Silverstone, 1990, p. 37)

However, within this broad overall trend there are considerable differences between social groups (at least in the UK) in terms of the scope of leisure-time activities and the locations in which they are undertaken:

> In a society where four households in ten still have no car, over half of unskilled workers and the unwaged have no holiday away from home, and attendances at the cinema and professional sports have dwindled, the home has become more than ever the necessary site of most leisure activities.
>
> (Golding and Murdoch, 1986, p. 72)

But even at the level of a household, recent developments have made possible greater fragmentation in the way that family members participate in domestic leisure activities. In 1990 almost all UK households (98 per cent) contained a television set and in nearly three-fifths of those households there was more than one set: about 12 per cent of homes with video equipment contain more than one such machine (Gunter and McLaughlin, 1992). Portable radios and personal stereos have become commonplace. As a result, many leisure activities are not collectively undertaken, but are individual, possibly private and in parallel with other members of the family.

During the 1980s there was an increase in the amount of part-time working (including home working) in the UK in response to a reduced demand for labour and an increase in the workforce. Many more women are employed on a part-time basis than men. However, outside working hours great differences exist between the activities undertaken by men and women and the amount of time spent on those activities. Men in full-time employment tend to have much more 'free' or leisure time per week than working women (both full time and part time), as they spend less time on essential domestic work - see Table 4.1.

For men in the UK, time spent in the home is primarily defined as leisure time, as distinct from the 'work' time of their employment outside the home; for women, home is defined as a sphere of work, whether or not they are also employed outside the home. Social relations within the household influence both the amount of time available for leisure activities and the pattern of attention and participation (i.e. uninterrupted commitment or fitted in when domestic responsibilities allow). Studies of family television viewing (for example, Morley, 1986) suggest that control over the choice of programme tends to be exercised by men, particularly when there is a remote-control device available, and video machines are usually operated by men and children.

There is also a tendency for many more men than women to engage in

Table 4.1 Time use in a typical week: by employment status and sex, GB, 1990–1 (hours)

| | Full-time employees | | Part-time employees | | |
| | Males | Females | (females) | Housewives | Retired |
|---|---|---|---|---|---|
| Weekly hours spent on: | | | | | |
| Employment and travel[1] | 48.3 | 42.6 | 20.9 | 0.3 | 0.7 |
| Essential activities[2] | 24.1 | 39.6 | 52.1 | 58.4 | 33.0 |
| Sleep[3] | 49.0 | 49.0 | 49.0 | 49.0 | 49.0 |
| Free time | 46.6 | 36.8 | 46.0 | 60.3 | 85.3 |
| Free time per weekday | 4.5 | 3.3 | 5.4 | 8.4 | 11.6 |
| Free time per weekend day | 12.1 | 10.3 | 9.5 | 9.3 | 13.6 |

[1] Travel to and from place of work.
[2] Essential domestic work and personal care, including essential shopping, child care, cooking, personal hygiene and appearance.
[3] An average of 7 hours sleep per night is assumed.
(*Source:* The Henley Centre for Forecasting.)

activities that are ostensibly technical, mechanical or electrical – for example, car maintenance, photography and the construction of electronic devices. Many of those pursuing these hobbies seem to derive at least as much interest and enjoyment from the process of undertaking the activity as from the outcomes of their efforts and skills. The activity is seen as an end in itself. In contrast, there is a tendency for the leisure-time activities undertaken by women to be related to outcomes, as means to an end.

How does part-time study fit within the overall pattern: is it seen as a leisure activity or not? It depends upon both the nature of the course content and the motivation of the learner: people may be studying the same course for very different reasons. In Chapter 2 the idea of an individual's 'orientation' to their studies was discussed. Some see their studies as clearly vocational; they seek enhancement or updating of the knowledge and skills required in their current occupation or they wish to prepare themselves for career advance, job change or a return to work. Students with such an orientation are unlikely to consider that their studies constitute a leisure activity. Others might be studying for personal or academic reasons that are almost totally unrelated to vocational interests. Such students might feel that their studies constitute a leisure activity. Then there are many others for whom studying is neither leisure nor non-leisure.

## Computers for Leisure in the Home

During the 1980s computer manufacturers expended a great deal of effort promoting computers as the multi-purpose device that no home could afford to be without. In the UK it was the arrival of the low-priced Sinclair machines and the BBC/Acorn models of the early 1980s that heralded the home-computer boom. Usually home computers were promoted as being particularly suitable for children: not only did they promise hours of fun and amusement by providing a wide range of games, but they also appeared to offer educational opportunities to complement the computing experience that schools were providing.

By the end of the decade between one-fifth and one-quarter of households in Britain contained a home computer (Office of Population Censuses and Surveys, 1991), although ownership was greater (over one-third) in households with children (Gunter and McLaughlin, 1992). But what are the reasons for wanting a computer in the home? Is the home computer a solution in search of a problem?

> Home computers are a triumph of latter-day capitalism. The product could be mass-produced, but there was no mass-market demand; so a mass-market demand was created . . . Often following nothing more than their own obsessions and fantasies, the entrepreneurs have managed to pick up our games and pastimes, our chores and anxieties, and sell them back to us in a brilliant new technology (expensive but affordable) – a technology so seductively advertised and promoted, by micromaniac friends as well as the so-glossy magazines that live off the advertising, that we might easily be persuaded that only has-beens and know-nothings could insist on carrying on with their lives in the old (cheap) fashion.
>
> (Rowntree, 1985, pp. 7–8)

This may seem rather cynical, but there is plenty of evidence to support the view that most home computers are used for little else than entertainment. Haddon's account (1988) of the development of home computers differentiates hobbyist machines, like the early Sinclair computers, from software players, like the Commodore VIC 20. The former were self-referential machines, without practical uses or benefits: 'You bought the machine for itself, to explore it, rather than for what it could do' (*ibid.* p. 28). The primary market for such machines was male – older children and young adults. Home computers that were capable of running a range of software were closer in conception not only to office computers but also to other domestic entertainment hardware, like record and cassette players. Most of the software that was available to run on these home computers was in the form of games, developed from arcade games and video games machines that were used in the home, again usually by young males. 'Serious' software was also available, providing adults with a justification for purchasing the machine, although for most (if not all) of the time the home computer was likely to be used for playing games.

In a survey of fourth- and fifth-year secondary-school pupils (Culley, 1986), 39 per cent reported that there was a computer in their home (56 per cent of boys but only 22 per cent of girls). Most of those boys (85 per cent) said that the computer had been bought for them or for another male member of the family – only 14 per cent of the girls reported that the computer had been acquired for them or for a female member of the family. Among younger pupils (ages 11, 12 and 13) the pattern was very similar: computers were in the homes of 37 per cent of children surveyed (50 per cent of the boys, but only 26 per cent of girls). While parents are keen for their children to learn about using computers, it seems that the actual activities undertaken with a home computer are almost solely for entertainment: 'In the vast majority of cases pupils reported that home computers were used for playing games. Less than 5 per cent of pupils referred to additional uses such as domestic accounts or some form of work-related activity such as record keeping' (*ibid*. p. 36).

Similar studies of computer use among teenage children (Fife-Schaw *et al.*, 1986; Mohamamedali, Messer and Fletcher, 1987) report that over 50 per cent of the schoolchildren in their samples had access to a computer at home and that the most popular use of the machine is for playing games, although the use of educational software and programming were also reported.

In order to make machines available at relatively low prices, the home computers marketed in the UK in the early 1980s usually needed to be connected to other domestic electronic equipment: a television set to act as a monitor and a cassette-recorder for storing and loading software. As a result, these machines were perceived by many as being 'toys' rather than real microcomputers of the kind that were increasingly being used in commerce and industry.

Although there remains a market for home computers, the boom years in terms of sales came to an end in the mid- to late 1980s. Figure 4.1 shows that the ownership of home computers has increased very little since 1987, while over the same period there has been a steady growth in the number of households with a video-recorder.

The lack of standardisation has been partly to blame; sometimes successive models from a single manufacturer were incompatible. People who were more than 'hobbyists' or 'enthusiasts' wanted a machine (or at least a standard) that would not become obsolete too quickly and for which there existed a wide range of software and support services. Also, the distinction between 'home' and 'business' computers became blurred in the mid-1980s

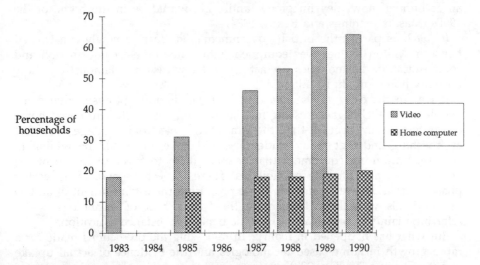

Figure 4.1   Households in Great Britain with video and home computer, 1983–90 (Source: *OPCS Monitor*, SS 91/1, Office of Population, Censuses and Surveys)

by the arrival of fairly sophisticated, but relatively cheap, machines that were compatible with the IBM PC. These were aimed at small businesses and home-based professionals and provided access to existing applications packages developed for professional or semi-professional users – for example, for text processing, databases and spreadsheets. As this sector of the computer market continues to develop, a greater diversity of software is likely to become available, with some intended primarily for home use and for entertainment.

## Whatever Happened to the 'Electronic Cottage'?

For the last twenty years or more, vociferous enthusiasts of computers and information technology (IT) have been predicting revolutionary changes in social arrangements brought about by the advances in microelectronics and telecommunications. These new technologies, it was claimed, would play a decentralising role in society by removing the necessity for people to move physically to their workplace or to commercial and shopping centres. Among others, Alvin Toffler (1980) offered a view of the future in which the home became the centre of society, a return to cottage industry on a new, higher, electronic basis. In the 'electronic cottage' not only paid work but also leisure and service consumption were mediated through new technologies. In the USA several large companies encouraged home working with computers ('teleworking' or 'telecommuting') and there were predictions that such activities would increase dramatically as the year 2000 approached. A number of prototype 'homes of the future' were built to demonstrate the electronic cottage idea, making possible not only home working but also the consumption of home-based services. For example, the Xanadu House (located near Orlando in Florida) inspired technological futurists to publish an account of how they imagined family life would be in the home of the 1990s (Mason, Jennings and Evans, 1984).

In 1982, as part of the British government's 'IT Year', a newly constructed house in Milton Keynes was equipped with state-of-the-art information and communication technologies to act as a show-case to demonstrate how ordinary homes might be adapted.

It was in the early 1980s, at a time of technological optimism, that some people at the OU began pressing for the introduction of student based home computing. They argued that the era of the electronic cottage was fast approaching and that many students would have, or would be willing to acquire, computing equipment that enabled them to take advantage of the new services and lifestyle possibilities. There are echoes here of an earlier phase of technological optimism: those proposing the establishment of an OU in the 1960s were keen to harness the 'white heat of technology' (then referring mainly to broadcasting) for the benefit of distance education.

But what has happened in reality? In reviewing the predictions made for a rapid growth in home-based technologies and the evidence of actual uptake to date, Forester (1988, p. 228) suggests that

Most writers on the subject tend to point up the trend to home-working and the consumption of home-based services (generalizing from a few well known examples); review the existing technology; state the vast potential for increased home activity; and then conclude with a technologically determinist prediction for future growth which entirely glosses over the many problems encountered by the actual participants.

Home working that involves the use of IT has not significantly increased for a number of reasons. First, not many forms of employment suit home working. Traditionally, paid work undertaken in the home has involved unskilled or semi-skilled assembly jobs, for example, garment manufacture or the assembly of cheap goods. Home workers of this kind are mainly female, unskilled and poorly paid. IT is unlikely to have much impact on this type of employment. The form of home working most likely to be made feasible by developments in IT is primarily associated with middle-class or professional occupations. These include jobs that involve information handling for clerical, administrative or management purposes or professional activities involving writing and design. Although the growth in such full-time home working has been modest, there appears to have been a significant rise in the number of people who are able to undertake some of their work from home using equipment supplied by their employers. Many companies, however, would be reluctant to sanction home working because it would entail a loss of their control over employees' time and the tasks they perform: management usually likes people to be at their desks throughout the day undertaking well regulated activities. What growth there has been in 'professional' home working may be related to the increase in self-employment and home-based consultancy work. In such cases, economic changes are likely to have been more influential than IT developments.

A second reason for the limited growth is that not many homes are suitable for home working with IT. Using a computer at home entails many practical problems in terms of the space required and arrangements that allow work to proceed without too much disruption (both to the home worker and any other people in the home). This implies the need for accommodation that is above average in size. But Forester (*ibid.*) feels that, above all, the technological determinists have totally neglected the psychological adjustment necessary to undertake home working. Many of those who have tried home working felt lonely and isolated, missing the social contacts provided at the workplace and some felt that they did not possess the self-management skills necessary to organise their lives efficiently: for example, motivation and discipline, effective time management and coping with stress. In addition, they had problems in segregating 'work' from 'home' life, experiencing tensions in relations with their family and spouse and with friends and neighbours. It seems clear that social change does not automatically follow technological change.

Life in the electronic cottage was also predicted to involve considerable use of IT for activities such as shopping, banking and information services. However, experiments in these fields have had only a small measure of success, partly due to the limited services that can be offered and their

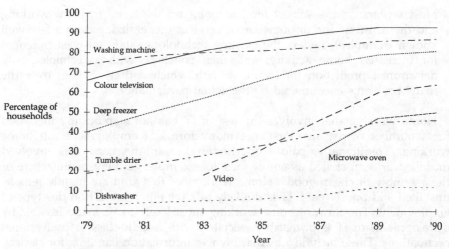

Figure 4.2 Domestic technology in households in Great Britain, 1979–90 (Source: *OPCS Monitor*, SS 91/1, Office of Population Censuses and Surveys)

inability to provide the social contacts. Most people simply don't want to remain at home unless they have no alternative.

Certain domestic technologies have become increasingly widespread in recent years. Figure 4.2 shows that a rising proportion of households in Great Britain are acquiring an expanding range of domestic technologies. In 1990 nearly all households had one or more television sets; and over 80 per cent contained a telephone, a washing machine and a deep freezer.

Gershuny (1978) argued that considerable social change could result from the transfer of technology into the home, with washing machines, dishwashers, freezers, food processors, microwave ovens, VCRs and the wide range of electrical equipment designed for 'do-it-yourself' in the home and garden providing a substitute for services otherwise obtained from launderettes, restaurants, cinemas, decorators and gardeners. However, at the level of the individual household, the effects of these technologies on social relations can be very different:

> It is important to distinguish between domestic technology, the so-called labour-saving devices, and entertainment technology. The home computer . . . comes within the latter category. What entertainment technologies demand of their user is *time*, this is particularly true of the home computer which requires an initial mastery of skill before it is to be of any use at all . . . Women have a lot less time for play in the home than men, and when they do they would rather spend it on what they see as 'productive' activities like knitting, sewing, baking and gardening.
>
> (Gray, 1988, p. 47)

The term 'home informatics' has been used to describe applications of IT products for use in the home environment. It includes not only home computers but also consumer electronics and 'smart' household equipment. Like Gershuny, Miles (1988a) suggests that home informatics have the potential to give rise to massive social change, but there is little evidence that it is really likely to revolutionise the lifestyles of the majority (Forester, 1988). Again, the technological determinists have failed to take account of social factors at play in families and households. However, Miles has acknowledged (1988b, p. 364) that home informatics could reinforce social inequalities when used to provide new forms of access to public services, such as education and preventative medicine: 'Privileged social groups could exercise more control over their circumstances by such means, and would be in a position to reproduce class structures by passing on advantages to their children. Apart from purely financial advantages, inequalities in educational performance and physical health might be exacerbated.'

Silverstone (1991) argues that information and communication technologies are unlikely to bring about dramatic changes to the existing social relationships in the home. Households constitute complex and powerful social and cultural environments capable of profoundly influencing the ways in which new technologies are introduced, used and possibly discarded. Any machine is capable of being used in a variety of different ways depending upon the social setting:

> There is very little evidence . . . of families being dramatically affected or disturbed by a new machine except perhaps in the brief period of its novelty: gender roles remain unchanged; the household division of labour is rarely disturbed; the sociability or unsociability of individuals rarely enhanced or compromised for long; and the arrival of the VCR, satellite or cable is more likely to reinforce the established patterns of social interaction than impose new ones.
>
> (*Ibid.* p. 11)

## Computers in the Homes of OU Students

Well before the introduction of the Home Computing Policy, the first indication of the level of access to a home computer among OU students came from a survey conducted at the end of 1982 (Grundin, 1983). It suggested that about 15 per cent of undergraduate students had some kind of computer at home, although many of those machines would not have been suitable for educational purposes (the Sinclair ZX80 and ZX81 models accounted for half of this total). A survey conducted at the end of 1986 (Kirkwood, 1988) asked students about their access to computing equipment, using a definition of the term 'home computer' intended to exclude low-powered 'games' machines. It revealed that among undergraduate students in all faculties of the OU, one-third had access of some kind to a computer that could be used for study purposes: over 18 per cent at home, the remainder at their place of work or in some other location.

It was clear that many students used computers for more than just entertainment in the home. The 1986 survey indicated that over one-third of students with access to computing equipment (at home or elsewhere) had already used it for their OU studies, with only some of the uses being *required* or *prescribed* by the University. Some courses, for example those intended primarily for school teachers, provided software that was sent as part of the course materials for students to run on suitable equipment. A further selection of courses included structured practical activities for students (to gain programming experience or to use computer-assisted learning – CAL – or other software packages) using the ACS mainframe computers. Access to the mainframes was normally achieved through the networked terminals located in OU study centres; however, students with suitable equipment were able to log on to the system using the public telephone service via a modem. However, in addition to these prescribed uses of computers a large proportion of students had used general-purpose software to support their studies in one way or another, particularly for wordprocessing, but also spreadsheet, database and graphics software packages.

As we saw in Chapter 3, many students had, over the years, experienced difficulties in gaining access to and using the University's networked terminals located in study centres throughout the country. Having access to suitable computing equipment in the home is far more convenient than having to make arrangements to use a computer located somewhere else. However, if students were to experience problems in making use of the equipment at times that are most appropriate for their OU studies, home access would be far less convenient than that afforded to those studying full time in higher education. Obviously, an ideal situation would be achieved if the computer were set up permanently in a quiet, private location like a study or a spare bedroom, but it is easy to envisage situations that are far from ideal. For example, the equipment might have to be assembled for use when needed for studying and packed away again afterwards. It might be set up in a 'public' part of the house, such as a dining or living room, where it can cause inconvenience to other members of the household.

However, the *quality* of access to home-computing facilities was found to be reasonably good among the general student body: in the 1986 study, nearly 60 per cent of those with a home computer had the equipment permanently set up, with fewer than a quarter having to set it up when needed. More than twice as many students used their computer in a private area, like a study, than did so in a 'public' part of the house. Overall, male students enjoyed a better quality of access than did female students in terms of these locational aspects.

The introduction of the OU's Home Computing Policy in 1988 meant that students enrolling for specified courses were required to arrange good access to a personal computer (PC), and for the vast majority that meant in their home. The first year of the policy saw about 4,500 students taking one of the three courses and, with the addition of two more courses in each year to 1992, the number of undergraduate students affected has grown to about 17,000. However, there remains considerable use of computers located in the home or at the workplace by students taking other courses that do not require 'home computing'. A survey of OU undergraduate students' access to computers was undertaken at the end of 1988 (Kirkwood, 1990). This replicated the 1986 study, but specifically excluded those students taking 'home computing' courses. Among the general student population, home access to equipment had risen to over 23 per cent (from 18 per cent in 1986), with a further 14 per cent having access at work or in some other location. Almost half (48 per cent) of those with access to a computer had used it in some way for their OU studies.

## From Home Computers to PCs

The University's policy made students on specified courses responsible for arranging access to an IBM-compatible PC. Research undertaken with those students has provided valuable information about the social impact of a PC in the home. Among the students taking the first three 'home computing' courses in 1988, most (over 85 per cent) of those with equipment at home had their PC set up permanently, with more than three-quarters having the equipment located in a 'private' area used for studying (Kirkwood and Kirkup, 1989). This pattern has changed little in subsequent years. However, those without a permanent location for their equipment can be seriously inconvenienced, as illustrated by this comment from one student: 'Moved from confined space close to phone point downstairs to bedroom and finally to dining room because working on the table top was more convenient than working on bedroom units' (Kirkwood and Dale, 1989, p.12).

Another important aspect of the *quality* of home access is the possible inconvenience caused to other members of the household when operating the computer. Use of computing equipment, particularly a printer, can generate noise that may disturb other people in the house. When in use the equipment may also monopolise space or facilities that others in the house might want to use, for example a dining table. (This is likely to cause greater concern where equipment is not set up permanently in a private location.) But it is also possible for other members of the household to inconvenience the student while using the computer. While studying, home-based students need peace and quiet and a minimum of distractions: this is just as necessary while working on a practical computing activity as when reading a book or writing an essay.

In 1988, over half of the students using a PC at home (57 per cent) felt that it caused no inconvenience to others. About one-eighth of students with home access (14 per cent) were concerned about the noise generated disturbing others, for example, 'set up in son's bedroom . . . late night usage can disturb him' and 'equipment in bedroom – can't work while spouse sleeps!' (Kirkwood and Kirkup, 1989, p. 23). A similar proportion of students were aware that the computing equipment monopolised space or other facilities that others may have wanted to use, while almost as many were concerned that their need for quiet, undisturbed use of the PC could inconvenience others.

Only one of the undergraduate 'home computing' courses involves obligatory computer-mediated communication (CMC). Students taking *An introduction to information technology* are required to use a modem and the domestic telephone system to link their PC with a mainframe computer at the OU to effect communications. Although the University loans a modem to each student taking this course, the need to connect with the telephone system has a number of implications. Until quite recently all domestic telephones in the UK were wired into a fixed telephone point. Newer installations provided homes with one or more sockets into which telephone equipment can be plugged. Students using a modem for communications purposes require a conveniently located plug-in telephone point.

In 1988 nearly half of the students taking *An introduction to information technology* needed to convert or extend their existing telephone point (Kirkwood and Kirkup, 1989). Although some needed simply to convert their telephone point to the plug-in type, about one-third of students on the course needed to install a new extension point close to the location of their PC in order to avoid the dangers of trailing long connecting leads from one room to another. Students had to bear the cost of these alterations to their telephone system as well as the call charges when engaged in communications.

## Use of the PC as a Household Resource

Part of the rationale for the Department of Trade and Industry granting the OU £2.25 million towards the initial costs of introducing the Home Computing Policy was the belief that this innovation would help spread computer literacy among the population, beyond just the OU's student body. Some students already had a PC they could use for their OU course work and it is highly likely that they were using that equipment for other purposes. However, very many students who had never previously owned a computer acquired a PC because of the requirement for the course(s) they were studying. Of the 4,500 students who took home-computing courses in the first year (1988), almost two-thirds purchased or hired a PC in order to undertake their course work. About 45 per cent of those who had acquired a PC for their course had not previously had home access to computing equipment (Kirkwood and Kirkup, 1989). With the inclusion of the technology foundation course in the Home Computing Policy from 1989, there has been an annual intake of very many students new to computing. So, has the arrival of a PC in the homes of students new to computing actually led to wider use of the equipment? Our surveys suggest that the spread of use has not been as extensive as expected.

At the time they registered for their first course with a compulsory practical computing component, many students felt that a PC in the home could be used for a range of activities other than course work and that it would be a resource for other family members to use. The anticipated wider use might also provide additional justification for acquiring a PC. In the first year of 'home computing' almost half (47 per cent) of female students indicated that the equipment they acquired was also intended for use by their spouse or partner; almost one-third of male students (32 per cent) responded similarly. Overall, 22 per cent of students felt that the PC would be used by their children. However, half of those who did not previously have a PC indicated that there was no intention that the equipment would be used by others; a larger proportion of men than women responded in this way (53 per cent compared with 39 per cent). Many of these students had hired a PC from the University's pool of machines for the duration of the study year and were likely to perceive the equipment as course specific rather than as a general-purpose tool. A very similar pattern of anticipated wider use of the PC was found in subsequent years for other courses (Kirkup, 1989; Jones and Singer, 1990; Dale and Kirkup, 1991).

The extent to which the PC was actually used by others was less than expected, although the equipment used by female students was more likely to be considered a family resource than that used by male students. Children used the PC much less than many students had anticipated, for school work or for entertainment, probably because the computer and the software are not of the kinds used most frequently in schools. Male students were more likely to use the PC for a variety of non-course-related purposes, for non-OU work and for entertainment. The partners of women are much more likely to use the PC than are the partners of men. However, it would seem that the longer the machine remains in the household, the more likely it is that other uses will become established as a wider range of software is acquired (from the OU or from elsewhere).

In a number of surveys (Kirkwood and Kirkup, 1989) students who had purchased or hired a PC in order to take one or more of the OU's home-computing courses were asked who had been consulted about the decision to acquire suitable equipment. Men were more likely to have made a decision about the financial outlay entirely on their own than were women (56 per cent of men compared with 39 per cent of women). Half of the female students involved their spouse or partner in the financial decision-making, compared with one-third of male students. When it came to deciding which particular equipment to acquire, women were much more likely than men to have discussed the matter with their spouse or partner, with children or with others in the household. The gender differences revealed here, in subsequent surveys and in interviews (e.g. Baines, 1991) reflect not only differences in levels of disposable income available to men and women but also different patterns of control and consultation over major items of expenditure in the household.

## Use of Computing Equipment Elsewhere than at Home

Up to about 15 per cent of students taking courses with an obligatory practical computing component start the study year with the intention of using a PC at their place of employment. Students able to arrange access in this manner avoid having to make the financial commitment of acquiring their own PC – an obvious advantage not only to those who are new to home computing but also to those whose existing equipment is not IBM compatible. However, many have found that the quality of such access was not as good as they had anticipated, making it difficult for them to use the equipment to optimum effect in their studies. For some, the location of suitable computing equipment proved to be inconvenient, while for others the times at which they could gain access or the length of time they could spend at the computer created difficulties. Very often the practical activities they had to complete for their course could not easily be scheduled to suit the other demands of their work situation. When exclusive use of a computer at work could be arranged, considerable advance planning and organisation might be necessary to ensure that all the required study materials were to hand for the practical work session (Morgan, 1989). It is not always easy to estimate the amount of time required to undertake some of the activities.

The problems that are encountered in trying to use a work-based PC for course work have resulted in many students acquiring their own equipment either part way through the study year or before commencing a second course with a practical computing component. Some students felt quite strongly that the OU had not provided sufficiently clear advice in advance about the nature and extent of computer usage; access to equipment elsewhere than at home was unlikely to prove satisfactory.

## Connections – Interactions between Learners

The main focus in this chapter has been the context of home-based learning and the impact of introducing a PC into the social and physical environment in which distance education takes place. It seems somewhat paradoxical that the advent of home computing enhances the individualised and isolating nature of distance learning, by reducing the need for learners to attend study centres or residential schools in order to use shared computing facilities, while it also provides the potential for individual students to communicate and interact with a very large and geographically dispersed academic community. The use of CMC in the OU course *An introduction to information technology* was discussed in Chapters 2 and 3. Evaluation studies (for example, Mason, 1989 and 1991) indicate that CMC can provide learners with not only a mutual support mechanism but also a learning environment that is interactive and non-didactic. It can help overcome feelings of isolation which can affect all distance learners, but particularly housebound and disabled students who may otherwise be unable to benefit from social and educational interactions.

## Conclusions

When the requirement for home-based student computing was introduced for specified OU courses, it was an innovation that was influenced by a diverse range of factors and circumstances. Home computing using PCs may have provided a technical solution to certain academic problems, but its implementation responded to and had consequences for changes in the domestic environment of students. This chapter has considered some of the economic, social and technological circumstances that accompanied the introduction of home-based computing. It has also reported and discussed the social and physical impact on students' households of the arrival of a PC, although a computer (often suitable only for leisure purposes) was already a familiar piece of equipment in some students' homes.

An important consequence of developments in domestic and information technologies has been the differing effects upon men and women and between various social groups. These differences have been reflected in the impact of home-based computing upon OU students and their social and physical environments. The issue of equal opportunities for student computing at the OU is considered in greater depth in the following chapter.

# 5

# Issues of Access and Equal Opportunities

## Openness to People, Methods and Ideas

In Chapter 3 we traced the pressures on the Open University (OU) to expand practical computing for students and discussed the reasons for the choice of a policy which relies on student-owned personal computers (PCs). The development of PCs and their use in education, although dramatic, was not the only major issue of concern to educators in the 1980s. Consciousness about the discrimination suffered by minority groups, and their lack of participation in post-school education and training, coupled with a strengthening of legislation on such equal-rights issues as sex discrimination, meant that in the UK (and other European countries) higher education institutions began to examine their access strategies, curriculum and teaching methods. The integration of student-owned PCs as a compulsory component of some courses has the power to confound access and equal opportunities objectives as well as facilitate them. This chapter looks at ways in which it has done both.

The OU's commitment to equality of opportunity in education dates from its Charter granted in 1969. Expanding opportunity through open access was the explicit reason for creating the OU. This commitment was summarised by Lord Crowther, the first Chancellor of the OU, in his inaugural address in 1969: 'We are open, first, as to people . . . we are open as to places. . . . We are open as to methods . . . We are open, finally, to ideas' (quoted in Woodley, 1981, p. 3).

Some educators and politicians of that time credited the OU with a radical social objective, which it was already being criticised for not achieving by the early 1970s:

> The Open University was founded in this country to mitigate social inequality. It is being taken up abroad for the same reasons. Here, it can be seen to have failed . . . Of course if the Open University were to succeed in educating the uneducated, either here or abroad, it would be all set to save the world; but it won't succeed.
>
> (Burgess, 1972, p. 178)

Burgess's statement was not based on student outcomes – the University had not been teaching for long enough to measure success by such means. He felt that the OU could never succeed in its more radical objectives *because* it was a university, with formal academic standards, and systematised knowledge. This forced it to operate a 'top down' model of education which transmitted and promoted the values of a social and educational élite. A university, he argued, could produce social mobility for some, but not change a system of inequality.

Others, although critical of the OU, felt that if one was realistic about what education could contribute to social change then the OU was having some success:

> That while we have to recognise the economic basis of social class and inequality, education is by no means an impotent force. Institutions such as the Open University serve to promote social mobility: but more importantly, point away from a selective towards a mass system of education. In this way education can provide people with the self awareness which will enable them to challenge the basis of the economic system which produces inequality and deprivation.
>
> (Woolfe, 1977, p. 82)

Initial surveys of students in the 1970s (McIntosh, with Calder and Swift, 1976) showed that the OU was recruiting a high proportion of people who fell into 'middle-class' social categories and who were likely to have engaged in education after the age of 16. However, if their parents' social class was an indicator, then the OU recruited more students from 'working-class' backgrounds (52 per cent) than did traditional UK universities at that time (29 per cent) (Woolfe, 1977). But, it could be argued, the University was supporting those who were *already* upwardly socially mobile by providing the chance to acquire an educational qualification.

It was also known that students with no, or low, prior educational qualifications were not only less likely to apply to the University but were also more likely to withdraw or fail if they entered (Woodley, 1981). McIntosh (1975, p. 174) coined the concept of the 'revolving door':

> If large numbers of students who enter an 'open' door discover that it is in reality a 'revolving' door and all that they are doing is entering it in order to be carried round and out again, then both the educational institution *and* society could be said to have erred.

An open-access system, i.e. requiring no formal entry requirements, subtly shifts the blame for failure on to the individual student, and an open-access system must take more responsibility than a selective system for supporting all students. The OU always recognised that open access alone was not enough – student retention and satisfaction were equally important. Foundation courses were designed as what we would recognise now to be 'positive action' initiatives, to help students acquire the kinds of skills and background knowledge they needed to succeed at undergraduate level. But apart from recognising the special needs of students with disabilities, before the late 1980s no other particular groups in the student population were supported in any special way.

The other aspect of the 'openness' of the OU, and one which was seen to be potentially very radical in the 1970s, was determined by the technology of the delivery systems used by the University: the very public systems of broadcast radio and television, to which any member of the public could tune in, and the presentation in published texts of academics' ideas and teaching techniques. Previously the content of higher education was very private; although academics authored books for public consumption, what they said in their tutorials and lectures remained accessible only to those selected in the first place to attend. This was part of the concept of academic freedom and, it could be argued, it was a barrier to the development of professional teaching skills amongst university academics: 'The struggle to present material for the Open University is an extraordinary attempt to make explicit the assumptions and processes of academic teaching. The Open University is doing what all university teachers should do but in fact do rarely' (Burgess, 1972, p. 178). The fact that teachers in many universities used OU course materials, unofficially, to help them teach reflected the recognised quality of the materials.

But the systems which in theory made the construction and transmission of knowledge visible and 'open' also, it was argued, made them rigid and 'closed'. This contradiction between technology as a liberating, flexible influence, and technology as an oppressive and highly structuring force is present in most debates about the influence of information technology (IT), and it is a key theme in this book. However, the debate raged around other forms of technology in education and pre-dated computers. Because a course was produced with an estimated life of five years (in the 1990s this has stretched to eight) the course materials, once they were produced, could not be flexible to criticism, or to students' needs, unlike (in theory at least) a tutor working face-to-face with a group of students (Woolfe and Murgatroyd, 1979). The OU seems to have been so successful in making public the content of higher education that the radical nature of this venture is no longer obvious. There is, however, now more debate about what has come to be called an 'industrial' model of education exemplified by the large-scale, technical systems by which the OU teaches. The issue of equal opportunity in a mass-education system in the 1990s is seen as being about how 'difference' is recognised and validated, and how to enable more negotiation to take place with the individual student over the content, level and style of their learning.

## An Equal Opportunities Policy

In 1989 a University-wide Equal Opportunities Team was set up to review policy and practices in employment, student access and the curriculum with respect to equal opportunities. Data on students in the 1980s suggested that the University was doing an excellent job in recruiting and supporting students with disabilities, but, although women were 48 per cent of the undergraduate body, they were under-represented in maths, science and technology subjects. There had been no systematic data collection about ethnic origin, but from sample surveys it seemed that there were significant ethnic communities from which the University was not recruiting whilst polytechnics were. The University was better at recruiting from working-class occupational groups than traditional universities – but not much. A pattern emerged from a geographical survey of one region of England which was likely to apply nationally: 'Recruitment is least successful in areas characterised by high levels of council housing, or high levels of working-class owner-occupation, unemployment above the national average and the presence of significant communities of Asian or Afro-caribbean households' (West, 1989, quoted in Open University, 1990, p. 24).

A new and extensive policy statement was developed with the following aim and objective:

> to create the conditions whereby students and staff are treated solely on the basis of their merits, abilities and potential, regardless of gender, colour, ethnic or national origin, age, socio-economic background, disability, religious or political beliefs, family circumstances, sexual orientation or other irrelevant distinction.

> The declared objective is a University which is truly open to all sections of the community, and in whose activities all individuals, whether staff or students, are encouraged to participate fully and equally.
>
> (Open University, 1991b, p. 1)

These are followed by five principles, the most important one for our discussion being that:

> Notwithstanding its significant contribution to the widening of educational opportunity, the University acknowledges that, as a community, it still reflects patterns of inequality that are widespread in society at large. It is therefore determined through programmes of legally acceptable positive action to increase the level of participation as students, staff and clients of those groups that are currently under-represented.
>
> (*Ibid*. p. 1)

The extent to which computers can hinder or help in attaining this objective was the focus of heated internal debate, and at least one of the authors of this book felt very pessimistic at the time:

> Many distance education institutions, like the UK Open University, were set up with the notion that they were improving equality of educational opportunity for adults, through providing teaching to those who – for a variety of reasons, including geographical location or educational level – could not study at a traditional institution of higher or further education; and newer developments in open learning are a continuation of some of these early principles. However there is a need for reflection about what we are achieving. For example, Harris (1988) argues that many of us have got ourselves into a position where there is a disjuncture between the theory of what we are doing (and the rhetoric that goes with it) and our practice . . . Yet at the same time, the development of policy and practice in the new information technologies races ahead at the OU. It could be argued that, at least at the moment, distance education is being technology driven, rather than being driven by liberal educational principles on which it was founded.
>
> (Kirkup, 1989a, p. 7)

## Computers: Barriers to Access or Aids to it?

The requirement to have, and use, a computer at home is a potential barrier to student access for two main reasons. First, as was discussed in the previous chapter, computer ownership is not evenly distributed in society. Low-income families and single-parent families are less likely to own a variety of consumer electronics, including an IBM-compatible PC. Even within families, men and boys are more likely to have access than women and girls. Second, there is not only the question of access to the machine but also the business of using it. Unfortunately, for some students, we know that computers are associated with mathematics, and we also know that many people avoid mathematics. For some students who have not used a computer, therefore, there is an additional fear to be overcome, and additional skills to learn. Paradoxically, computers can also be helpful in just these access problems. For example, statistical analysis packages can reduce the amount of grappling with mathematics. Another example is the computer-assisted learning (CAL) numeracy programs for the technology foundation course which were described in Chapter 3. However, none of these can be used unless the student has reasonably easy access to the machine and once having access to the physical machine, can use the software he or she wants with reasonable ease.

The University's student computing provision prior to 1988 has been discussed at some length. The alternatives that a course could include were: use of a terminal linked to the mainframe at a study centre; use of a computer (which could be a terminal linked to the mainframe or a micro) at residential or day schools; use of small microcomputers classed as home experiment kits (HEKs) and loaned to students as part of the course; and, for some non-undergraduate courses, use of the student's own machine or a work machine (e.g. in the 'Micros in Schools' project). *These were not alternative options available to a student.* For example, if a course was designed so that all practical computing happened through terminal activities at study centres (which was the most popular option for all course designers) then this was the *only* way a student could do those activities. This kind of access was known to be problematic.

Surveys of OU students during the 1980s revealed that over a third of undergraduate students not studying computing courses had access of some kind to a PC suitable for OU study. By this was meant 'a reasonably sophisticated microcomputer-based system, which can be realistically used for home study purposes' (Kirkwood, 1990, p. 5). This is a significant proportion of the student body, but it must be remembered that these PCs included many which did not fit the Home Computing Policy specification. Less than a quarter of the sample (23.3 per cent) had a PC *in their own home.*

To recap from Chapter 4. A variety of OU surveys showed that men were more likely than women to have access to computing equipment at any location, with 43.4 per cent of male students having access compared with only 31 per cent of female students; men were also in a better position with respect to access in their homes, with 25.8 per cent having access compared with 20.5 per cent of women; differences were also found between different age groups with older students (aged 55 and over) being much less likely than their younger colleagues to have access; and between regions of the country, with students in rural areas of Scotland and Wales being less likely to have access than those in south east England. Not surprisingly, students taking courses mainly in mathematics or technology were more likely to have access than students in other disciplines.

In the first year of the policy a pool of rental machines was established. It was estimated that 40 per cent of students would want to rent, and this was, in fact, nearly correct. The pool was set up with 4,241 complete sets of equipment funded mainly by the UK government's Department of Trade and Industry and included a much smaller contribution for disadvantaged students from the Department of Education and Science. When the technology foundation course entered the policy in the second year, priority was given to foundation-year students. The pool was seen as a way of alleviating students' costs for early home-computing courses. As the ownership of computers grew, and the number of courses using a student-owned PC grew, it was expected that a bigger proportion of students would be willing to purchase machines. The idea was that the rental pool would eventually not be necessary. By 1992 the rental pool had been significantly restricted and is now only available to students on the technology foundation course and students with special disadvantage. It is unlikely that the OU will ever receive enough funds to re-establish the pool with new PCs, so as the present ones come to the end of their life, the pool will shrink accordingly. The future is one where, apart from a very small number of specially disadvantaged students, all others who need computer access will be expected to provide their own. This means that the issue of access to computers will be more stark in the future than it is at present.

The two major questions raised by the interaction of a policy to promote equal opportunities with a policy to promote student-owned PCs are as follows:

1. Does the demand for access to a PC create an extra barrier in the way of student access and retention, or does it provide new facilities which help overcome previous educational barriers?
2. Does the incorporation of PCs as tools for distance study open up an industrialised system and make it more flexible and responsive, or produce more 'distance' and require more central control?

In the rest of this chapter we look in detail at the first question through a discussion of categories of students who have been recognised as suffering from educational disadvantage. We address the second question briefly as an unresolved philosophical discussion, but an interesting one at that. We begin with a group of people for whom computers have been identified for many years as a technical aid to overcome disadvantage, and an area where the OU holds a distinguished international research reputation.

## Students with Disabilities

The University's equal opportunities report made the well-founded assertion that 'the OU has claimed for itself a near monopoly of higher education provision for the adult disabled population in the UK' (Open University, 1990, p. 35). From its inception the University acknowledged a special responsibility to the disabled in the population. A 1975 OU policy statement on students with disabilities made a number of recommendations about action; the following have special reference to computers:

- To give special consideration in its admissions policy to disabled students.
- To take all possible practical steps to enable full participation to disabled students in all aspects of University life.
- To treat disabled students as equal members of the University for whatever programme of study they may be registered and to make special provisions only to enable participation (so far as it is practicable) on equal terms with other students.
- To pay attention as part of the University's institutional research programme to the educational needs of disabled people, both because of the University's involvement and as a contribution to knowledge in this specialised area of education.

(Quoted in Taylor, Vincent and Child, 1992, p. 49)

In 1990 OU undergraduate students with disabilities numbered almost 3,000 and made up 4.1 per cent of the total undergraduate population. Comparison with the numbers of students with disabilities in other educational institutions demonstrates the special level of commitment of the OU. A survey by the National Bureau for Handicapped Students quotes polytechnic figures as 0.12 per cent, and in all higher education institutions in the UK (excluding the OU) 0.19 per cent. The OU's population with disabilities has increased by 65 per cent between 1978 and 1988, while that in other institutions has remained largely the same.

Table 5.1 shows that the range of disability amongst OU students is wide, and a number of students suffer from more than one disability. The picture is also complicated by the fact that students with disabilities are more likely to register for courses in some subjects rather than others. In 1990, 33 per cent of undergraduates with disabilities had registered for courses in the arts faculty and 27 per cent in social science but the numbers in maths, science and technology (where most of the 'home computing' courses are located) were much lower: 12.2 per cent, 12 per cent and 8.9 per cent respectively. If students with disabilities in these faculties are seen as a percentage of the total number of students registered for courses then students with disabilities are 6 per cent of students on courses in arts, 5.6 per cent in social science, 3.5 per cent in science, 2.6 per cent in maths and 1.9 per cent in technology.

Home-computing courses have not been completely unpopular with these students, and although they remain a small proportion of the total population on these courses, students with disability comprise a large body

Table 5.1 Causes of disability among OU undergraduates

| Cause of disability | Number of students |
|---|---|
| Arthritis | 479 |
| Visual impairment | 306 |
| Hearing impairment | 314 |
| Cardiac condition | 258 |
| Polio/spinal injury | 323 |
| Neurological disorders | 245 |
| Cerebral palsy | 32 |
| Asthma, bronchitis | 104 |
| Diabetes | 107 |
| Phobia/mental illness | 325 |
| Kidney/blood disease | 210 |
| Epilepsy | 116 |
| Muscular dystrophy/atrophy | 34 |
| Stroke/brain disorder | 164 |
| Dyslexia | 133 |
| Muscular/joint/skin | 338 |
| Other disability | 213 |
| *Total* | 2,946 |

*Note*
Up to two causes of disability can be noted on a student's record.

of people who want to use a PC, who may have special uses for one and who, in many cases, need special help to use it. In 1991, 97 students were studying the foundation course in technology (3 per cent of all students on that course), 81 were studying *The fundamentals of computing* (3 per cent), 17 were studying *Programming and programming languages*, 43 were studying *An introduction to information technology* (3 per cent), and 15 were studying *Analogue and digital electronics* (2 per cent).

Distance teaching has been especially appropriate for the student with disabilities because it made study possible in the student's home environment when their disability was such that accommodation in many educational environments would have been very difficult. Also the distance-teaching mode meant that students could work at their own pace, resting when necessary, rather than at scheduled intervals between lectures, taking as long as they needed to complete study tasks, such as note taking or essay writing. Only a small proportion of course material is delivered in an auditory form, through tapes or radio, which are inappropriate for students with a hearing impairment (who make up about 10 per cent of all OU students with disabilities). The OU has always provided a transcript of all such material for the use of deaf students. Greater problems are faced by visually impaired students, who register as students in numbers similar to hearing impaired students, since so much of any course is delivered as printed text. These students have in the past been provided with audio-tapes containing the written content, and experiments have been made to present diagrams, etc., in some tactile form. Courses with integral computing raise new problems for these students in particular but, for other kinds of disability too, some kind of 'enabling' device is necessary:

> In some cases the standard computer and software might be immediately accessible; in others, there might be a simple solution such as a keyguard placed over the computer keyboard that helps a person with limited manual dexterity to more easily press individual keys. Finally there are students who need a sophisticated adaptation, often through the addition of co-resident software, to make the standard application accessible. The use of this type of technology is termed 'enablement'.
>
> (Vincent in Taylor, 1991, p. 1)

Tom Vincent and his research team at the OU have worked since the late 1970s on ways of 'enabling' computers for students. For example, synthesised speech is at a sophisticated enough state of technical development to be a valid option for at least some material. Other software can 'split' a screen and show enlarged text in one half for students whose visual impairment allows them to cope with large type. For students with very limited manual dexterity who cannot hold down two keys simultaneously there is software which can lock the shift and control keys.

The adoption of electronic publishing for course material makes it feasible

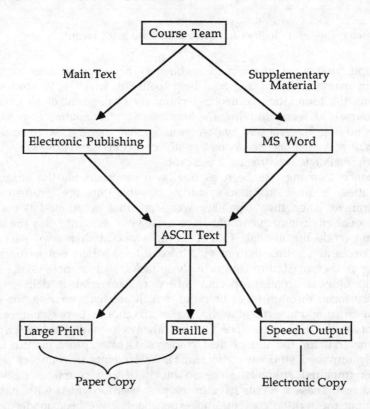

Figure 5.1  Conversion paths for text (from Taylor, Vincent and Child, 1992)

to produce at some point in the process alternative computer-based versions which can be accessed in various ways. Figure 5.1 shows possible conversion paths for text. One of the most flexible possibilities is the use of a hypertext program (Hyperbook) linked to a speech output, or a Braille device. This addresses the problem that if text material is simply presented to students in forms of linear text files these have to be scrolled through to access any particular place (a problem similar to that faced by a student listening to course material on audio-tape). Hypertext allows a user to make quick jumps between different areas of material, because the software does not treat it as linear text. However there is still a problem with screen material that is not text, and with icon-based operating systems which cannot easily be converted into speech. This problem is likely to become more significant as it appears that sighted people find the 'window, icon, mouse, pointer' (WIMP) command environment more user-friendly than the text command system, and more software is being produced with this environment. Some of the newly developed multimedia systems we discuss at the end of this book will, unless special versions are available, increase the difficulties of students with visual impairment while at the same time they increase the sophistication of CAL for fully sighted students.

The possibilities of some of these devices for students can be seen in individual histories. One student, for example, with an untreatable loss of vision, had studied an access course at a local college and gone to a social science degree course at a polytechnic which he had to abandon because he could not get the amount of print material he needed to study recorded on tape. He now studies with the OU: '[He] uses an Amstrad 1512 PC with HAL Speech and an Apollo speech synthesizer (dolphin systems). He had used this equipment, supplied by the Open University/National Federation of Access Centres scheme for 2 years' (Taylor, 1991, p. 4). At the moment it is still expensive to produce this kind of material. Taylor estimated that it would take two full-time person months to take the text from one OU undergraduate course (about the equivalent of half a year of a full-time course) in its electronic publishing form and put it into hypertext form. Each student would need the one-off cost of a version of the software (about £60 at 1990 prices), as well as one day of face-to-face training to install the software and learn how to use it. She also suggests that ideally there should be some special telephone support available for students working in this way, extra to their usual tutorial support. The special student-based costs are mainly one off and are small relative to the overall cost of a PC.

Although distance study has been the only option for students who are housebound (through disability, or other causes such as caring for children or sick relatives), their inability to attend face-to-face meetings with students and tutors is a disadvantage. This produces a sense of isolation and deprives these students of at least one other medium of learning. Computer-mediated communication (CMC) appears to hold out the possibility of alleviating at least some of the isolation of these students. In 1990 a trial of CMC was carried out with a group of ten students whose disabilities made them housebound (Dyer, 1991). These students were not studying courses which included the use of a PC, so they were loaned PCs, modems and communications software specifically for the purpose of communication. A special electronic conference named 'Link' was set up for these students to participate on a variety of topics, and it was open to all others on the network. During the year the number of messages the housebound students put into the conference was very small, only 15 in total; another 20 messages were submitted by other students, and the conference moderator input 20. However, the students were still enthusiastic when asked about the facility, and most had at least 'eavesdropped' on many of the other conferences that were available to them. This has been seen as perhaps the most successful part of the project, and CMC is seen as having potential 'to empower and reduce the social isolation of remote and housebound students' (Dyer, 1991, p. 27). The OU intends to expand the project to more housebound students as far as funding will allow, but economic and technical problems remain, such as the cost to the student of telephone calls, and to the OU of providing PCs and any enabling devices and the relative 'unfriendliness' of the software to novice computer users.

As far as students with disabilities are concerned, student-based PCs with enabling devices do offer real technical solutions to some of the physical disadvantages such students face, and CMC does appear to have the potential to reduce the isolation of housebound and remote students. There is therefore a good argument, even for courses that do not normally have any computing component, that students with disabilities be offered a PC for optional CMC (although if able-bodied students on the course are not using CMC the scope of interactions will be limited) and a PC-based version of course material, for use where necessary with enabling devices.

## Age

The OU has always deliberately recruited older students. Although there is no lower age limit for entry, in general the majority of students are over the age of 30. In 1990 roughly 60 per cent of all undergraduates were between the ages of 30 and 49. The age of students is related both to the area of study and to course completion – in the OU and in higher education generally. In the OU, arts and social science students are older than students doing maths, science and technology courses. For example, in 1990 only 22.7 per cent of students beginning the foundation course in arts were under 30 years of age, and 18.5 per cent were over 50; in social science this was 28.3 per cent and 9.2 per cent, while in maths it was 34.9 per cent and 6.1 per cent, and in technology 31.2 per cent and 5.7 per cent. There is a national trend for older higher education students to choose arts and social science courses. This appears to be due partly to the fact that older graduates have fewer prospects of changing their employment and entering new fields, except to teach (Woodley, 1991). They therefore choose less directly vocationally oriented courses. This is an equal opportunities employment issue, since it results from industry's preference for younger graduates, combined with less geographical mobility amongst older people. But it has a direct impact on education.

Figure 5.2 shows that in general students on home-computing courses are

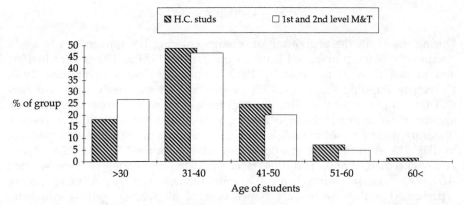

Figure 5.2 An age comparison of students on home-computing courses with all those on first- and second-level maths and technology courses

older than those studying other maths and technology courses. This is a surprising finding since computing and IT are associated in people's minds with youth. One explanation for the OU data might be that people in their twenties have less disposable income than those in their thirties and forties, and the requirement to purchase or hire a computer on top of their course fee is a significant disincentive for these students.

General OU figures show that students under 30 and those over 50 are the least likely to complete a course successfully (Open University, 1991a), but this is not the case on most home-computing courses. Once registered, younger students are more likely to complete than older students. Table 5.2 gives the pass rates by age group of some second- and third-level home-computing courses.

Table 5.2 Course completion rates by age (1990)

| | Per cent of total registered | | | |
| Year of birth | M205 | DT200 | M353 | T202 |
|---|---|---|---|---|
| Before 1911* | 0 | 0 | 0 | 0 |
| 1911–15* | 0 | 0 | 0 | 0 |
| 1916–20* | 50 | 100 | 100 | 0 |
| 1921–5* | 50 | 86 | 67 | 0 |
| 1926–30 | 45 | 64 | 50 | 50 |
| 1931–5 | 61 | 64 | 76 | 60 |
| 1936–40 | 69 | 67 | 56 | 77 |
| 1941–5 | 71 | 74 | 58 | 77 |
| 1946–50 | 71 | 74 | 71 | 73 |
| 1951–5 | 75 | 79 | 68 | 77 |
| 1956–60 | 75 | 75 | 72 | 77 |
| 1961–5 | 76 | 66 | 76 | 84 |
| 1966+ | 75 | 54 | 83 | 81 |

*Note*
\* Numbers of students in these age groups is extremely small.

## Gender

During the 1980s the proportion of women entering UK universities to study computer science courses fell from 24 per cent in 1979 to 15 per cent in 1984 and to less than 10 per cent by 1989 (University Grants Committee, 1988; University Funding Council, 1990), despite special schemes to train teachers and encourage pupil use. The statistics look even worse when they are seen against a background of the increasing participation of women in university undergraduate courses overall – from 42.4 per cent in 1985–6 to 44.4 per cent in 1989–90. A similar trend appears to have happened in the USA (Banks and Ackerman, 1990), and this is complicated by issues of race so that African-American women and Hispanic women were even more poorly represented – they were only 5 per cent of all women getting computer science degrees.

Chapter 4 discussed how computers were marketed for the male leisure industry (Haddon, 1988). They also have associations with mathematics – which is traditionally a subject preferred more by boys – and with military applications – which also structure the form of some of the programming applications and computing jargon. It has been argued (Haddon, 1988; Kirkup, 1992; and others) that these things have combined to 'gender'

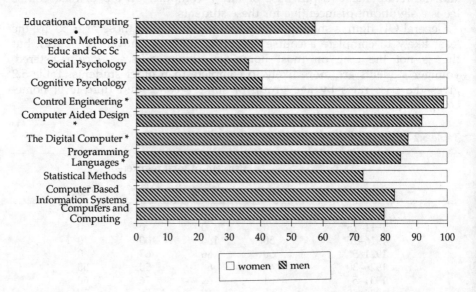

* On these courses a computing device was supplied for use in students' homes by the University.

● On this course students were expected to get access to a BBC microcomputer themselves.

On the other courses access was provided through a study centre terminal or at summer school.

Figure 5.3 Registration of women on computing courses *prior* to the Home Computing Policy

computers. In the mid-1980s in the UK, the most important variable connected with ownership of a computer in the home was the presence of an 11–14-year-old boy in the family. Culley's work (1986, 1988 – see Chapter 4) demonstrates how few women and girls had a sense of ownership of, or access to, computers in their own homes.

In the light of this international trend the participation of women in computing courses in the OU suggests considerable success. Figure 5.3 shows the situation in the year prior to the implementation of the Home Computing Policy. Even then women were less likely than men to register for courses with a compulsory computing component even if the computing facility was provided via a local terminal link to a mainframe, or in the form of a machine on free loan from the University. In the mathematics and technology courses shown in the figure, women form a smaller proportion of students than they do in those faculties in total. On the two psychology courses, women are over 60 per cent of the student body, and this is influenced by the fact that these two courses were compulsory for students wanting recognition from the British Psychological Society, demonstrating women's interest in pursuing a career in psychology rather than an interest in computing itself.

By 1991, four years into a policy of student ownership, women were 28 per cent of all students on the foundation course in technology, 20 per cent of students studying *Fundamentals of computing*, 35 per cent of those studying *An introduction to information technology*, 16 per cent of those studying *Programming and programming languages*, but only 3 per cent of those studying *Analogue and digital electronics*, a figure not much larger than the proportion of students with disabilities on the course (2 per cent)!

Two courses, *The fundamentals of computing* and *Computational mathematics*, had replaced similar courses which had required students to use a local terminal link for their practical activities. Although about 25 per cent of students taking the pre-'PC-based' versions were women, under the Home Computing Policy the proportions fell to less than 20 per cent. For the first three years of the policy a fee-reduction scheme operated for students on home-computing courses, and there was a rental pool where students could get the equipment they needed for a hire fee of £150 per year. (The foundation course had a specially reduced hire fee of only £50. This was justified in terms of the importance of student access at foundation level.) Data was obtained about how students acquired equipment and, although buying was the preferred option to hiring, women were much more likely to hire, and men were more likely to have already owned appropriate equipment at the beginning of the course. The most significant difference between men and women was on the *Computational mathematics* course where 50 per cent of men already owned suitable equipment compared with 33 per cent of women, and 40 per cent of women hired equipment compared with 25 per cent of men. On all the other home-computing courses the differences have been in the same direction but smaller. The problem with a subsidy scheme in these varied circumstances becomes obvious. Because more men were studying these courses, the subsidy to male students as a group was over four times as big as that to women as a group. Kirkup (1989a) estimated

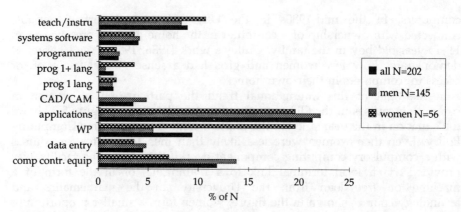

Figure 5.4 Job-related computing experience: men and women studying the foundation course in technology

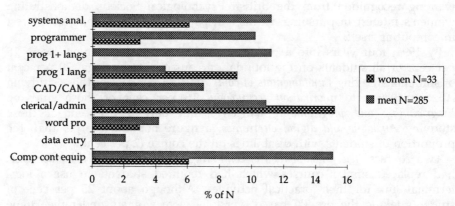

Figure 5.5 Job-related computing experience: men and women studying *Fundamentals of computing* (M205)

that in the first year of the policy male students received roughly £236,000 and women £58,000. The students who gained the most financially from the scheme were those who already had access to equipment – again much more likely to be men, since they had no initial outlay and they were getting computing courses cheaper than any other course. For those who rented – more likely to be women – the subsidy provided one-third of the cost of the hire fee, leaving them still with almost £100 to pay for hiring; the course fee remained the same, and at the end of the year the computer had to be returned. General positive action initiatives like this can often have an unintended effect on particular groups, or operate in an unintended inequitable way.

The future restricted nature of the hire pool means that although hiring is not inexpensive, the costs of hiring will be kept as low as possible and targeted at the most disadvantaged students. In the OU students whose income falls beneath a particular level are able to apply for financial assistance from a special OU fund. This assistance can be for the hire of equipment. In the past, family income was assessed, so that many women who were not wage earners themselves were excluded from applying, even if it was well known that they had no access to the family income to pay for their study. The advent of the equal opportunities policy has changed this bar, so women can now apply for financial support based on their own personal income. It is now recognised that women do find it harder to get access to equipment than men, and positive-action initiatives to alleviate this are being developed. These are in general small and localised (for example, regionally, OU staff have solicited money from the University and from local industry to buy a small number of machines that can be lent to women, or put in locations where they can be accessed easily by women students, such as at local women's centres).

However, access to equipment is not the only problem faced by women. Women in the OU have had less experience of computers either through work or through leisure activities. A sample survey of students on the foundation course in technology showed that only in data entry and wordprocessing did women have more experience with computers than men (Figure 5.4). This has been the case on all home-computing courses, and is perhaps most crucial on computer science courses like the *Fundamentals of computing*, where men were much more likely already to have professional skills in computing at the beginning of the course (Figure 5.5).

Students were also asked to assess their level of expertise on a ten-point scale at the beginning and end of their course. Women students always

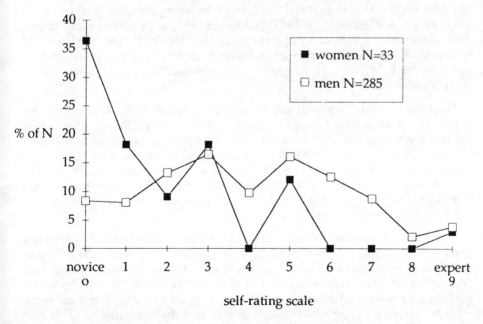

Figure 5.6 Self-rating scales of expertise: men and women on entry to *The fundamentals of computing* (M205)

rated their level of expertise much lower than that of men on the same course (see Figure 5.6). These are the same students as in Figure 5.5.

Interviews carried out by Sue Baines in her research with OU women students suggest that whereas many mature men got their first experience of computers in the home-computer boom of the early 1980s, purely as a hobby interest, this was not the case with women:

> Women's initial interest in PCs was almost invariably related to the specific and significant events in their personal lives, principally changes at work or children's needs. The strong but unfocussed desire to be involved in a modern technology which men report was not described to me by any woman. However, although women rarely seem to embark upon computing as a personal hobby as many men do it does not seem to follow that their use and enjoyment is puritanically restricted to the practical. Despite their busy lives some of my female interviewees admitted to sheer pleasure in computing . . . However for the women I spoke to male hobbyist computing was irrelevant rather than excluding or threatening.
>
> (Baines, 1991, p. 11)

This suggests that the OU has, for many women, opened a door to pleasure with computers that they might not have had opened in any other way. It is the enthusiasm to open it even further that has caused women staff within the University to question the content and style of computing courses and suggest ways in which content and method could be further improved to make the material even more 'women friendly' (Kirkup *et al.*, 1991; Shipp and Sutton, 1991). This touches on the importance of content and curriculum for equal opportunities, and the fact that the issue of whether some subjects are gender exclusive is one that has not been resolved generally and certainly not in the OU course teams Shipp and Sutton (1991, p. 178) wrote about:

> Three male academics held the view that it was unnecessary to consider female students whilst writing course material. They felt that the subject matter was asexual and their aim was to write good teaching material. They did not think of students as being male or female, and considered that students of both sexes would be best served by concentration on the subject matter rather than on the sex of the reader. These men experienced a degree of irritation with members of the team who were consciously trying to encourage women.

Sophisticated theories are being developed about the relationship between gender and computing. For example, it is suggested by Turkle and Papert (1990) that the domination of the computing profession by men has led to a privileging of particular styles of thinking which are often not the styles preferred by women. Turkle bases her argument on her own empirical work with young people and children learning to use the computer, and that of Gilligan (1982) who found that there were important differences in the way that men and women reason about morality. Together their research suggests that *one* model of mental development is inappropriate to describe men and women, and that there is not one *correct* model of using a computer:

> Several intellectual perspectives suggest that women would feel more comfortable with a relational, interactive and connected approach to objects, and men with a more distanced stance, planning, commanding and imposing principles on them. Indeed we have found that many women do have a preference for attachment and relationship with computers and computational objects as a means of access to formal systems. Yet in our culture computers are associated with a construction of science that stresses aggression, domination and competition.
>
> (Turkle and Papert, 1990, p. 150)

Recruiting and supporting women in computing and other non-traditional areas is an activity that University groups such as the Women into Science and Engineering (WISE) Group and the Women into Computing (WIC) Group have been active in for some years. They have taken on board the feminist analysis of people like Turkle and are trying to design new ways of using the computer that will fit better with the preferred thinking and learning styles of women. Some of their positive-action initiatives will be discussed in the last section of this chapter.

## Occupation

Amongst OU undergraduate students there is a significant difference in the occupational categories of students who study arts and social sciences and those who study mathematics, science or technology, and it is no surprise to see these differences reflected in students on home-computing courses. In mathematics, science and technology courses fewer students are out of paid employment: about one-fifth compared to one-third in arts and social science (this also reflects the lower numbers of women on these courses); fewer are in professional occupations (16–18 per cent) compared with 20–25 per cent in arts and social science; and many more are in technical and manual occupations (between 35 and 41 per cent, compared with fewer than 10 per cent in arts and social science (Ashby, 1991)).

Figure 5.7 shows occupational pie charts for the total undergraduate population and for students on the foundation technology course (T101), *Analogue and digital electronics* (T202), *Fundamentals of computing* (M205), *Programming and programming languages* (M353), and *An introduction to information technology* (DT200). These illustrate that on all these courses the largest occupational groups are technical personnel and skilled trades. However, DT200 has a larger proportion of clerical and office workers and shop personnel than do the others. It would be justifiable to assume that the other courses are being studied for explicit vocational reasons. Taking home-computing courses there are fewer unemployed people and housewives, fewer people employed in the medical profession or social services. Shop workers and clerical and office workers are generally under-represented too.

**Legend**

■ 1 □ 2 ▦ 3 ▦ 4 ▦ 5 ⊟ 6 ▥ 7 ▧ 8 ▨ 9 ▩ 10 ▩ 11 ⊟ 12 ▥ 13 ▧ 14 ▨ 15 ⊞ 16 ▩ 17 ■ 18

| | | | | | |
|---|---|---|---|---|---|
| 1 | housewives full-time | 7 | medical prof. | 13 | other manual |
| 2 | housewives part-time | 8 | social services | 14 | comms and transport |
| 3 | armed forces | 9 | other prof in arts | 15 | clerical and office |
| 4 | admin and managers | 10 | science and eng. | 16 | shop and personnel |
| 5 | school teachers | 11 | tech personnel | 17 | retired and unemployed |
| 6 | teachers HE and other | 12 | skilled trades | 18 | in an institution |

**NOTE THAT CATEGORIES 1 AND 18 BOTH SHOW AS SOLID BLACK ON THE CHART, BUT IN EACH CASE THE PERCENTAGE FOR EACH CATEGORY IS PRINTED.**

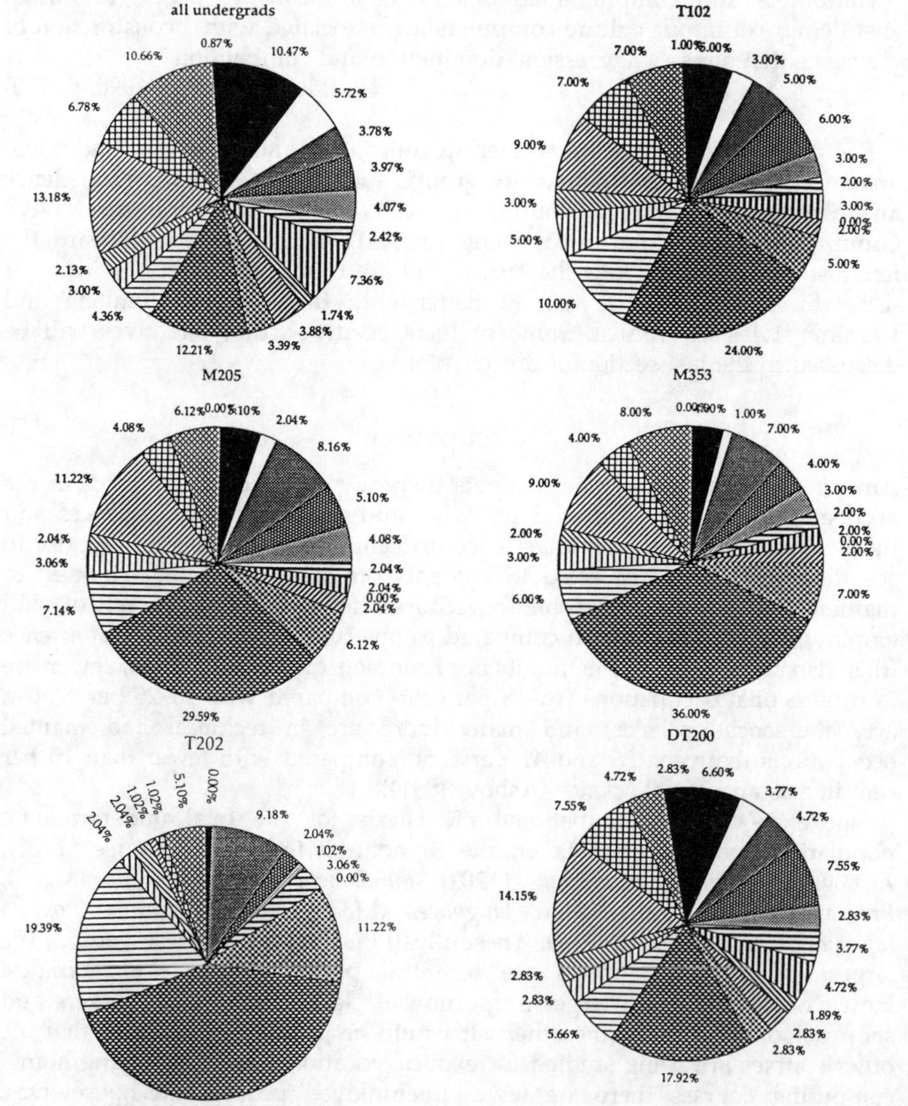


Figure 5.7 Occupations of students studying home-computing courses

Since computing skills are vocationally relevant it is disappointing to see the smaller proportion of unemployed students.

Earlier it was noted that in the early years of the course *Fundamentals of computing* there was a high proportion of students with computing and programming skills, and that there was a relationship between experience and final course result. This reinforces the sense that this course is perceived by students as very vocationally oriented and discriminates in favour of students who are working in the industry. But this is not true for all home-computing courses. Few students entering *An introduction to information technology* in its first year had professional experience in computing, but many more had 'end user' experience, having used a machine for clerical packages (20 per cent) or wordprocessing (almost 10 per cent) and another 10 per cent had used computer-controlled equipment. There was no relationship between the pre-course experience of these students and their final course result. This course did not discriminate in favour of students working with computers. There will always be computing and programming courses which are designed to be directly vocational and there will continue to be a relationship between students' professional experience in computing and their performance on such a course.

However, students studying the foundation course in technology had very similar prior experience of computers in their workplaces as did a group of maths and technology students who had not chosen to study computing courses (Jones and Singer, 1992).

Jones and Singer found that there were usually a number of reasons why students who first consider taking a course in the Home Computing Policy decide against it, but cost was a reason mentioned more frequently than any of the others. In the early years of the policy, Saxton (1989) surveyed students in the London area who had applied to do the technology foundation course but then decided against it. She found that cost was a significant reason; she also found that they were insecure about the rental pool. Many said that they would have taken the course if they could have been guaranteed a machine from the rental pool; however, some could not be given this guarantee when they made their application and, since they were afraid that in the end there might not be a machine for them, chose another course rather than wait and see. In 1992, cost remains a serious barrier for some students, both employed and unemployed.

The OU's mission, and its equal opportunities policy, means that more effort needs to be put into overcoming financial barriers for courses with PCs, and this will mean targeting financial help.

## Educational Level

There is no evidence that students with low educational qualifications are being discouraged from taking courses with home computing. Students entering home-computing courses are approximately of the same educational level as the general body of undergraduates. For example in 1991, 42 per cent of all OU undergraduates had qualifications higher than A-level. On home-computing courses this figure ranged from 36 per cent on *An introduction to information technology* to 42 per cent on *Fundamentals of computing*; only on *Analogue and digital electronics* was there a significant difference with 53 per cent of students having higher than A-level qualifications. This is explained by a very large proportion of students on this course (43 per cent) having a higher-level vocational qualification (Higher National Diploma or Certificate – HND/C).

The performance of students with no or low educational qualifications on entry is significantly poorer across the whole undergraduate programme. In 1990, of new students entering foundation courses, 71 per cent of those with 'low' qualifications (GCE O-level and lower) completed their course, 80 per cent of those with 'medium' qualifications (A-level and HND/C), and 84 per cent of those with higher-level qualifications (higher than A-level). On second-level courses and above the comparable figures were 66 per cent, 74 per cent and 76 per cent (Ashby, 1991). This is of great concern to an institution with no entry requirements, and the University is looking for ways in which to better prepare students with low qualifications on entry to the University, perhaps in some cases counselling students against beginning an undergraduate course. It is more difficult to see how to overcome the problem of performance on higher-level courses. The question with respect to home-computing courses is whether students with low qualifications are particularly disadvantaged on these courses and, if so, could the practical computing contribute to poor performance? There is, however, no consistent pattern of performance across courses in the home-computing policy. In two, *An introduction to information technology* and *Programming and programming languages*, there is little difference in performance between any of the groups of students. On the other courses the pattern is consistent with that of the University, with students in the 'low' group achieving a pass rate between 60 and 70 per cent and students in the higher groups achieving a 10–20 per cent better performance. There was also no indication from surveys of students studying these courses that difficulty with practical computing work was related to educational level – it seemed related more to previous experience with computers and to gender. The technology foundation course in particular has demonstrated that it is possible to produce distance-teaching materials that can teach students with low prior education how to use the computer for a variety of applications.

## Ethnic Origin

In 1992 very little can be said about the ethnic origins of students at the OU. Data only began to be collected from all applicants to undergraduate courses in 1990, and the data-collection procedure is such that the information on ethnic origin is separated from a student's personal details. The personal details are stored with a student's personal identifier number, but the details of ethnic origin are only collected cumulatively and cannot be related back to individual students. Also, because data is collected from applicants when they first enter the University, it is only possible to relate it to their preferred foundation course, which is a good indication of their preferred area of study but gives no indication of whether they go on to study home-computing courses at second and third level. Unfortunately many people also regard monitoring with great suspicion, and 8 per cent of new applicants choose not to disclose their ethnic origin. From the available data we know that Asian students account for 3 per cent of new undergraduates and black students 2 per cent. The majority of Asian and black students live in the London regional area where 12 per cent of students are Asian and 9 per cent are black. Amongst ethnic minority students, social science is the most popular foundation course (37 per cent of black students and 24 per cent of Asian students). Maths is also popular with Asian students (24 per cent) and technology with black students (23 per cent). This is an optimistic figure with respect to getting computers into the black and Asian student population, although anecdotal data from regions suggests that women are a very small proportion of these populations.

## Positive Action

Some common threads of disadvantage run through this chapter. The most obvious one is to do with money. Three years after the beginning of the policy the cost of MS-DOS machines has not dropped significantly and the UK has experienced a major recession. Buying a computer remains financially extremely difficult for some students – in fact studying with the University at all can be financially difficult. However, because of the expansion in the number of courses using home computers, the rental pool is now only available to very few students. There is therefore for many students no cheap option, and there is no longer any subsidy for course fees. Many staff in OU regional offices have been concerned enough about this issue to try to recruit funds from local industry to buy machines which can be put into local libraries or meeting places so that students who cannot afford their own machine will be able to have access to one for as many hours in the week as possible. The availability of such machines will help, but course material is really designed with the expectation that computer access will be constantly available, and if it is not students will find their study sequence interrupted. They are also likely to run into all the problems that students found when they used terminals in study centres. Ways have to be found to put machines into students' homes – ways that will involve money from somewhere.

The issue of women's under-representation in using computers is being addressed by positive-action groups in the University. For example, a special bursary scheme for women studying technology courses has now run for ten years. Between thirty and sixty women, who have been out of paid work for at least two years, have been funded each year by the various UK government and European initiatives to study a vocationally relevant course in maths or technology. (This is known as the Women into Technology Scheme – WITS.) Every year some of the women study courses in the Home Computing Policy and the rental of a machine is provided in the bursary. This scheme, along with addressing the issue of cost, also addresses that of confidence. All the women attend a residential weekend course before they begin their course proper. At this weekend they get a chance to discuss all sorts of issues that concern them about beginning their study, and they also begin to form a support network for each other. The success rate of women on this scheme has been very high (Swarbrick, 1986).

In another attempt to address the issue of confidence among women, special, women-only 'introduction to the computer' sessions have been run in local study centres. These have usually been run by women staff who have attempted to introduce the computer in ways they think will be more user friendly to women. At the OU this initiative has been a very personal one for the women staff concerned; however, in other institutions, such as the Open Universiteit of The Netherlands (project team: Crutzen, Vlas and Joosten), special courses have been written for women-only tutorial groups. An evaluation of these projects is underway, but the anecdotal evidence of the women who attend them is that they enjoy them very much.

Many computing courses will continue to be vocational in nature and, as well as recruiting more women, other under-represented groups such as black and Asian students, and unemployed students, would benefit from such courses. The issue of recruitment of ethnic minorities is being addressed in the regional offices of the OU through special outreach programmes and by networking with organisations in ethnic communities. For example, Judy Emms, a maths Staff Tutor in the Nottingham area, ran a computer workshop with an Asian community worker in a black and Asian women's centre. Unfortunately these kinds of positive-action programmes are very small compared with the size of the problem.

While there are groups in the UK population who for some time will not be able to enjoy high-technology distance education, there are even more people in other areas of the world for whom, as yet, PC-based learning is an impossibility. The danger of these developments is that they have the potential to increase the educational and economic gap between the rich and the poor. It is not apparent that this has happened yet in the OU; demographic statistics do not show that the University is recruiting richer students to its undergraduate programme, but then there is still only a minority of courses for which a PC is required.

Finally, it is important to end this chapter with some of the positive features of the effect of the use of student-based PCs. The new technical capabilities do seem to offer the potential to aid students with disabilities in a variety of ways. Some of the ways in which computers can be used as new media make possible a more flexible system of mass distance education, with more chance for contact and communication and more possibility of producing individualised learning packages without entailing the isolation and fragmentation which usually come with individualised learning. Chapter 9 includes a more extensive discussion of the nature of these new technical possibilities and their potential educational impact.

# 6
# Teaching Practical Computing Work – at a Distance

## Introduction

This chapter is concerned with two home-computing issues: the kinds of problems and difficulties that people have when they are learning to use computers by means of distance-teaching materials, and the design of instruction for learners in this position. These two issues are intimately connected: in order to design effective teaching materials students can use on their own, it is essential to find out about the kinds of problems students have in learning about computers and the kinds of errors they make. Problems to do with learning to use the computer and computer applications are the next hurdle after the problem of gaining access to the computer itself has been solved.

Before the Home Computing Policy was introduced, evaluation studies of some of the computer-assisted learning (CAL) programs used in Open University (OU) teaching had been carried out in the late 1970s. In one paper summarising some of these evaluation studies, the authors concluded that

> students have a realistic view of the benefits of CAL but usage is low because their view of the practical problems is also realistic. It can be summed up as a number of barriers or layers to get through ... Our studies show that the first two barriers are currently the major limiting factors. They include the practical difficulties of accessing a terminal, and the problems of accessing programs, which for novices include their fear and embarrassment, the problems of logging in, and possibilities of the machine malfunctioning. The real breakthrough here must be in providing home terminals. Not only would access cease to be a problem, but it would allow a radical re-think about the role of CAL, permitting it to occupy a central role in the learning process, instead of being merely an optional extra.
>
> (Scanlon *et al.*, 1982, pp. 74–5)

Access to CAL was described in terms of a Chinese box (Figure 6.1). In a sense, what providing (or requiring) home access has done is to attack the first barrier, allowing the second barrier to be looked at more closely. It has long been recognised that learning to use a computer is not unproblematic. Computers are used to carry out a variety of tasks ranging from programming in various languages to using such applications tools as spreadsheets and wordprocessors. Such tasks are very different, but they all

Figure 6.1   Barriers to the use of CAL (from Jones and O'Shea, 1982)

involve learning complex knowledge domains and skills, and will therefore require some effort and time to learn.

There are now research findings in two important areas related to student computing. Firstly there are studies of learning to use computer applications (such as wordprocessors) in commercial environments, and on designing self-instructional training materials for these applications. Many of the same issues arise in producing distance-education materials for teaching practical computing as in designing self-instructional materials; in both cases the learner is almost completely reliant on the packaged teaching material. This material, therefore, has a crucial role and will affect the ease with which the student is able to learn. Secondly there is research on learning to program, including a study of learners using OU instructional materials carried out by one of the authors (Jones, 1990). The studies on wordprocessing and learning programming at a distance are both important for informing the design of instructional material for carrying out home-computer-related activities at a distance. The remainder of this chapter will draw on these areas, and on past and current practice in instructional design for practical home-computing work to consider issues of learnability and instructional design.

## Learning to Use Wordprocessors and Text Editors

Several studies have been carried out on learning to use such applications as wordprocessing in commercial environments using self-instructional materials. As with distance teaching, learners are largely on their own in this situation. Carroll and his colleagues have carried out a number of studies in this area starting in the early 1980s, the results of which were used to inform the design of a manual for self-instruction. Carroll (1990, p. xvii) explains his approach and goals in his preface:

> One of my professional concerns has been to understand how people acquire competence at using new technology . . . Our analysis of specific learner problems exposed fundamental flaws in the standard systems approach to instruction . . . and exposed an alternate instructional model,

which we call the minimalist model. . . . The essence of the minimalist approach is to obstruct as little as possible the learner's self-initiated efforts to find meaning in the activities of learning.

On the face of it, this approach would also seem to address some of the fundamental issues (and offer possible solutions) for students learning to use information technology (IT) at a distance. This section will discuss the problems Carroll's learners experienced, before going on to consider his proposed instructional model.

In an early study the participants, who were temporary office staff, learnt one of two text-processing systems (Mack, Lewis and Carroll, 1982). They used self-study manuals for about 12 hours over four half days, and in the testing phase they were asked to type and revise a letter. They were asked to think aloud while they worked and all their interactions with the computer were recorded.

The learners had a lot of difficulties with the task. They often attempted to carry out tasks, such as logging on to the system, without reading the manual, and complained about the amount of material to read and remember. They lacked basic knowledge and had problems with terms such as parameter, queue and pagination. Some of these were problems in misinterpreting words the participants were familiar with but which, in the context of the computer application they were learning to use, now had a different specialised meaning. For example, one of Carroll's learners wondered who the printer was. Another problematic term was 'default', which elsewhere is a legal term.

They did not know what was relevant and so were influenced by superficial connections between what they did or perceived and the problems they were trying to solve. They were also very active in their learning: 'Complementary to learners' lack of knowledge about what is relevant is their ability to go beyond the information given by constructing and elaborating ad hoc interpretations of experiences . . . In explaining away puzzles, learners can convince themselves that all is well when the odd happenings they have noticed are really evidence of disaster' (ibid. p. 7). For example, one learner was attempting to enter her password when she made a typing mistake which caused the system to stop and await correction. An indicator light marked 'input inhibited' came on. The learner attributed both the delay and light to a heavy workload on the system. Another learner had made an error in issuing a 'file' command and wondered whether her work had been filed. She interpreted the message, 'INPUT MODE 1 FILE' as meaning that it had.

In another paper (Lewis and Mack, 1982) such explanations are described as abductive reasoning, where a hypothesis is generated to account for one or more observation. One implication of abduction is that the consequences of errors are explained away and learners do not realise they have made a mistake. They are influenced by superficial resemblances between what they think they need to know and what they see or do. Such abductions are often wrong and are not tested out. Lewis and Mack (ibid.) suggest that such reasoning has value in interpreting future events where there is no alternative to abductive reasoning. Often such complex learning is characterised by incomplete and ambiguous information and if learners are to try to understand the process that might lie behind what they experience then they have to use abductions. What Lewis and Mack are in fact talking about is learners *building up mental models*, which will often be wrong, as they are based on fragmented, ambiguous information (as perceived by the learner). This notion of mental models will be taken up a little further on in the chapter.

One response to problems such as those experienced by the learners Carroll studied is to consider them as the teething problems of introducing new technology into the office for the first time. If this is the case, then it should be expected that later systems (and accompanying instruction) would benefit from the experience of earlier ones. However, Carroll cites similar problems in learning the later Macintosh-like Lisa system. The Lisa was, at the time, a new user interface with a high-resolution display, a reliance on graphic presentation and applications and was mouse driven. It was highly regarded and highly acclaimed in a review: 'Lisa has made giant steps in saving the user both time and frustration' (Chin, 1984, quoted in Carroll, 1990, p. 50).

In the study of learners using the Lisa, there were six volunteers drawn from various professions. These participants were not computer professionals but did have a reasonable amount of computer experience and, furthermore, they had experience of different systems (an average of four systems over three years). As in the previous study, the participants worked on their own, using the self-instructional manuals. These included an online tutorial, although not all the participants tried this. Carroll concluded that overall there was a rather lower level of success than expected. The participants did not finish all the tasks suggested and the same types of problems occurred that had been seen in the previous study. They also took far longer than estimated on the instructional materials: for example, the five who tried the online tutorial spent over an hour and three-quarters on it: three times the time estimated by Apple. One complaint made by all the participants was that the tutorial placed them in too passive a role.

These participants said that they were going to read the manual carefully before doing anything – but none of them maintained this strategy for long; instead, they started to try out activities on the computer. When they did read they had trouble finding what they were looking for in the manuals and in co-ordinating the display with what they were reading in their books.

## Designing Minimalist Instruction for Teaching Wordprocessing

The learners in these studies can be viewed as being active in their learning, making use of their prior knowledge (which often led to misunderstandings), and having great difficulty in recovering from errors. The problems experienced by the learners in these studies led to a critical analysis of the design of the self-instructional materials.

The style of the self-instructional material the participants had used throughout the studies was very structured. The design followed a standard systems approach which involves hierarchical decomposition of learning objectives. However, Carroll argues that learners have problems because such materials do not relate to their own goals, and because learners are very active in the learning process. He argues (1990, pp. 74–5) that the systems approach does not work and describes how

> Systematic drill and practice materials present learners with a motivational double bind with respect to meaningful interaction. If they succeed at following the steps . . . the success is hollow. They have little control over the situation and cannot feel seriously responsible for the outcomes. However if they eschew the prescribed path – for example, correcting a real typo – they are likely to become snarled in a tangle of errors, which the system and training do not anticipate and recovery from which they do not support. The learner will fail in some sense no matter what the choice.

On this basis, the idea of minimalist instruction was developed, which aims to avoid these problems, first, by allowing learners to start immediately on meaningfully realistic tasks; second, by reducing the amount of reading and other passive activity in training; and, third, by helping to make errors and error recovery less problematic and more pedagogically productive.

The minimal instruction approach was first tried out by producing a set of cards which replaced the self-instruction manual and which adopted a 'guided exploration' approach. These were tried out with a group of learners. Although the cards worked well, and this group did better than a group using the standard training manual, it did not ameliorate all of the standard problems. In particular, the learners wanted a more traditionally structured manual, and so a self-instructional manual was designed, based on the minimalist model. It attempted to have topics of interest to the learners – for example, chapters had headings such as 'Typing Something' – and learners were able to start learning to use the system (as opposed to reading about it) quite early on: hands-on training begins after 7 pages compared with the systems-style instruction manual where it began after 28 pages.

Two experiments carried out on the use of the 'minimal manual' indicated that it was substantially and reliably better than the commercial self-instruction manual (Carroll et al., 1988). An important concern to those designing distance or self-teaching material for students using computers is the best way of carrying out the design process itself. Interestingly, the design process for the minimalist manual described by Carroll is similar to the standard process adopted for OU teaching material which is described in the next section. It is an iterative design process where the material is designed, empirically evaluated and then redesigned. In particular, producing the minimal manual involved three stages of different empirical testing. Pilot testing was incorporated into a design-analysis stage which drew on knowledge of how users went about tasks and their typical errors. Following this, particular design elements were empirically tested in qualitative detail by observing typical users at work with the manual (or parts of it). The final version of the manual was tested in the two experiments described earlier.

## Design of Instructional Material for Novices at the OU

In earlier chapters we saw that the very structured approach to distance learning offered by the 'industrial model', of which the OU is an example, was criticised for being too prescriptive and didactic and for promoting a one-way model of teaching, where the student has little opportunity to engage in a real dialogue. Such criticism is consistent with Carroll's (1990) data where learners felt they were cast in too passive a role. (However, it should be noted that, unlike the manual Carroll describes, few OU courses offer drill-and-practice exercises.) One alternative to this kind of approach for practical work is a more student-centred 'discovery' model. Such an approach has often been used with children learning the language LOGO, which was briefly mentioned in Chapter 1. Some of the claims made for LOGO are that it can teach people to reason, problem solve and plan, or rather, help people to learn these things for themselves. The best exposition of this LOGO philosophy is given by Papert (1980, p. 5) in his book *Mindstorms*, where he says:

> In my vision the child programs the computer, and in doing so, both acquires a sense of mastery over a piece of the most modern and powerful technology and establishes an intimate contact with some of the deepest ideas from science, from mathematics, and from the art of intellectual model building.

This philosophy assumes an open approach to learning where the sequence of concepts learnt will depend largely on the learner, and the judgement of the teacher.

One manual produced to accompany a version of LOGO developed by the OU did adopt such an approach, where the learner is invited to explore and discover LOGO. In line with LOGO philosophy, the manual adopts a style which is rather less structured than many programming instructional manuals. However, a study of adult learners using this booklet showed that some problems arose because it was *not* prescriptive enough (Jones, 1990). For how long were they supposed to explore? Had they got a 'right' answer? The adult learners in this study found learning LOGO hard and the difficulties they had led to problems with the exploratory 'diagnose your bugs' style of the tutorial manual. Where they have made more than one mistake, and these may interact in a programming language, and their processing models are faulty, students are unlikely, themselves, to diagnose the problems. In this style of teaching, programming is not taught because the learner is supposed to discover it.

Too unstructured an approach can feel very uncomfortable for adults who are not used to working in this way: moreover, in practical work at a distance, it can leave them without sufficient support when things go wrong as, when students explore, things inevitably will! The LOGO curriculum, in attempting not to be prescriptive, failed to meet the needs of the intended audience, and was criticised both for misjudging the audience and for therefore presenting both inappropriate material and for using an inappropriate style. It is interesting that Carroll's learners also found the unstructured style of the guided exploration cards uncomfortable, and asked for a more traditional manual.

To a large extent, the kind of iterative process employed by Carroll *et al.* (1988) is already built into the production cycle of most OU materials. Courses are produced by a course team which will typically include academics, a course administrator, a member of the academic computing service, a television/audio producer, an editor and designer and an educational technologist. Drafts of particular parts of the course are produced and circulated around the members for comment. Typically a unit of course material will undergo three full drafts before it is finalised and handed over to the editor. In addition to this internal commenting, there will be one or more external assessors who will also receive and comment on all the drafts. Depending on the course, it may also undergo formative evaluation, which usually involves a number of students working through the course materials and commenting on them. The stage at which this happens is quite critical: if it is too early, the materials will have gaps and they will not resemble the final product closely enough to be a realistic simulation; if it is too late, then there will be insufficient time to make changes following the feedback.

## Designing Practical Work for Training Teachers to Use Computers

The formative evaluation process described above is not applied to every course. However, it is particularly important to test out any element of practical work, whether it is a laboratory-style home experiment or the use of a computer, as students will be on their own if and when any problems occur. We know that learners are likely to have difficulties when starting to use computers for the first time, and in developing one set of materials for novice computer users, the course team adopted a particular design process to ensure that the material was as accessible as possible for students. In this case what was being developed was training materials for teachers as part of the 'Microcomputers in Schools' project. The project team responsible for these materials decided that the empirical evaluation process was so important that it should be carried out twice. Before describing the process it is necessary to describe the courses and their design.

The 'Microcomputers in Schools' project produced five standalone but linked 'packs' of course materials aimed at teachers, ranging from complete novices to those with some experience of computers. Its background, aims and design process are described in more detail elsewhere by the project director (O'Shea, 1984). At the time, the early 1980s, it was clear that there were teachers who were very frightened by the idea of using computers, and the first pack produced was the 'awareness pack' which assumed that the student (a professional teacher) had no knowledge whatsoever of computers and, moreover, might be very nervous. To help students with the very real problem of getting the computer they were using connected up in order to start, different-coloured and coded labels were provided which could be attached to the leads and their connections.

In the text material, all the practical work was laid out in a three-column format, where the first column gave the keypress required, the second gave a photograph of the screen display that appeared as a result of that action, and the third column provided a commentary. Clearly in this style of very structured instruction it is imperative for the text and the screen photograph to match exactly what was happening on the student's screen. For the courses in the 'Microcomputers in Schools' project, the empirical testing was extensive. External 'critical readers' were employed to comment on the first drafts of materials in addition to the project members. The second draft, which incorporated the feedback from the first, was evaluated by students working through the whole course in detail. Following comments from other team and project members and the evaluation feedback, a third draft was produced. Before this was handed over to the editor, a final round of testing was carried out to ensure that all the steps in the practical work corresponded to the screen photographs and that these, in turn, were an accurate representation. This final round of testing came to be known as 'catastrophe testing'!

This formula proved to be very successful for complete novices, and was also appreciated by students with some experience. It is quite structured, and allows the student relatively little freedom to decide what to do in the practical hands-on material, although in other parts of the course there is much more open-ended work where the student applies what he or she has learnt to his or her own situation and carries out project work. Figures 6.2 and 6.3 give a flavour of the style of instruction. They are both taken from the awareness pack. In Figure 6.2, at step 17, the student is learning particular commands and is told what to do. In Figure 6.3, however, the student is invited to explore and the screen display shown is just an example.

These two figures illustrate how exploration, and the learner's own goals, can be encompassed within this model: it does not need to be the kind of step-by-step approach criticised by Carroll for leading to passive learning, and which seemed to contain a lot of drill-and-practice. A further way of

**17** To find the number of children under the age of 14 who were at school (as before) and find their average age, it is easiest to make use of an additional MicroQUERY command, 'MEAN'. Type:
M E A N [SPACE] A G E [RETURN] and then
G O [RETURN]
When the search is finished your display should look like that shown in Figure 31(a). Press the [SPACE] bar to obtain the results shown in Figure 31(b).

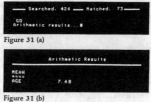

Figure 31 (a)

Figure 31 (b)

MEAN AGE specifies that during each subsequent search performed, the average value of the contents of the AGE field for all the matched records should be calculated. At the end of the search, the message Arithmetic Results... is displayed.

Typing N or pressing the colon key now suppresses these results, and gives the usual colon prompt for a further command.

Pressing any other key, such as the SPACE bar, produces the required average value followed by the colon prompt. (As usual, only one key needs to be pressed in either case; RETURN is not needed.)

The average (or 'mean') value of any number of numeric fields can be found in this way. If more than one field is specified, they should be separated by commas or spaces.

To revert to the 'default' state, i.e. no calculation of average values, just type the command:
M E A N [RETURN]
on its own.

Figure 6.2 Searching in MicroQUERY: an extract from the 'Microcomputers in Schools' awareness pack (p. 83)

**14** Spend 15 minutes or so exploring the BIBLIO database, looking for items of interest in your own subject area. You may find that in some cases you prefer to stick with FORMAT 1, particularly where you don't mind losing some information off the right-hand edge of the display. In such cases, the command GO 16 is often of great value, as it provides an automatic pause every time the screen display becomes full. The sample screen display shown opposite depicts what would happen if you were looking for titles of articles about Computer-Assisted Learning (CAL), using FORMAT 1 and GO 16, assuming that you typed in the following:

[Q][U][E][R][Y] [SPACE] [K][W] [SPACE]
[S][U][B] [SPACE] [˹][C][A][L][˼] [RETURN]
[P][R][I][N][T] [SPACE] [T][I][T][L][E] [RETURN]
[G][O] [SPACE] [1][6] [SPACE]

(The FORMAT 1 specification is in effect by default whenever you begin using MicroQUERY. You only need to type in
[F][O][R][M][A][T] [SPACE] [1] [RETURN]
if you have changed the specification to FORMAT 2, as in step 13 above).

```
TITLE
CAL AT ST. PATRICK'S.
COMPUTER AIDED LEARNING
AN INTRODUCTION TO THE NAPCAL
GUIDELINES FOR DEVELOPING EDUCATIONAL C
GETTING STARTED WITH COMPUTER BASED LEA
FOCI FOR COMPUTER BASED LEARNING IN THE
MYTHS AND MYSTICISM IN COMPUTER ASSISTE
WHERE NEXT IN COMPUTER AIDED LEARNING?
AN APPRAISAL OF COMPUTER ASSISTED LEARN
DESIGN CONSIDERATIONS FOR CAL PROGRAMS.
SILVICULTURE AND COMPUTER BASED LEARNIN
FINDING OUT ABOUT CBL
EDUCATIONAL PARADIGMS
A COOL LOOK AT COMPUTER-AIDED LEARNING.
INTERACTIVE MATHEMATICAL PROGRAMMING US
PRINCIPLES OF INSTRUCTIONAL DESIGN APPL

— Searched. 65 — Matched  16 —

.GO 16
Continue?▮
```

Figure 28

After 16 lines have been displayed using the GO 16 command, MicroQUERY will ask you 'Continue?' at the bottom of the display. If you press [N] or [n] it will abandon the search, whereas if you press any other key it will continue the search. This pausing remains in effect as a specification for all future GO commands until you explicitly change the number (e.g. GO 12) or eliminate the pause by typing in
[G][O] [SPACE] [M][A][X] [RETURN] the next time.

Another useful tip for doing your own exploration is that MicroQUERY will accept three-letter abbreviations of commands. Thus, instead of typing
[P][R][I][N][T] [SPACE] [T][I][T][L][E] [RETURN]
you could type
[P][R][I] [SPACE] [T][I][T][L][E] [RETURN]
The abbreviation facility only applies to the names of the commands themselves (e.g. PRINT, FORMAT, QUERY, etc.), not to the names of fields (e.g. AUTHOR, TYPE, etc.).

Figure 6.3  Exploring the database: an extract from the 'Microcomputers in Schools' awareness pack

increasing the amount of time that students spend following their own goals is by including more open-ended project work.

There was also an attempt to avoid the problems of the step-by-step approach, where students lose the global view and can end up recipe-following with little understanding (as was seen in Carroll's studies) by including the third 'commentary' column which provides some rationale and an overview.

The three-column style of the activities book, along with the case study and project book which accompanied it, appears to fulfil the same criteria as Carroll's minimalist instruction. Students are quickly in a position where they are engaged in hands-on activities; the guided exploration which happens in some places encourages students to be active and to engage in the activities they want to; and recovery from the errors they make should be supported by the troubleshooting guide supplied in the appendix. As far as keeping the reading down is concerned, the booklets are quite slim with little extra verbiage or repetition and little in the way of overviews and prefaces, etc. In fact, the OU has a built-in disincentive against producing too much reading material because of the high cost of extra print – and the extra study time required of students.

This approach is not completely successful in all cases, however. A study of students carrying out practical work with such an approach, on quite a different course, indicated that, for these students, the problem of learners operating at too low a level (taking a micro-level approach, like the surface-level processing) has not altogether been avoided (Jones, 1990). The course was analysed as part of a study in which four different curricula for teaching novices to program were evaluated. Three of these texts guide the student quite closely by structuring the material very carefully, two of which adopted the three-column format discussed above. It would seem that in some cases, however, this style of instruction, although it does provide an overview, may still encourage the learner to adopt an over-dependent attitude towards the text.

The experiment book for one of the courses examined in the study, *Microcomputers for Managers* (Open University, 1979), adopts a step-by-step 'recipe'-type approach and contains relatively little work of a less structured and open-ended nature. Students instead carry out 'experiments' and are working in assembler, a low-level programming language where it can be quite hard to 'step back' and get a global view. One danger, therefore, is that as the experiments consist of very structured steps, they can be followed and yield the correct answer without a deep understanding of the process being developed. There was some evidence of this happening in the study. It seems that it is important therefore to consider not only how the material is presented (e.g. Is there enough guidance? Is the amount of structure right?) but also the domain and the task involved.

The 'Microcomputers in Schools' awareness pack was very successful. The same design was followed by the next level of pack – aimed at students with some experience of microcomputers (or those who had completed the awareness pack). Subsequently some of the material from the packs was incorporated into an undergraduate course, for which it was much more

The **keyboard** is used to give commands to the system. Figure 1 shows a picture of the keyboard I used, though yours may have some differences. It has three sections: the typewriter section; the functions keys, on the left; the numeric key pad, on the right.

*Figure 1 Keyboard layout.*

The typewriter section is laid out like a standard typewriter, but with some extra keys. These have special functions:

The **RETURN** key tells the computer that you have finished typing and want it to respond to your instructions. It is located on the right-hand side of the typewriter section of the keyboard.

The **BACK SPACE** key erases the last character (letter, number, punctuation mark, etc.) that you typed. It is just above the **RETURN** key.

Figure 6.4   Keyboard layout: an extract from the computer book part of *Teaching and learning technology in schools*, ET 887/897, Module 3 CB, OU, 1988, p. 8

To create a spread sheet you need to use the 'Create' menu.

| | | |
|---|---|---|
| 1 | Press **Ctrl**, hold it down. | It's next to the A key. |
| 2 | Press **C** while holding down **Ctrl**. | In future I shall write **Ctrl  C** to indicate this. |

Your screen should now look like Figure 3.

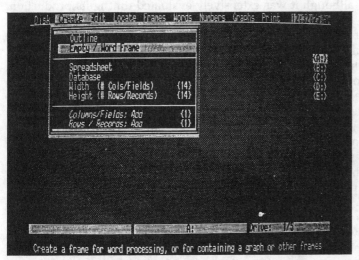

*Figure 3 The 'Create' menu showing one option highlighted.*

As you can see, one of the rows of the menu ('Empty/Word Frame') is highlighted. You can move this highlight by using the direction keys on the key pad.

| | | |
|---|---|---|
| 3 | Move the highlight up and down. | Use the up and down direction keys. |
| 4 | Now move the highlight to 'Spreadsheet'. | |
| 5 | Press **RETURN**. | |

You now have a spread sheet on the desktop, but enclosed within a **frame**. The first task is to give a name to the frame. You will see that the highlight is flashing at the top left-hand side of the frame and you can simply type in a name of up to eight characters. For reasons that will become apparent, I suggest you call it U4SAQ13.

| | | |
|---|---|---|
| 6 | Type in U4SAQ13 and press **RETURN**. | You press **RETURN** to tell the computer you've finished the name. |

Figure 6.5  Creating a spreadsheet: an extract from the computer book part of *Teaching and learning technology in schools*, ET 887/897, Module 3 CB, OU, 1988

difficult to decide whether to have the three-column format. Providing screen photographs of every step is expensive, and requires rigorous testing. Furthermore, in the awareness pack, every keypress was boxed (to avoid the all-too-familiar problem of knowing exactly what to type – learners can all too easily interpret 'Type PRINT RETURN' as meaning that they type in every letter in RETURN). It was not clear that such expense could be justified for the undergraduate course which was not aimed at complete novices. An equivalent amount of 'hand-holding' was not adopted with this undergraduate course, although it was extensively evaluated during its production.

Later courses have evolved their own particular styles of teaching and methods of instructional design. There is no one design philosophy at the OU to which all course teams adhere, although the course-team model ensures that each course is exposed to considerable comment and feedback during its development. The approach to teaching practical work in courses within the Home Computing Policy varies considerably. However, if they are introducing students to new applications, most include step-by-step guidance plus commentary, although the level of detail and support will vary, as shown in the following examples. Figure 6.4 shows an extract from the computer book part of a module of a course on teaching and learning technology in schools. It takes students through from the very beginning and even includes a photograph of the keyboard. In this respect it is reminiscent of the detailed hand-holding guidance given to the students of the 'Microcomputers in Schools' awareness pack.

Figure 6.5 shows an extract from a little further on in the same booklet. A screen photograph is included.

Figure 6.6 shows an extract from the course *An introduction to information technology*. In this section, students are being introduced to CoSy MAIL – the MAIL facilities for the computer-conferencing system on this course. A brief overview of the purpose of the exercise is given, followed by numbered instructions for the student to carry out. At the end of the third step there is a commentary. Note that the typography and layout carry quite a lot of information. The numbered steps help to reduce the cognitive overload by allowing the learners to see where they are, quickly. Everything that appears on the computer screen is in bold type, and the commentary section is prefaced by its own icon.

The next example is also taken from the same course, but is rather different. Here, the learner has just found out how to select a desktop function by single clicking the mouse, working with the GEM desktop program. Next, double clicking is introduced, and here a screen image is given so that the learner can check whether the action has been carried out correctly (Figure 6.7).

One point to note about the difference between the two examples shown in Figures 6.5 and 6.7 is that the amount of detail, guidance and illustration will vary according to the task being carried out, and also according to the consequences of making errors. Unfortunately, the MS-DOS operating system and many of the applications that run on it are not very 'forgiving' of errors and do not give useful error messages. In these cases, uninformed exploration can be very frustrating, or even disastrous, and learners will

## EXERCISE 4: AN INTRODUCTION TO CoSy MAIL

This exercise will introduce you to the use of CoSy's mail facilities. You will learn how to check what mail you have in your in-basket on CoSy, how to read it, how to send in a message that you have prepared off-line (the test message that you prepared in Exercise 3) and how to delete mail. At the same time, you will learn how to record a CoSy session onto your data disk, so that you can peruse any recorded message at leisure, either on screen or on a printed copy.

◀ 1  Turn on your workstation modem, and cassette player, and set Audio cassette 0 to the beginning of Band 6 ('CoSy mail exercises').

◀ 2  Load the communications software and, at the A> prompt, type menu. Then select OUCom from the DT200 Communications menu, followed by the appropriate option from the PC Disk Combinations menu. This will load OUCom for you and leave you at the Connect Options menu. Use the up and down arrows on the cursor keypad to select Auto to CoSy and then hit <Ret>.

◀ 3  Check the Communications protocols window. Your student identification number and password were already entered in Exercise 1 and should still be there, although masked by asterisks. Make sure the speed is set at 1200/75, and that the phone number is correct. Finally, assign a Rec.File name for this session, and toggle the Record: switch to Yes.

▷  The details of your password, student identification number, phone number etc. which you enter in the protocol window are stored on your data disk. So, if you start a new data disk (because your original one becomes full or corrupted) you will need to re-enter this information in the protocol window, or transfer the file(s) containing this information onto the new data disk.

The filename you supply will be used by Kermit to create a disk file in which it will record a transcript of your use of CoSy. To help you keep your visits to CoSy organized on your data disk, we suggest as a general rule that you use the date as a file name, with csy as the extension. This must be done in a valid MS-DOS format, of course, (i.e. up to 8 alphabetic characters or numbers, followed by a three character extension). So 15mar89.csy would be valid (whereas 15.3.89.csy or 15/3/89.csy would not). In this and the following exercises, we will use the

Exercise commentary
Audio cassette 0, Band

Problems? – See 'Ten useful tips', pp. 13–14
p. 43

Figure 6.6   CoSy MAIL: an extract from *An introduction to information technology: social and technological issues* (practical workbook), Block 1

need to be told the basic commands, and work through them, before exploring for themselves.

Students with differing amounts of experience will also need a different approach. One approach used in the technology foundation course, where it is reasonable to assume that most students are novices with respect to computing, is to introduce the operating system and the applications through audio-cassettes. This reduces the number of physical items students have in front of them, which can be a real problem. It also means the learner does not have to keep alternating between referring to a book and looking at the screen. The instructions on the audio-tapes were recorded in 'real time', so the student can carry out the instructions whilst listening to the tape, although of course there are places where he or she will need to pause the tape in order to try out some activity and then re-start it when finished. Some students have found this way of introducing them to the practical work invaluable. Others have used it in ways that were certainly not anticipated by the course team, e.g. listening to the tapes whilst driving to work! However, once students have worked through the tapes, they are not a good vehicle for reference. Trying to find where particular commands are dealt with on an audio-tape is not easy and, similarly, for students who are not complete beginners, using tapes is not so helpful, as what they need is a quick and easy reference system that reminds them about particular

### 4.4.5   SELECTION BY DOUBLE CLICKING

Now you know how to select a Desktop function by single clicking, let's move on to another technique: *double clicking*. Here the left-hand mouse button has to be clicked twice – *quickly*. (If the interval between the two clicks is too long, GEM treats the two clicks as two separate clicks and just activates the icon twice.) Place the mouse cursor onto the a: disk icon in the upper window and double click.

If you get the speed right, the icon's outline will darken and the cursor will change into the hour glass shape, telling you to wait a few seconds. The window will then display the contents of the root directory of the disk in the a: drive as icons, as in Figure 2. If this doesn't work the first time, try again – you are probably too fast or too slow with your double click action.

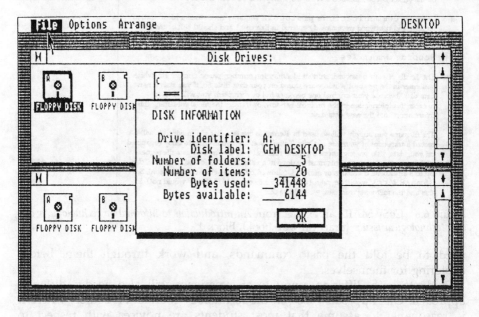

Figure 6.7   Selection by double clicking: an extract from *An introduction to information technology: social and technological issues* (practical workbook), Block 1

commands, and also ways of relating information to what they already know. For example, if a student already knows one integrated application package (i.e. a program that combines a wordprocessor, database, spreadsheet, etc.) he or she does not want to learn a new one from scratch. The student already has very useful knowledge: he or she knows the kinds of tasks that can be carried out, and how to do them with the package with which he or she is familiar. What the student needs to know is how the new one is different from the one he or she knows.

Another important factor in distance learning and practical work the three-column format may not take fully into account is that learners actively interpret the text and form mental models. This is inevitable and necessary in order for them to learn and assimilate the material they are encountering. Carroll's studies provide examples of how learners will seek to be active in their learning even when discouraged from doing so.

# Conceptual and Mental Models

In the previous sections, the term 'mental model' has been used to describe how learners represent the system they are learning to use. The idea of learners using such mental models has been around for some time, although different researchers have used different terms. It can probably be traced back to at least 1981 to a statement made by Young (1981, p. 51):

> system designers and applied psychologists are increasingly coming to believe that people deal with complex interactive devices by making use of a conceptual model of the device, and that the fostering of this model is an important consideration for the designer. The notion of a user's 'conceptual model' is a rather hazy one, but central to it is the assumption that the user will adopt some more or less definite representation or metaphor which guides his actions and helps him interpret the device's behaviour. Such a model, when appropriate, can be helpful, or perhaps even necessary for dealing with the device, but when inappropriate or inadequate can lead to misconceptions and errors.

This then is the idea of the mental model learners use when operating a device. It has also been argued that the system itself should be taught using a similar model. This idea applies throughout learning complex devices or domains, and when teaching about computer systems or applications it is particularly important to consider how they are presented and represented to the learner, especially given that learners will be active in their interpretation.

Du Boulay, O'Shea and Monk (1981), for example, argue that a major problem in teaching novices programming is describing the machine the novice is learning to use at the right level – as the novice usually does not know what the machine can be instructed to do or how it does it. They suggest overcoming this problem by basing the teaching on a 'notional machine', which is an idealised model of the computer based on the programming language. The notional machine helps learners by providing a descriptive model which they can use to plan programs and to interpret the machine's response. As this idea, and similar ones, are usually referred to as 'conceptual models' by other researchers, this is the terminology that will be used here from now on.

## Criteria for Designing Conceptual Models for Novices

Du Boulay, O'Shea and Monk (ibid.) advocate two principles upon which to base the conceptual model: simplicity and visibility. One aspect of simplicity is that there should be a set of instructions and commands which is small enough to be learnt readily by a novice. Another example of simplicity is that the language is suited to the task in hand. Syntactic simplicity 'is achieved by ensuring that the rules for writing instructions are uniform, with few special cases to remember, and have well chosen names' (ibid. p. 238).

Visibility means that wherever possible, methods should be provided for the learner to see the workings of the conceptual model in action, for instance the effects of commands. One way of doing this is by means of a commentary, a 'glass box' through which novices can see the workings of the machine. As the area they discuss is programming, it is not surprising that most of the examples of visibility which are given concern highlighting flow of control. Help for novices to decide what state the machine is in is also mentioned, and the importance of choosing names that do not conflict with novices' previous knowledge. In the context of distance education where learners have little support, it is clearly important to consider how to make learning such skills as easy as possible.

To help illustrate these ideas, an example of a conceptual model will be discussed which embodies the principles of both simplicity and visibility. The discussion is necessarily rather more technical than previous sections of this chapter, and readers who don't want to follow through the example in detail should miss this section and go on to the last part of the chapter, the conclusions. The conceptual model is a for a microcomputer, 'DESMOND' (DESMOND is an acronym standing for Digital Electronic System Made Of Nifty Devices). The conceptual model is essentially provided by the machine itself – it is its own model and has been designed so that its workings, at the appropriate level, are visible (Open University, 1984). DESMOND is the name given to the microcomputer used as part of two OU study packs: *Inside Microcomputers* (Open University, 1984) and *Learning about Microelectronics* (Open University, 1985), and was in fact sent out to students as a home experiment kit (HEK – see Chapter 3). This is shown in Figure 6.8.

In accordance with the principle of simplicity, DESMOND has a limited set of just 16 instructions, of which the three instructions given below are typical:

LDI     LDI xxx     Load Accumulator with xxx
ADD     ADD xxx     Add to Acc from memory location xxx
JZ      JZ xxx      Jump to memory location xxx if zero flag set to 1

DESMOND can be operated in three different 'modes'. In the first, monitor mode, the user can inspect different memory locations and change the contents. In order to increase the machine's simplicity, there is an attempt to make the workings of each mode easy to understand. In monitor mode, for example, the display is divided into three parts, each giving different information: the first part gives the address of the memory location, and the second and third parts give the contents in two different forms. Arrow keys are used to move backwards and forwards through memory locations.

To fulfil the criterion of visibility, all the circuitry and chips are visible, and devices are grouped together according to their function. The battery box is on the top right. On the top left are various switches and below these are the sensors. Together these make up input devices, as shown in Figure 6.8. The output devices are grouped together on the right. On the right, below the battery box, are five different-coloured lamps; below these are a buzzer and a motor. The keypad has two sections: the left side contains digits from 0 to 9, and the right has two rows of keys, of which the top four are keys for changing *mode*, for example, going into assembly mode (by pressing A for assembly) where programs can be entered in assembly language, or into run mode by pressing R for running a program.

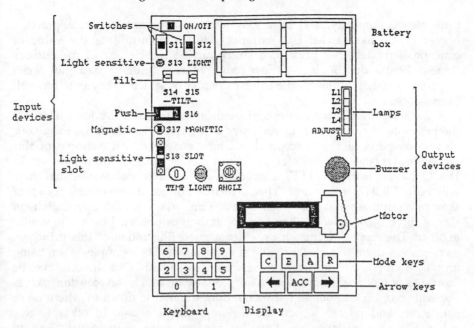

Figure 6.8    The DESMOND microcomputer

A detailed analysis of the design of DESMOND in terms of visibility, simplicity and additional criteria is given by Jones (1991). Here, one further example will help to illustrate the attempt to make the conceptual machine as visible as possible and to help the learner keep track of where he or she is. This is visibility by making the contents of memory locations visible, for example by making it easy to inspect the 'address' of a memory location (i.e. its label) and its contents. An earlier example was given of how in one mode, monitor, the display shows the address of the location and its contents; in another mode, assembly, we see the program line (e.g. 10), and the two parts of the instruction (e.g. LDI 001). In run mode, when programs are being executed, the contents of different locations are not usually shown, but there is a facility for running a program step by step and being able to inspect the contents of the relevant memory locations after each step has been executed by the computer. This helps the user to see what changes are happening at each step.

Keypresses are given for most of the experiments in the practical book, except for the final experiments where it is assumed that this level of guidance is not needed. The instructions are given in the three-column format described previously where the first column gives the keypress, the second shows what will appear in the screen and the third gives the commentary.

## The Criteria for Designing Conceptual Models in Use

One important problem with such criteria is that there may not be a clear correspondence between what appears to be good design, according to the principle of simplicity, and how easy such systems are to use in practice. Mayer (1975) has carried out empirical work demonstrating the value of conceptual models, but prior to a study carried out by one of the authors (Jones, 1990), du Boulay, O'Shea and Monk's criteria had not been empirically tested, although the three examples of systems they give have all been in use.

A further principle for conceptual models is introduced by Jones (1991) – the principle of consistency. Consistency is the extent to which the behaviour of various parts of the conceptual machine is related. An example of this would be whether a particular command can be inferred from another. In LOGO, having learnt the LEFT instruction, one can reasonably infer that there will be a RIGHT instruction. This principle applies in environments other than programming and may even be more important in such applications in that, if there is consistency, then one application can be used by analogy with another. The Apple Macintosh provides a good illustration of this principle, as it enables users to transfer between applications. For example, when using an unknown piece of software, a user can assume that he or she can take the mouse to one of the headings at the top (many of which stay constant across applications), click to obtain the menu, drag the mouse down to where he or she wants and release to activate the appropriate action. In other words, using a new application is done by analogy with a previously known application. There is also another more general type of consistency, which is whether the conceptual model is always presented in a consistent way. The conceptual model is not solely presented through one channel, such as the instructional text, but through error messages, what appears on the screen, etc. All these should be consistent.

It has recently been argued (Jones, 1991, p. 8) that the criteria offered by du Boulay, O'Shea and Monk are not sufficient for evaluating conceptual models for novice programmers as they do not give enough emphasis to what happens when novices are learning programming, and therefore do not predict the problems novices have in practice. This is also true for learning any interactive domain, although the analysis suggested to overcome this deficiency was originally applied to programming languages. Jones's argument is that, for an analysis which is helpful in designing conceptual models for novices, and which also has some predictive power, it is necessary to combine such criteria with a different approach, which categorises the conceptual model in terms of state, function and procedure. The analysis she advocates combines three criteria for a conceptual model (simplicity, consistency and visibility) with the identification of which of three views of the system (function, state and description) are most prevalent in practice, and this is described next.

## Views of the Machine

The three different views or descriptions of the system are given briefly below. A full description is given by Jones (1991):

State description        This is the state of the machine at any point in time, and will include for example, the values of variables, or in the case of DESMOND, the contents of particular memory locations.

| | |
|---|---|
| Functional description | A description of the system in terms of the goals of the task and a description of the methods for achieving the goals. The goal could be expressed at various levels of detail. In some languages (such as used in DESMOND) such a goal might be to 'add 2 numbers', and the method for achieving it would be described in terms of the contents of particular 'registers' or memory locations. In another language the goal might be to sort an unordered sequence of numbers into ascending order and the way to do this might be to use a SORT routine. Some goals might be achieved by a single statement or command, e.g. a LOGO repeat statement has the function of repeating commands. |
| Procedural description | A description of the machine in terms of the set of operators and their pre-conditions for carrying out a task. In LOGO examples include the commands for moving the turtle or for printing on the screen. In order to have a complete procedural description for drawing a square, the necessary pre-conditions include the position of the turtle on the screen. In a low level language (such as used for DESMOND) an example is the command for incrementing the contents of a register. |

Thus the functional view is distinguished from the procedural because it describes the problem in terms of goals rather than in terms of a sequence of operations. A conceptual model is unlikely to give equal emphasis to these three different views. Which of the three views is emphasised will depend on a number of factors which include the language, the types of examples given, the style of the instruction and the representation used.

There may well be examples for which it is difficult to decide which view is being given. This is not a serious problem: what is important is which aspect is emphasised or highlighted. So, for example, a functional description emphasises the function or role of the code whereas a procedural description gives the steps for carrying it out. This emphasis is important for the novice. The usefulness of the categorisation lies in identifying the different kinds of knowledge which are necessary to understand the conceptual model. It provides a way of assessing whether the conceptual model offered gives these different views, or whether it is emphasising only one or two views. For example, a conceptual model offering only a state description will not be helpful, because the steps for carrying out the solution are not fully specified – though listing the intermediate states when presenting a procedural model may be helpful since it gives the learner confirmation that his or her mental model is correct.

For the example considered earlier, DESMOND, it was the functional view which was the weakest. For example, the two main problems for students learning to use DESMOND were identifying the appropriate 'plans' to use, and flow of control. This is consistent with the lack of a functional view of the machine: students were required to use such plans as counting routines or testing the keyboard, yet such plans were not acquired by most of the students and even the simplest was not given in the DESMOND manual. Instead, the instruction manual gives examples of the plans in the form of short programs but does not give the plans themselves.

The indications, therefore, are that it is important for the novice to have a functional view of the machine, as this will help in developing programming plans. However, in the conceptual models studied it was this view which was often missing. Fortunately, such a deficit is not too hard to remedy. Wherever possible, a functional description could be displayed in addition to the state descriptions and procedural descriptions.

In a language such as DESMOND, the best way to give a functional description of the conceptual model is to give the plans. By giving the learners a functional model, their task would be made less demanding, and their chances of successful learning increased.

In spite of the concern that learners become too dependent on them, it is clear that the students in the study mentioned above (Jones, 1990) were active in their learning – interpreting the text and making connections. It seems, therefore, that the designer of distance-learning or self-instructional material for the programming novice is faced with a dilemma. The material needs to be structured and much support provided such that the novice can confidently negotiate the material, but it should not lead the novice to place too much reliance on the text. The novice needs to develop the abilities to solve the problems that will undoubtedly occur, and have faith in his or her ability to do so. However, encouraging (and indeed requiring) students to interpret the text actively means allowing them to make their own mistakes, form misinterpretations and incorrect models. The issue is not about preventing them from doing this, which is neither possible nor desirable, but about how to support them when they have made mistakes.

## Conclusions

This chapter has tried to draw together what we know from the studies of learners carrying out practical computing work at a distance, and from current and past practice in designing associated teaching material. First it seems clear that any rigid approach where learners follow step-by-step guidance and carry out activities that do not relate to their own goals will not be successful. Learners are active in their learning, and enterprising in using what knowledge and information they have to hand (and interpreting it the best they can). They are also impatient to get their hands on the system. The needs of novices and learners with more relevant experience are also likely to be different, and novices often welcome a guided step-by-step approach. However, such an approach does not need to be at the expense of providing an overview, or allowing learners to choose their own activities which fit their own goals, as exemplified by the 'Microcomputers in Schools' examples.

Students with rather more experience have different needs. They need to be able to relate the new information to what they already know. All learners (no matter what their expertise) will make errors and ways need to be found to make these errors productive rather than irritating (at best), or at worst leaving the learner in a tangle from which he or she is unable to recover. Thinking about productive errors leads to a consideration of the design of the system itself that the learner is using: even the very best instructional material cannot protect the learner from, for example, unhelpful and meaningless error messages. Also, the further the learner moves from a path determined by the instructional material, the less easy it is to give specific help in error recovery as the circumstances in which the error occurred will not be known.

One way to help learners, therefore, especially in their error recovery, is to provide a good conceptual model of the system they are using, which will give them a representation within which they can search for information, locate new information and relate different pieces of information. It has been suggested that one way of doing this – that of du Boulay, O'Shea and Monk (1981) – is limited in that it gives insufficient consideration to how learners actually use such systems and it does not provide a way of checking whether a balanced view of the conceptual model is provided. However, combining the modified du Boulay, O'Shea and Monk's criteria with this second way of analysing the different views of the conceptual model would partly overcome these problems.

The only way to know how learners will use a particular program or system is to study them. Perhaps this is the most important issue. Having designed the best possible instruction which incorporates a conceptual model, finding out what happens in practice when students are engaged in using the material is imperative. As has been discussed, learners are active and interpret what they learn in the light of the knowledge they already have. We can therefore never assume that a piece of instructional material, studied by a learner at a distance, is being used or interpreted in the way the designer intended or hoped. This is true for all self-instructional or distance-teaching material, but it has particular consequences for practical computing activities. The only way to find out how learners will use specific instructional material is to study them: there is no design process or method that can predict the outcomes or pre-empt all the learner's problems. So the design process *must* be iterative: the material must be tried out on students, and refined, and then tried again, and the cycle continued for as long as necessary.

# 7
# *Institutional Support for Home-Based Computing*

## Introduction

In Chapters 3 and 4 the introduction of home-based computing for many Open University (OU) students was described and discussed, while Chapter 5 considered how the implications varied for different groups of students. Each year since 1988, thousands of OU students have used a personal computer (PC) for the first time in order to undertake the practical computing component of courses for which they have enrolled; for a large proportion of those students it is their first experience of computing. This chapter will discuss the institutional support necessary for the introduction and maintenance of home-based computing in the OU: support not only for students but also for tutorial staff and course writers as well. This examination of the OU experience aims to draw out some of the wider implications of home-based student computing for other institutions (in distance or conventional education) that may consider implementing such a strategy.

## Supporting Students

A great deal of support is available to OU students. When they register for courses at undergraduate level (and in most of the other programmes of study), students are allocated to a 'local' tutorial group with about 25 members. The course tutor is responsible for marking and commenting upon students' assignments and for running group tutorials. They also monitor the progress of their group and provide academic support for individual learners. Tutors are, for students, the human point of contact with the OU and most expend a great deal more time and effort for the benefit of their students than they are contracted to do by the University. In the OU's system of producing and presenting distance education, many individuals remain associated with the course they tutor long after the team of course writers has disbanded and moved on to prepare other courses. (This is in contrast with 'dual mode' institutions, at which academic staff offer basically the same courses to students on campus and to those learning at a distance.) In addition, a number of other support mechanisms are available for students: for example, counsellors provide general study-skills advice and guidance on the selection of further courses and schemes, and can provide copies of television and radio programmes that have been missed and audio-taped materials for blind students. The introduction of home-based computing made it necessary for some of the OU's support systems to be adapted, while some new ones had to be created.

Enrolling for a course with an obligatory computing component presents a double challenge for students who are not already familiar with using a PC. They take on not only the intellectual demands of studying their chosen subject but also the need to learn the practicalities of using a PC and a variety of software packages. Having decided on a specification for the computing equipment students were to use (IBM PC compatible), the OU established or adapted a number of mechanisms or procedures for supporting the practical computing activities of students. These included schemes to help students acquire suitable equipment, guidance for setting up and starting up the PC, the provision of back-up facilities and an array of arrangements to provide help and guidance to overcome problems and difficulties. Individual courses included guidance on the use of specific software packages that were provided by the University as part of the course materials. Many of these are described and discussed in the following sections.

## Acquiring Hardware and Getting Started

Chapter 5 describes the options open to students who need to ensure that they have good access to a PC in order to undertake the practical computing required as part of their studies. Individual students could purchase suitable equipment or use a PC they already owned (or to which they had good access). Alternatively, it was possible to hire for the duration of a study year a machine from the pool of PCs acquired and maintained by the University, at least during the first three years of the Home Computing Policy. The OU arranged a number of discount schemes to enable students and staff to purchase a PC. A finance arrangement was also negotiated offering credit at a competitive rate. In the first year of the Home Computing Policy, about 30 per cent of the students whose studies required use of a PC purchased through a University scheme, while almost 40 per cent hired equipment from the University's pool.

In the process of getting the PC set up and running for the first time a small proportion of the students who had acquired a PC specifically for their course work found that there were faults in the equipment they received:

> I had an initial fault with the monitor. As this powers the whole system, I had to wait [for it to be replaced] before I could test everything else. When the monitor was replaced I discovered that the disk drive was also faulty.

> Computer arrived in an unserviceable condition; took 8 weeks to get three different faults corrected.
>
> (Quoted in Kirkwood and Dale, 1989, p. 6)

Students are not only concerned about receiving faulty equipment but also about the implications of being without a PC, and therefore being unable to undertake practical computing activities and complete assignments, during the tight schedule of a study year. Although the OU did locate PCs in each of its 13 regional centres to provide back-up facilities to cover such eventualities, the contingency plan was not well known by students in need and, in any case, regional centres are not conveniently located for many students.

To assist students with setting up and starting the PC, the OU provides guidance in the form of a booklet to supplement the computer manufacturer's instructions and course-specific guides. Initially these were sent with machines purchased or hired through an OU scheme and related mainly to the Amstrad 1512 and Akhter computers. In the first year of home computing the documentation and the software provided by the OU were suitable for Amstrad PCs, but many students with other IBM PC compatible machines had problems getting software to run. Students trying to run OU software on a PC with a hard disk also experienced difficulties, for example, 'The biggest problem I have had is getting the floppy disks onto hard disk. Much time and effort, and success only when a fellow student sent me a 7 page instruction sheet which he had acquired after much difficulty' (quoted in Kirkwood and Kirkup, 1989, p. 17).

These relatively minor difficulties were dealt with for the individuals concerned and in subsequent years guidance on a wider range of equipment options was provided to students. Initially, all students were supplied with software on $5\frac{1}{4}$ inch floppy disks; students using machines that take smaller disks were required to send back the large disks they had received to exchange them for $3\frac{1}{2}$ inch disks. This somewhat cumbersome procedure used up valuable time for students, as illustrated by one student's comment:

> The computer I bought took some time in arriving. I then had to send back the $5\frac{1}{4}$ inch disks and swap for $3\frac{1}{2}$ inch disks. When the $3\frac{1}{2}$ inch disks arrived, I had just finished 'copying' them when the monitor of my PC faded. I sent the monitor back and have not yet received another.
>
> (Quoted in Kirkup, 1989, p. 39)

These various incidents highlight the fact that for home-based computing, the lack of standardisation remains an issue, even when ostensibly 'compatible' equipment is being used. Supporting a variety of equipment is difficult for any institution.

Although some students managed to set up their equipment without referring to any of the written instructions, most consulted one or more of the guides. However, some required additional, more personal contact in order to get them going or to sort out problems. Computing novices and others with limited experience are likely to have difficulty diagnosing the nature of their problems. As they are working independently it is hard for them to know whether the problems they experience result from their own actions (for example, setting up the equipment incorrectly or giving inaccurate commands) or are due to hardware faults or errors in the software or course materials.

At the beginning of the first year of home computing, 1988, there were a number of special 'computer induction' meetings arranged for students in several parts of the UK. These were intended to provide practical help and hands-on activities for students with little or no computing experience. However, attendance was low and did not justify the time and costs involved. While some students seemed unaware of these special meetings taking place, many others found them unnecessary because they were held too late to be of assistance – any problems with getting the equipment set up and running had already been sorted out. In the second year of the policy, tutors for some courses were encouraged to provide an early tutorial meeting at which practical computing problems could be discussed. Although these were intended primarily for novices, students with much experience of computing also attended and some tutors found it difficult to cope with a mixed audience.

It was consistently found that women were more likely than men to seek advice and guidance from other people (for example, fellow students, family members and friends) about setting up their equipment and getting it running (Kirkup, 1989; Kirkwood and Kirkup, 1989; Jones and Singer, 1990). However, women were more likely than men to have had little or no experience of computing prior to starting their course. Students who considered themselves to be computing novices needed time and support from any available source to learn how to use the PC and to build up their confidence in its use.

## The Help Desk

Many students approached their local course tutor for help with practical difficulties, the tutor being the most familiar source of advice within the OU. However, tutors are not necessarily well informed about problems with computer hardware and software and it is not really their responsibility to provide help of this nature. The Academic Computing Service (ACS), which develops and supports computing facilities for students throughout the OU, operates a central Help Desk that students can telephone when they need assistance with computing difficulties. In 1989 up to 130 calls per day were handled by the Help Desk (Loxton, 1989) and, although the service provided is primarily of a technical nature, it is often necessary for Help Desk advisers to spend time counselling frustrated students who may have invested a great deal of time trying to overcome their difficulties by themselves. With a growing number of courses and equipment options available for home computing, it has been necessary to create a database of known problems and their solutions to assist the advice-giving process.

However, the fact that students' computing activities are primarily home based has introduced some new problems, so that providing a help service is more difficult than it was when student computing was achieved through the use of terminals at local study centres linked to a central mainframe computer. Previously, ACS advisers were able to respond to a request for help during a computing session by calling up the student's file from the mainframe on their own monitor. They were then able to see precisely what the student had done. Now the Help Desk adviser has only the verbal description given by a student to work from. In some cases this is given from memory some time after the student has switched off the machine in desperation (Loxton, 1989).

## Financial Support for Student Computing

Some students received financial assistance for the purpose of acquiring a PC for their studies. Although employers were unlikely to provide assistance for students to purchase a PC, many students received aid with the cost of hiring equipment. In 1988, about one-quarter of the students who hired a machine from the OU's pool received assistance from their employer, although men were much more likely than women to get help of this kind (Kirkwood and Kirkup, 1989).

In an attempt to retain the notion of open access to all OU courses, funding was obtained from the Department of Education and Science for the purchase of about 350 PCs to provide a free loan pool for 'disadvantaged students'. This category was taken to include students with disabilities (taking home computing or other courses) and those who were receiving financial assistance from the University's funds for unemployed or low-income students.

## Supporting the Use of Software

The software provided by the OU for students as part of their course materials includes general-purpose packages as well as specially prepared computer-assisted learning (CAL) programs and other course-specific software. Proprietary software is supplied to students under a licensing agreement and is normally accompanied by the manufacturer's documentation. Students' use of software that has been specially developed or adapted for a particular course may be introduced and supported within the main teaching texts, in separate documentation or by the use of audio-visual media. In the preceding chapter (Chapter 6) some of the key issues relating to teaching practical computing at a distance were discussed and the particular problems of catering for learners with differing levels of expertise were considered. In this section, a number of the strategies adopted by OU course teams to introduce home-based computing will be examined.

Novices to computing are more likely than other learners to spend considerable amounts of time undertaking practical work. Some courses, including the technology foundation course, have introduced practical computing sessions by means of a commentary presented to students on audio-cassette. This approach, which was discussed in Chapter 6, has proved to be extremely helpful for complete novices, of which there are many at foundation level, as it guides the learner through a computing activity step by step and helps build confidence. Even so, some students experienced difficulties co-ordinating their progress on the PC and the audio-cassette – for example, forgetting to switch off the tape if they lost track of the computing operation (Kirkup, 1989b). However, as was mentioned in the previous chapter, this method involves a real-time linear progression, which more experienced students find rather slow. It is also very difficult to locate and review particular sections of the material. Clearly an alternative form of guidance would be appropriate for students with more computing experience.

Some courses relied upon specially prepared booklets to introduce or support the practical computing activities. Many of the issues concerning the design of suitable text-based support were considered in Chapter 6. Where students are instructed simply to follow a procedure by undertaking a series of keypresses, there was little scope for them to understand the nature of the problem if any difficulties were encountered. In practical work, developing an understanding of the process can be as important as achieving the outcome:

> Many of the activities gave step-by-step instructions. These are extremely unhelpful and provide little understanding of what you are doing or how to do it. When things go wrong it is very difficult to correct. A clear explanation of the aim of the exercise and the information needed to complete it would be much better.
>
> (Quoted in Kirkwood and Dale, 1989, p. 21)

## Familiarity with Software

While it is obviously necessary to support computing novices in the use of software, there were many students with considerable experience and expertise in using particular applications packages (e.g. for wordprocessing) who need to transfer their skills to the software provided by the OU. In some cases students may be resistant to learning how to use a new package when they are familiar with one that does the job at least as well, if not better. For such students it may be necessary to do more than just offer alternative guidance to that provided for novice users; it may be appropriate to consider whether use of the same software by all students is essential to the course aims.

As the range of courses requiring home-based computing increases, there is a growing number of students who have studied several such courses and are familiar with some of the software that is common to several courses. Although the use of familiar software reduces the workload for experienced students, there may be implications for the preparation of instructional materials that address very different levels of student expertise.

## Supporting Tutorial Staff

If students are required to arrange access to a PC in order to study certain courses, then it is also necessary for their tutors to be familiar with both the equipment and the software used in teaching a particular course. Without such knowledge and experience course tutors would be unable to provide academic support and guidance to their students. In the OU, course tutors are the 'local' point of contact for students: they are responsible for marking and commenting upon students' assignments, providing optional group tutorials and supporting individual learners in their studies. Most tutors do not work full time for the OU; many are normally employed in other institutions of higher education. However, it could not be assumed that those appointed to tutor courses requiring home-based computing would already have good access to a PC or would have the appropriate computing expertise. Although people appointed to tutor courses on programming and computational techniques would be expected to have relevant computing skills, those appointed to courses that used the PC as an educational tool would be selected for their knowledge and skills in the subject area rather than for their computing experience.

Although students are advised to contact the ACS Help Desk rather than their local course tutor for help with computing problems, tutors report heavy demands being made of them for technical assistance. This is hardly surprising, as students tend to regard their tutor as the human face of the OU: their first line of communication and source of advice. The majority of tutorial staff for courses with an obligatory computing element have been very enthusiastic about the potential of the technology as a teaching tool. However, most tutors for these courses are not highly experienced computer users; in fact many have had to develop new skills in order to use a PC for the purpose of tutoring their OU students. Very many experienced OU tutors have incurred extra expense as well as significant extra work when tutoring a home-computing course, particularly during its first year.

The demands upon tutors in terms of computing activities obviously vary from course to course. Findings from studies of tutors' experiences on two courses will be used to illustrate some of the problems they experienced, the advantages they perceived from the introduction of home-based computing and their own needs for help and support.

## The Computer as a General-Purpose Tool

Students taking the technology foundation course are required to use a PC as a general-purpose tool, making use of software packages for wordprocessing, outlining, spreadsheet and database. The course also includes some CAL material (see Chapter 3 for a fuller description). A large proportion of the 4,500 students taking this course each year are new to undergraduate study with the OU and for many students the course provides their first experience of using a computer. There are more than 300 course tutors spread throughout the UK, many of whom have many years' experience of tutoring technology subjects at foundation level and above.

A survey of tutors' use of PCs was undertaken at the end of 1989, the year in which the course was first presented to students (Kirkup and Dale, 1990). Like the students, many tutors had little or no experience of using a PC and few (about 14 per cent) had previously owned suitable equipment. Although some tutors acquired a PC immediately prior to the course (about 16 per cent), almost two-thirds obtained a machine from the OU's rental pool. During the study year, most tutors had spent a considerable amount of time using the PC – typically between 2 and 4 hours per week, although use tended to be higher at the beginning of the year when it was necessary for tutors to familiarise themselves with the equipment and the software (Kirkup and Dale, 1990). Many were using a PC for the first time and some had no previous computing experience. Learning to use the equipment and the software gave them a very valuable experience that enabled them to understand problems and difficulties students encountered. Many felt that it was essential for them to share the students' experience in order to undertake their role as tutor, as illustrated by these comments:

> I had to learn DOS from scratch (and 'unlearn' the user-friendliness of the Mac I use every day). The same applies to the software provided. So I spent, I guess, the same amount of time as a student on this aspect (worked through all [assignments]). I consider all this was necessary.

> I like to go through all the material so that I can empathise with the students and be more able to answer their questions and understand their problems. . . . In some of the [assignment] questions I needed a computer so that I could try and emulate their solutions, and so find out where they went wrong.
>
> (Quoted in Kirkup and Dale, 1990, pp. 7, 9)

Many tutors felt that using the PC and software in the same way as students gave them more confidence in their tutoring. Furthermore, having a PC at home enabled them to provide advice and to answer students' queries without unnecessary delay. A number of tutors indicated that they had taken their PC to tutorial sessions (there would be no access to equipment at study centres) and some had run special sessions for students who experienced difficulties with their computing activities.

Some tutors indicated that they had used the PC for other aspects of their work as a course tutor, for example in preparing handouts, notes, examples and question sheets for use in tutorial sessions, and for administration (letters to students, student records, etc.). Several mentioned the value of extending students' awareness of the potential for using the PC constructively in other parts of this course and also in higher-level courses.

The OU provided financial support (in the form of an annual allowance) to tutors of the technology foundation course who were using their own PC, while the majority who did not possess suitable equipment were able to hire a machine from the University's pool. Many of those in the latter category were unwilling or unable to buy a PC simply for their OU tutoring, so continued access to the hire pool was seen by many as essential (Kirkup and Dale, 1990).

## The Computer as a Communications Device

One of the first three home-computing courses was *An introduction to information technology* and this remains the only major undergraduate course that requires students to use a modem for communications and conferencing using CoSy software. Although computer conferencing is only a small component of the course, the course team felt that it was essential for students actually to experience the use of various types of information technology (IT) rather than just learning about them from printed or audio-visual materials. In addition to the communications facility, students learn about the MS-DOS operating system and use wordprocessing, spreadsheet and database software packages provided by the OU as part of the course materials. The course has a complex, inter-disciplinary structure, bringing together social and technological issues related to IT and it requires tutors to possess a wide range of knowledge and skills. However, it is the use of the

PC for communications that has particular implications for the role of the tutor, and this was the subject of evaluative studies in 1988 (Mason, 1989; Thorpe, 1989).

Each year OU courses are allocated a number of hours for face-to-face tutorial sessions. Because computer mediated communication (CMC) was to be included in *An introduction to information technology*, the time for face-to-face sessions was reduced to less than half the normal allocation for a full credit course. A notional 20 hours was allocated for online tuition using the CoSy system, a diagrammatic representation of which appears as Figure 3.3 in Chapter 3. Only two or three of the 65 course tutors in 1988 had experienced computer conferencing prior to the course briefing that was held a few months before the start of the course. They were expected to welcome their students to CoSy, to put items into the tutor conference for their own local group and to log on around the time of each of the eight assignments. However, in the first year most tutors spent at least double that amount of time working on and with CoSy. As well as online time, this included learning how to use the system, preparing material for online use and reading material downloaded to avoid online charges. Perhaps it is because the tutors for *An introduction to information technology* tend to work in IT-related posts and to have a personal or professional interest in the practical aspects of the course, that they spent more time preparing for and using CoSy than specified in their contract.

Although it was necessary for all tutors to spend time learning how to use the CoSy system in the first year, there is no reason to believe that in subsequent years significantly less time was devoted to CoSy: having mastered the basics of CMC, tutors would be able to develop their skills and improve the uses made of CoSy.

There is great potential for e-mail and computer conferencing to ease and improve communications between tutors and their students, particularly for administrative or course-related matters. Instead of writing to (or telephoning) each individual in their tutor group about such matters as tutorial dates and topics, assignment deadlines, holiday absences and 'stop press' information, tutors can create a single message that can be sent simultaneously to all group members. However, until students log on regularly throughout the year (and many do not), use of CoSy increases tutor workload because it remains necessary to duplicate urgent or important messages for contact by telephone or by post.

Few tutors felt that CMC had affected the way they handled their tutorials or marked assignments. They felt that most students wanted more face-to-face tutorials and did not consider CoSy to be a substitute for group meetings: this feeling was particularly strong among those who were struggling with the course. While CoSy made it easier to contact students who logged on regularly, progress chasing relied on traditional methods for those who made little use of CMC.

When it comes to using CMC as a means of engaging in academic interaction and discussion, data from an evaluation of CoSy use in 1988 indicate the importance of tutors' contributions to the progress of discussions: 'Tutors who continued to input messages – cajoling, informative, chatty or substantive – produced the largest number of messages. Tutors who put in opening messages in each topic and then expected students to carry the ball were disappointed' (Mason, 1989, p. 141). A subsequent qualitative analysis of messages in a number of conference topics suggests that significant educational interactions can and do take place within CoSy and that tutors play a crucial role in the process (Mason, 1991). By 1990 CoSy had been structured so that each tutor had responsibility for a closed conference with his or her own tutor group (about 25 students) to discuss local matters: in addition, there were regional conferences (with 200–300 students) for the discussion of course issues, and a number of optional national conferences for technical assistance and extra discussion. Some tutors had responsibility for monitoring and organising large regional conferences, initiating, stimulating and attending carefully to the flow of the discussion, removing messages that were in the wrong topic and reminding students to keep their comments within the relevant subject area. Other tutors were free to contribute to topics and conferences that were of interest to them. To contribute effectively, tutors need to develop conferencing skills that are similar to interactions in a face-to-face seminar. From the analysis of messages in certain topics,

> it is apparent that tutors are providing a substantial input to the discussion – they stimulate new topics, they contribute new material and they redirect and focus the flow of conversation. However, [the messages] show clearly that this is not a 'chalk and talk' situation. Tutors are facilitating learning; they are not controlling it.
>
> (Mason, 1991, p. 166)

Conferencing enables dialogue between tutors and students (as well as between students) to develop in an open manner, as the status of contributors is not displayed as part of the message: everyone is able to participate equally. All participants can draw upon their knowledge and experience when contributing to a discussion topic; in the social learning process conventional teacher–student relations need not apply. However, the success of a conference can depend on the quality of its moderator. Conference moderation is time-consuming and requires skill in undertaking a range of activities. In some ways the moderator's functions are similar to those of a committee chair, a seminar leader or a facilitator, but 'the text-based, asynchronous nature of computer conferencing places entirely new demands on the moderator, for which proper training and familiarisation is needed' (Kaye, Mason and Harasim, 1989, p. 39).

It is clear that working with CMC not only requires the development of new skills to promote the active involvement of students, it can also challenge established relations. In addition, effective tutoring with CoSy necessitates a different pattern of working, as one tutor commented: 'CMC tutoring can be far more time consuming than conventional tutorials and effectively takes place on a continuous basis throughout the course rather than as three or four well defined sessions' (Davies, 1989, p. 30).

## Implications for Supporting Tutors

When courses are introduced that require home-based computing, additional demands will be made on the tutorial staff. Good access to suitable equipment is essential and arrangements must be made to ensure that a PC is readily available, preferably located in the tutor's home. Allowance must be made for tutors to learn how to use the particular hardware and software in order that they can understand students' problems and provide appropriate guidance. If a course is using the PC as a general-purpose tool, tutors are unlikely to be appointed primarily for their computing expertise; some may have little or no previous computing experience. Opportunities must be available for them to become familiar with the hardware and software before they have to deal with students' queries. For courses teaching about computing and programming, some difficulties may be encountered in recruiting suitable tutors, because people with the appropriate knowledge and skills are able to command a higher level of remuneration than is likely to be available for part-time tutoring. As well as having the subject-based knowledge and skills necessary for the course, tutors will need to develop skills for supporting students who experience difficulties with the practical aspects of computing.

If tutorials are to be held at local study centres, suitable computing equipment must be made available in sufficient quantity to support the practical activities planned for students to undertake. (There are implications for the transportation and insurance of equipment if it is to be located only temporarily at a study centre.) The nature of the course may alter the distribution of time spent tutoring. Instead of tutors concentrating their efforts around a pattern determined by a limited number of assignments and face-to-face tutorial sessions, practical computing may lead to a more continuous demand for tutors' participation, especially if CMC are involved.

The institution must provide the necessary resources and support tutorial staff with appropriate briefing and training to enable them to fulfil their enhanced role. In the OU the responsibility for supporting tutors is shared between the course team and the full-time staff (academic and administrative) in regional centres throughout the UK.

## Supporting Course Writers

As was described in Chapter 3, the ACS has overall responsibility for the development and support of non-administrative computing in the OU. The service was originally established to oversee the hardware and software requirements of student computing based upon mainframe computers and a national network of terminals located at regional study centres. The activities of ACS widened as the range of equipment and the opportunities for students to undertake practical computing increased: the latter includes computing at residential or day schools as well as home-based computing (Bramer, 1980; Butcher and Greenberg, 1992). Within ACS, the Educational Software Group is responsible for developing the software that enables academic course writers to achieve those of their teaching aims that involve the use of a computer. Despite increasingly rapid technical developments over the 1980s, it is the educational value of programs and activities that remains the most important element; good ideas for educational computing can long outlive the hardware and software that support them:

Many of the original computer developments for summer schools from the early part of the decade are still supported, now all on MS-DOS based PCs. The original Beam design program from the Materials Science summer school has been updated twice to reflect changes in the course and changes in computer hardware.

(Butcher and Greenberg, 1992, p. 214)

The educational purpose of computing activities should always be paramount. At the OU the course-team approach to preparing teaching materials enables academic course writers to plan their proposals for educational computing with technical advice from members of ACS. Course-team members work with the Educational Software Group to acquire or develop the desired software. This needs to be done as early as possible in the course preparation process, as the practical computing activities can only be fully integrated within the course if teaching materials can be written around the software. An early start on the development of computing activities should also ensure that sufficient time is available for testing the software and associated materials in as many ways as possible in order to anticipate or correct any problems. (The iterative testing of instructional materials for computing activities is discussed further in Chapter 6.) Even if proprietary software is to be used by students under a licensing agreement, it may be considered inappropriate to rely upon the commercial manual, so there will be a need for more specific guidance and instructions to be prepared and tested.

As far as possible, the production schedules for different types of course material need to be co-ordinated, as the lead times for the various components may differ considerably. For example, the production of audio-cassettes may take less time than the development of software and printed materials, but the commentary to be recorded may require the other components to be in their completed form to ensure accuracy.

Over 4,000 students registered for the first three home-computing courses in 1988 and over 13,500 students were taking seven courses in 1990. On this scale, the production of software to send to students (and tutors) as part of their course materials became a major operational issue. Like all materials prepared for distance education, the software for home-based computing needs to be produced in large quantities after it has been written and tested. It is then necessary to make multiple copies from the masters, and for the copies to be warehoused, assembled with other course materials and despatched. In 1988, 47,000 floppy disks were distributed to students; by 1990 the annual figure had risen to 180,000 (Butcher and Greenberg, 1991). Strict quality control procedures are obviously necessary during the production stages and some members of ACS were transferred from normal software design duties to undertake quality assurance roles.

## Supporting Computing for Distance Learning

If students are to undertake computing activities in their own homes (or at their place of work) a variety of support mechanisms must be put in place. Not only is it important to help students to acquire suitable equipment and software but they must also be given guidance on its use. However good the written instructions on the use of the PC and associated software, students with little or no previous computing experience are likely to need help and guidance of a more personal kind, as they need to develop not only competence but also confidence in using a PC. Those who are responsible for tutoring courses which include home-based computing need to be familiar with the hardware and software used by students in order to understand and deal with any problems. This is particularly important if a course is using a PC as a general-purpose educational tool, as tutors for such courses may have limited computing expertise. If a course is to include CMC, tutors will require briefing and training on the successful use of this facility, particularly if they are to encourage active student participation and the development of dialogue. Support is also likely to be necessary for academic course writers, primarily to ensure that their ideas for educational computing are technically feasible, although materials must also be tested thoroughly to ensure that activities can be undertaken successfully by learners working in isolation.

However, these issues don't only apply to distance-teaching institutions. Increasingly, students at conventional universities, polytechnics and colleges are being expected to arrange their own access to computing facilities. The kinds of support services provided by the OU for its students are likely to be necessary in cases where students are expected to undertake home-based computing.

Of course, the model of home-based computing adopted by the OU is not the only one possible. The OU strategy is primarily concerned with achieving uniformity in terms of the hardware and software used by students and tutors, to the extent that much of the support and guidance provided aims to overcome problems arising from the use of non-standard hardware and software. One alternative approach would be to establish clear educational aims to be achieved by the use of a PC and to let students decide which particular pieces of hardware and software were most suitable and accessible for them to achieve those aims. In this case, support would assume diversity and greater individual responsibility for achieving the educational goals. Such an approach may be unsuitable for some courses – for example, ones on which there are likely to be a high proportion of complete novice users, or for which there is a considerable amount of specially written CAL material. However, the increasing use of commercial software (word-processing, spreadsheet, database, etc.) for educational purposes and for communications (with other users and with remote databases) makes uniformity less of a necessity.

Another alternative approach is necessary when one institution offers its students courses that have been prepared and produced by another. For example, the Open Learning Institute in Hong Kong offers a number of distance-education courses that have been prepared elsewhere: one of these is the OU course *The fundamentals of computing*, which requires students to undertake home-based computing activities. Although the course materials are acquired from the OU, the Open Learning Institute is responsible for providing tutorial and other forms of support and for assessing its students. In cases where whole courses are used by other institutions, the nature and level of support that can be provided for students and tutors has to reflect the local circumstances.

The strategy for home-based computing adopted by the OU provides a large-scale example of institutional changes made in response to educational innovation. The next chapter examines the nature of educational and institutional change, particularly in relation to IT innovations.

# 8
# *The Process of Institutional Change*

> The university is among the most traditional of all institutions of our society, and, at the same time, it is the institution most responsible for the changes that make our society the most changing in the history of man.
>
> (Hesburgh, 1971, p. 3)

This quotation sums up the contradictory attitude towards universities that has been common for at least a hundred years. Universities are seen as defending class privilege and perpetuating outmoded and sometimes offensive forms of behaviour and arcane areas of study that seem merely to be vestigial remains of a previous world. Yet they are also seen as hot houses for new and sometimes dangerous ideas. And, as Seymour (1988) argues when he quotes Hesburgh, the fact that they continue to exist at all when many of them had their foundations in the medieval world is an indication of their ability to adapt and change. Why and how does innovation and change come about in universities? – especially if, as Seymour argues, they have a high 'comfortability index' and 'operate with no great sense of urgency or uncertainty' so that a 'climate for innovation is therefore not a natural happenstance. It must be orchestrated' (Seymour, 1988, p. iv).

Studying the adoption of student-based personal computers (PCs) in the Open University (OU) will illustrate the combination of forces that were involved in directing educational change in one particular institution. Generalisable points can be made, some relevant to the wider UK university context and others to the international distance-education context, but the OU also has special features. It has always seen itself as an innovatory institution with a mass higher-education mission that is only more recently being adopted by other UK universities and by distance-education institutions in other countries. It was also one of the first universities to exploit a variety of technologies to teach. A former OU professor, Tony Bates, argues strongly (1986, p. 2) that the OU is an important agent for technological innovation in both education and the world at large:

a) by creating *courses* which encourage innovation: these courses not only influence *specific target groups*, but through their method of dissemination these courses also bring to the attention of *the general public* important technological developments

b) by using teaching *methods* and *media* which are themselves technologically innovative, influencing not only the students who study in this way but also the educational world at large

c) by itself being a *system* which is designed to be innovative, adaptive and productive.

This chapter will examine why the OU adopted the policy of student-based PCs when it did through an examination of the process of innovation that took place in the University. In doing this it will also look in contrast at some potentially innovatory technology which was not taken up. In Chapter 3 we gave the history of the development of computing at the OU as if it was driven almost solely by internal pressures, and was dependent simply on the technical development of the *right* solution. But no educational institution operates outside a social and political context and, if theorists like Cohen, March and Olson (1972) are correct, then there is no guarantee that the 'organised anarchy' that characterises the decision-making processes of most universities will come up with any solutions at all, never mind good ones.

## The Political and Economic Context of the 1980s

The early 1980s were an unhappy time for UK universities. The higher education system of the 1960s and 1970s had appeared to ally itself with the left in British politics. It had thrived with expansionist educational policies, including the creation of new universities and polytechnics in the 1960s, and had received relatively generous government funding. But the 1970s brought with them a shrinkage in the population of 19-year-olds and the beginning of a series of recessions which have plagued the UK economy ever since. They also brought with them a Conservative government who, for both economic and political reasons, wanted changes made to British higher education. These included cuts in funding, increases in student numbers, more vocationally oriented courses, and a closer relationship with industry, which it was hoped would increasingly provide the funding that was being cut by central government. In this environment the OU felt itself to be particularly threatened.

Politically it was an institution with a specific ideological mission, a child of socialist politics, expected not only to offer education to many who had never before had the opportunity but, as we discussed in Chapters 3 and 5, it was also hoped by some that it would bring about social change by doing so. Also the fact that all its course material was in the public domain meant that it was scrutinised and in some cases criticised for political bias: specifically for Marxist bias – not a comfortable position during a period when universities were seen by right-wing critics as hot houses of Marxism and communism. Economically the OU was criticised as expensive because of the large block grant it received each year from the government. OU staff began to talk guiltily about the OU's 'Rolls-Royce' model of course production. This had been one of the proud trademarks of the University in the early 1970s and a factor which contributed towards its reputation for quality, but in the 1980s it looked to many people like an extravagance that could no longer be justified. However, it should be noted that it cost only about one-third as much to produce an OU graduate in the 1980s (Bates, 1986) as it did to produce a traditional graduate, and the OU graduate was likely to have been carrying on an occupation, or managing a family, at the same time as they studied.

In the 1980s universities all over Britain implemented strategies of voluntary severance and early retirement, along with 'frozen' posts and reduced staff costs. Wherever it was possible, budgets were reduced, for example on library stock and accommodation. Courses were 'rationalised' and 'modularised' to cope with more students at less cost, and the number of vocationally oriented courses was increased, especially in business and management studies. The OU had to cut course production costs and all media components of courses had to be produced more cheaply. Some solutions to this have expanded the influence and reputation of the University, for example the co-publication of some course texts with major publishing houses which then market them internationally through bookshops. Other solutions, such as student fee increases, have meant that students have borne an increasingly larger share of the financial costs of their study. Each new strategy was debated fiercely in the University Senate or at faculty level and course team meetings where the content and structure of new courses was decided.

The OU also faced new challenges from other institutions. Once it had been one of the few UK universities to cater for mature (over the age of 23) students; the others, for example Ruskin college in Oxford, were small and highly selective. In the 1980s all higher education institutions began to recruit larger numbers of mature students to replace the shrinking numbers of 18-year-olds. Once the OU had been the only higher education institution in the UK to have no entry requirements to its degree programmes. In the 1980s polytechnics in particular adopted policies of widening access to students (often mature students, and often women) by providing pre-degree 'bridging' or 'access' courses for those students who did not have the traditional entry requirements. Once the OU had been the only recognised higher education institution in the UK to use distance teaching but during the 1980s the UK government established the Open College, which produced vocational courses through a network of local institutions. This development in particular was seen within the OU as being potentially very threatening, because it showed that the government was experimenting with a different model of national distance education in which there was no specially funded central organisation employing its own academic staff. These new developments provided potential competition for the OU, and there was no guarantee that the expanded pool of potential higher and further education students was large enough to support them all. On any 'comfortability index', the OU and its staff would have scored very low during the 1980s. The University had to re-assess its aims and its mode of operation urgently, and make decisions about the directions it wanted to go in for the 1990s and beyond. In fact government attitudes were more favourable than most people had anticipated, and many traditional institutions fared much worse in terms of their financial health. The government of the time seemed to appreciate the potential of the OU as a national system which could provide updating and training in a period when these were seen as part of the prescription for recovery from recession. Also, more pragmatically, the OU received its funding directly from central government, and was therefore more responsive to targeted funding and government criticism than other UK universities who were funded through a central funding body (the Universities Funding Committee) which served as a buffer between them and central government.

## The Creative Forces of an Institution

However, the explanation of why the OU has historically been such an innovatory institution cannot be explained solely as a result of economic pressures and its relationship to government. External pressures and internal anxieties can as easily tip an institution into crisis and paralysis as into innovation and energy. Like most universities, but perhaps more so than many, the OU is an institution full of creative people looking for outlets for their ideas and their energy, many of whom joined the University in its early stages with a commitment to this innovatory area of education, and with a desire to help build its reputation. The structure of universities is such that the management of this creativity is problematic. As has already been said, universities have been characterised as a form of 'organised anarchy' (Cohen, March and Olson, 1972). During the 1980s when UK universities and polytechnics went through a longer and more extensive period of innovation and change than many commercial businesses, this form of anarchy produced results. Yet much of the literature on innovation in education discusses it in terms of the institutional *barriers to change* rather than the *creative potential of the institution*. For example the following, from Brown in a book on *The Electronic Campus* (ed. Brindley, 1989a), lists what he sees are the strategic issues facing universities adopting new information systems:

- Our limited conceptual capability to anticipate the changes that are likely in our environment as a result of new technologies
- Inertia of both individuals and institutions
- The organisation, which can either facilitate or throw up barriers
- Resources, a scarcity of which can impede or even preclude the adoption of new technologies
- Standards in operating systems, communication, protocols, interfaces, computing language etc . . .
- Conflicts resulting from traditional academic, teaching and publishing structures and practices and the necessity to recognise new modes of economic and professional reward in an increasingly non-print environment; and published information overload and its increasingly reduced use
- Insufficient knowledge of how we learn and how computer technologies can effectively be used in the cognitive process
- The complexity and cost of software development and maintenance
- The changes for faculty, administration, publishers and others in coping with the rapid obsolescence of constantly changing hardware and software

(Brown, 1989, pp. 29–30)

This kind of list, although included in an article which was exhortatory about adopting information technologies, concentrates on the weaknesses and pitfalls faced by universities without also examining their strengths and opportunities. The OU had a history of technological innovation in its research and in its teaching. Some of this technology was never implemented on a large scale, usually because of apparent economic issues. A short discussion of some of these projects gives the impression of an institution where innovative ideas were nurtured but where sometimes the resources for them, or the institutional will to adopt them, was lacking.

## Computing Innovations which Were not Adopted

The story as we presented it in Chapter 3 might suggest that all OU technical developments in information technology (IT) and computing led towards the establishment of the Home Computing Policy. This was not the case. Since the 1970s research groups within the University developed experimental ITs, some of which in 1992 still have potential for the future, while others, discussed below, have been overtaken by developments. The first of three initiatives we will discuss, Cyclops, never got beyond experiments internal to the institution, but what it was trying to achieve in terms of a graphical interface and audio interface for students and tutors to communicate with each other is very sophisticated. The second, interactive videodisc, still has great potential and the OU continues to experiment with it, but it remains too expensive to be a regular educational medium. And finally there was Optel, an experiment in which the technological problems were solved, but the human costs of maintaining the system were too high.

### Cyclops

Cyclops is like a long distance overhead projector with a TV screen acting as both the writing surface and the projected display, so any black pen picture that can be drawn on an overhead projector transparency can be transmitted via Cyclops.

(Sharples, 1987, p. 66)

'Cyclops' was a device developed at the OU in the 1970s by three academics: Graham Read, Chris Pinches and David Liddel. It had interesting educational aims, some of which are now being explored by more established forms of computer-mediated communication (CMC), and others by newer developments. The potential of a Cyclops-like system would enormously enhance any computer-based communication system.

McConnell (1984) described Cyclops as a 'telewriting' or 'audiographics' system, in which a number of individuals in different locations could make input on to a 'shared' display screen, linked over the public telephone system. Technically the system consisted of a Cyclops terminal, which was a medium-resolution graphics terminal with a 6800 Motorola processor, with a light-sensitive pen, an electronic digitising pad, two telephones (one for speech communication attached to a loudspeaker and one attached to the

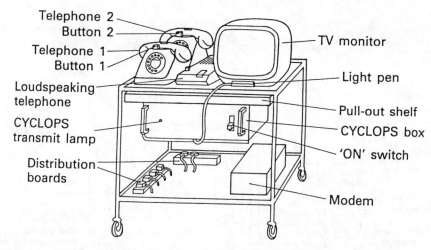

Telephone 2
Button 2
Telephone 1
Button 1
Loudspeaking telephone
CYCLOPS transmit lamp
Distribution boards
TV monitor
Light pen
Pull-out shelf
CYCLOPS box
'ON' switch
Modem

Figure 8.1   Cyclops: the user's view (from Jones, Scanlon and O'Shea, 1987)

modem to transmit pictures) and a standard TV screen. Figure 8.1 shows what the system looked like to the user.

Cyclops provided both a writing and a drawing facility. The light pen could indicate menu commands on screen and it could also be used for drawing on screen and on the digitising pad. Cyclops could operate in 'local mode' where an individual or group had complete control over what was on the screen, or when linked via the modem the screen became a communal picture area to which anyone could contribute. The parallel verbal communication over the telephone in what was effectively a telephone conferencing facility provided, in theory, a highly interactive system. A tutor could lecture to students and use illustrations at the same time; students were able to interrupt both the speech and the visual display if they felt the need. An even more interesting feature was that a group discussion could include shared visual materials that were either drawn during the discussion or prepared ahead of time and transmitted, since line drawings could be made and stored on cassette-tape.

The Cyclops system was never developed beyond its research and development phase. Sets of equipment were only available at some study centres and were therefore usually used by groups of students linked to a tutor and other groups of students in other centres for planned tutorials. This is shown in Sharples' (1987) conceptual model of the system (Figure 8.2).

Although the evaluation of the system demonstrated its enormous potential, its major drawbacks were that it was expensive both in terms of the equipment and also in the advance preparation of material. Tutors needed training to prepare material and to get the best from the system in operation. As long as it was restricted to study centres it suffered from all the disadvantages that students faced in organising attendance. Sharples (ibid.) also found that students came up against many difficulties in using the equipment. Some of these were technical faults to do with connecting both

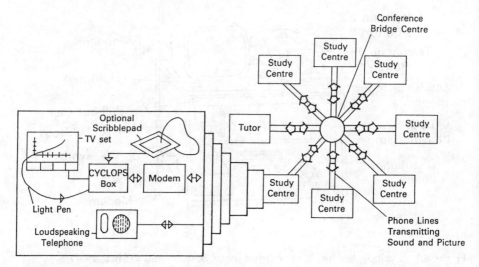

Figure 8.2   Cyclops: the conceptual model (from Jones, Scanlon and O'Shea, 1987)

sound and vision links, not unlike those found by students using study-centre computer terminals, but compounded by the fact that two links had to be made. Other problems were caused by students being unable to follow operating instructions and behaving in a way that seemed to them intuitively correct but that often did not correspond to the correct operating procedure they had been asked to follow. We have already discussed this, in Chapter 6 in particular, as a common problem when students are learning to use computer systems.

But the main reason for the failure of Cyclops was that it was impossible to get development money to manufacture the hardware:

> Development is at least as important and as difficult as research – especially finding adequate funds for development. The intermediary stage between research and full-scale manufacture and use requires substantial funds, and is a high risk activity. This is a particularly difficult area for a university or a teaching institute, and consequently external funding from industry or research bodies is essential.
>
>   For this reason, it is easier to innovate using existing manufacturing equipment which can be bought off the shelf, rather than developing one's own equipment.

(Bates, 1980, p. 15)

Bates drew that conclusion in 1980, but it had not become an obvious one for others in the OU. In the early 1980s the OU was producing a basic PC, the Hector, which was specifically designed for students on a digital computing course and then used as a home-based terminal to a mainframe for a programming course. In the early days of designing the policy for home-based computing, one of the options considered was that of mass-producing Hectors which would then be borrowed or bought by OU students. That turned out not to be feasible since, as with Cyclops, it wasn't possible to get the necessary investment. But that realisation was only made after experiments with these devices.

## Interactive Videodisc

The first interactive videodisc the University produced in 1984 in collaboration with the BBC achieved a certain fame and has been quoted frequently in the literature. It was used in a materials science course and explored the reasons for the failure of materials in the construction of a teddy-bear's eyes. Students had to respond to prompts in the system in the role of an expert witness (Laurillard, 1985; Butcher, 1986). The system was composed of an Apple II computer containing the interactive software which operated a Phillips videodisc player with a teletext generator, and the output was displayed on a television screen. What the student saw in response to their keyboard input was text and TV images, both dynamic and still.

Videodisc technology has remained very expensive, both in terms of the production of the interactive disc and in terms of the cost of the equipment to play it back. Another disc was produced in 1987 (Bolton, Every and Ross, 1990) in collaboration with the BBC and Phillips/Acorn, who produced the hardware. At present (1992) there is no intention to produce videodiscs for individual student use. They have been produced for group use at residential school and to some extent with the aim of being sold to other users. The production costs are very high and it is necessary to have financial support from elsewhere. Laurillard (1987b, p. 141) writes very pessimistically about the impact of financial constraints on future production of educational videodiscs:

> A number of unlikely conditions must be fulfilled if interactive video is to be implemented efficiently and effectively. Institutions that wish to develop the medium must put together a team of people experienced in video production, CAL design, graphics design, text design and educational design, as well as subject matter experts. They must find financial support for the necessary research projects on form of presentation, means of access, and the relevant aspects of student learning. The resources required for development are therefore considerable and the enterprise only makes economic sense if the product can be used by a large number of learners – over several years and/or over several institutions.

In the case of interactive videodisc, even when the hardware was already developed and commercially available, the costs of developing good teaching to use on it were too great for an educational institution to bear. This does not appear to have been the case for training in industry where, in the boom years of the late 1980s, companies were willing to commit large budgets to training. However, in our experience, the quality of these interactive training videodiscs was variable.

## Optel

Optel was modelled on the UK Prestel system, part of what is known generically as 'viewdata' in the UK or 'videotex'. A database of University information, mostly about courses, was set up on the Dec 20 system. This was updated frequently so that accessing it would give the best information on, for example, course application rates, or 'stop press' bulletins about courses and events. This kind of information is very useful for students, but is normally only available when it is mailed at intervals. With Optel information was transmitted to the regional offices and areas of the central Walton Hall site. Had it been successful, the intention was to expand it and also to use it to transmit software. However, after its main trial in 1983, it was found to be too labour intensive to update the database relative to the amount of use it received and it was discontinued. Developments in remote data access through PCs led to the early prediction (Bacsich, 1984) that distinctions between viewdata, computer, telewriting and facsimile (fax) terminals will vanish. This has yet to happen, and the problem remains that it is the cost of maintaining the database which is too great for the University to bear, regardless of how that database is accessed.

## Reasons for Failure to Implement and Innovate

These three examples reinforce an argument which was made in Chapter 1 about the development of educational software, which is that the educational market may be big in terms of the numbers of individuals involved, but it is not financially very profitable as far as manufacturers of software and hardware are concerned. Educational needs have not driven developments in either of these markets, and educational systems and institutions have learned that they must 'piggyback' on developments for the commercial or domestic market. Certainly as far as hardware was concerned this was what the OU realised and, although there is a large Academic Computing Service designing tailor-made software, it was apparent that the University would need to buy in commercial software and that on some courses this would be the majority of the software used.

However, another equally compelling argument can be made for why these three innovations failed to be adopted: their designers and their champions were not as skilled at rallying the University's support and resources as were the architects of the finally adopted Home Computing Policy.

## Agents of Change

Adams and Chen (1981, from pp. 267–70) list six criteria for the acceptance and persistence of an innovation:

- The initial acceptance of an innovation is a function of the relevant power that can be marshalled in its support. The greater the relevant power, the greater the likelihood of acceptability . . .
- The initial acceptability of an innovation is a function of the extent to

which, as a change, it is seen to threaten the power of existing groups. The less the perceived threat, the greater the acceptability . . .

- The initial acceptability of an innovation is a function of the extent to which the benefits expected to result are thought to be in excess of the costs entailed. The greater the benefits (relative to costs), the greater the likelihood of acceptance (and vice versa) . . .
- The initial acceptability of an innovation is a function of negotiation protocol. The greater the violation of protocol, the less the likelihood of acceptability . . .
- The initial acceptability of an innovation is a function of the rhetoric used. The more the rhetoric conveys the impression of difference between the innovation and the status quo, the greater the likelihood of rejection . . .
- The persistence of an innovation is a function of the innovation's credibility. The greater the gap between promise and performance, the less the credibility. The less the credibility, the less the likelihood of persistence.

Those who proposed and promoted the policy of a home-based PC for OU students managed to fulfil every positive criteria on this list. There were two phases to the Home Computing Policy: the first part, described mainly through the history given in Chapter 3, involved getting home-based PCs for students studying courses which included computing, in the traditional mathematical or programming sense; or for courses about IT. The economic and operational aspects of this were significant, and the principle of students having to ensure their own access to a particular medium was a radical change. But it involved only a limited commitment to a small content area and to a relatively small body of students and staff. In 1989 the Head of the OU's Academic Computing Service, who was instrumental in designing the technical specification, specified this limited phase of the policy:

*What the Home Computing Policy is not*

(i) It is not a policy aimed at every Open University student. Courses within the programme are either teaching about the technology or its direct application. Computer assisted learning on its own is never a justification to have a course included in the programme although many courses have a computer assisted learning element.

(ii) It is not a policy aimed at changing the way the University teaches in any fundamental way. I believe that computer technology will eventually fundamentally change the way the University teaches and offers its student support services. That however can only happen when the University can assume that *all* students can have easy home based access to the necessary technology.

(Burrows, 1989, p. 1)

But there were other people who had a much more radical view of the role of home-based computing. Their aim was, ultimately, to have a computer on the desk of every OU student, and the very limited definition of the policy described above was for them not the sum total of home computing but the first step. The next and more radical phase began when the course team of the foundation course in technology argued that their students should use a home-based PC because it was a *necessary tool* for any present-day technology student. Once this notion of the PC as a student tool was accepted more widely in the University then the technology foundation course became the thin end of a wedge in which courses in a variety of faculties could, if they wished, also argue for the importance of a PC as a tool in their disciplines. This expansion of the purpose of the policy was no accidental effect, but part of a vision and a very deliberate strategy carried out by a small group of academics.

What follows in this chapter is our interpretation of the events which led to this grander vision becoming incorporated into OU policy. It is always invidious to pick out particular individuals and discuss the importance of their role in events, because it diminishes the role of others who were also involved. As an innovatory idea permeates through an institution many people take ownership of it and it is impossible to say whether it ever was any one person's original idea. But some individuals played a very public role which makes it impossible to understand the process of the adoption of home computing without explicitly identifying and examining what they did.

In any innovation people play different roles: they will be agents of change or targets of change (Seymour, 1988). There are also different roles for those who are agents of change, the main ones being the innovator (the person with the vision) and the champion (the person with the power to support the vision). It is interesting to look at the role of two particular individuals, members of the technology faculty: John Naughton and Professor Jake Chapman, who were major change agents in getting this more radical stage operationalised. This is not to suggest that the vision of PCs for all students was not held by other members of the University – it was, but it was these two academics who understood the operation of the University well enough to see how to get a vision adopted as institutional policy.

They are both long-standing members of the University who are known as much for their ability to produce good teaching material, and interesting and popular courses, as they are for their scholarship. They had a reputation for being able to turn their ideas into practical teaching material. They were also seen as being strongly committed to the University and its special mission as both an open-access and a distance-teaching institution. They were aware of the development of competition from other institutions and both felt strongly that unless the OU could incorporate the potential of the new ITs into its teaching systems, it could no longer hold its position as one of the world's major distance-teaching institutions. For them the solution lay not, for example, in desktop publishing or in increasingly powerful computer-based management systems, but in putting the power of personal computing into students' homes, and then using them as multi-purpose distance-education tools.

They had themselves been using PCs in their own work for some time, and had tested out a variety of commercial applications packages, such as spreadsheets and wordprocessing packages which they felt would be useful for any student. They had even made contact informally with the producer of their preferred package to see whether a formal deal with the University would be welcomed. Naughton was a public and dynamic member of the various committees involved in discussing new technology policy in the University from its very early stages, which ensured that he played a central role in the debates and discussions. Chapman on the other hand was not initially such a public protagonist: he wrote discussion papers from an apparently more objective position. These fed into the debates which were going on with some energy during the 1980s, and contributed to the fact that the vision of home-based PCs for students became 'owned' by a large and diffused body of people in the University, and 'owned' particularly by the technology faculty.

The technology faculty at the OU has always had problems with its teaching. There is a severe limit to how much practical work can be taught to distance-education students when their only laboratory experience is at a week-long summer school, or briefer weekend schools. This was always perceived as a threat to the external credibility of technology courses and particularly with industry at a time when higher education was being criticised for its lack of industrial relevance. It was partly the reason why so many technology courses were innovatory in other ways such as their content, or the design of the teaching materials and special home experiment kits (HEKs). The possibility of technology students all having a powerful PC at home on which they could do calculations, modelling, designing, simulation as well as write reports would provide a new kind of credibility to OU technology courses. This was recognised and embraced by members of that faculty very quickly, and the Dean of Technology became a public defender of the idea that the PC should be introduced on the foundation course of that faculty.

Outside the technology faculty there was hostility to this expansion of the policy from a variety of areas, but basically around one issue: how far the obligation on students entering their first year in the University to ensure access to a PC would prove a major barrier to access. As long as PCs were only obligatory for specialised second- and third-level courses, then it was possible for any student who could not or would not get a PC to do a degree in any discipline, apart from computing, without using home-based computing. Once a PC was obligatory on a foundation course then students wishing to do a degree in any field in that faculty would have to get access to one, and effectively all students in that faculty would be obliged to learn some computing skills. This policy was significant enough to become a major item of debate for a meeting of the University Senate.

## Persuading the Institution

Like all traditional universities, the OU has a Senate, and all academic teaching staff are members by right. Other categories of staff, such as research staff, and students have representative members and the right as individuals to attend but not to vote. It is the place where major policy issues of the University are finally voted on after they have been discussed throughout the University through various committee and discussion documents. It is the democratic forum of the University and the place where any issues that concern members can be addressed because any member may get an issue on the agenda by putting a question to Senate. The Senate is chaired by the Vice Chancellor, who has no more voting rights than any other member, and sometimes the Senate has used its power to censure the Vice Chancellor when it has been unhappy about strategy or actions.

When the issue of home computing on the technology foundation course came to Senate, the nature of the debate and its outcome reflected the careful groundwork already carried out by its proponents, and just how far they had understood the criteria necessary to have an innovation accepted. Proponents (such as the Professor of Information Technology in Education, Tim O'Shea) had already organised University-wide public workshops where there was a forum for those antipathetic to the whole idea, or who wanted a different specification adopted, such as Apple Macintosh PCs, to engage in debate. This spread enthusiasm for the idea, but it also spread a sense of ownership of it amongst those who became publicly involved. By the time the Senate debate occurred there could be no one left in the University who was unaware of the issues, and a great many people had developed well-argued opinions. In the actual debate popular and powerful individuals such as the Dean of Technology and the then Deputy Vice Chancellor, Professor Norman Gowar, publicly supported the policy, and the technology faculty presented a united front through its Dean. The role of the Deputy Vice Chancellor as 'champion' of home computing in the OU was crucial from an early stage. He was the main person responsible for negotiating the funding from the Department of Trade and Industry (DTI) and the Department of Education and Science (DES) which supported the student subsidy scheme and provided machines for the rental pool. Without his championship and negotiating skill the original policy could not have been implemented in its final form, and without the subsidy and the rental pool hostility to the policy would have been much greater. It is possible that if those 'failed' innovations discussed earlier had been championed in a similar way then the resource problems which finally halted them might have been overcome.

It is traditional amongst academics that if one discipline wants to go ahead with something that apparently involves only themselves and their students then other disciplines are loath to interfere. The one important individual who spoke against the policy was the then Vice Chancellor, Dr John Horlock, who felt strongly enough to hand over his chairmanship of the Senate meeting for that particular item to someone else so that he could speak against it. However, his arguments were not strong enough to counter the forces on the other side, and with respect to his role in Senate, neither was his power.

The policy was also not presented as a first step in a larger vision, but as something special and crucial to technology courses. In this way it was not presented as a threat to others. If a large group within the University, such as the regional staff *en masse* or the Academic Computing Service, had spoken against it the critics would then have had an identifiable and threatened group to rally round. As it was even the student representatives, the Open University Students' Association (OUSA), did not have a consistent position. They seemed split between support and criticism of the principle, but were mostly concerned about cost. In fact it is possible that some faculties felt that they would benefit if the policy deterred students from studying technology since this could mean students coming to study courses in their faculty instead.

The benefits of the policy to the University were presented as great while the costs were presented as relatively small because students would be bearing the cost of access while being supported by the subsidy scheme and the loan pool. Therefore no group could argue that resources were being taken from them to fund this project.

In terms of protocol – in this case the decision making systems of the University – the proponents of the policy had carefully worked through the official committee and public debate structure as well as privately through other networks. It was not possible for anyone to attack them or the policy because they felt that proper procedure had not been carried out.

The rhetoric presented by the proponents (and it has to be said that they were all excellent rhetoricians) argued that the policy was not a radical change of direction for the OU but a logical extension of the OU's mission as an innovator in distance education, and that, as the general Home Computing Policy was already in place, all that was being discussed was the addition of another, although an admittedly special, course.

The outcome of the debate was an interesting one and one that could have blocked the policy. It was that the foundation course in technology could be included in the Home Computing Policy but only if the cost to students of getting access to a PC at home could be kept to £50, which was the upper limit for the costs of set books for any course. It was quite obvious to most people by 1988 that the cost of PCs was not going to drop to £50 by 1990, and at that time the costs to students of renting from the pool was £150. However, the Deputy Vice Chancellor was so committed to the vision that he was able to get more central government funds in order to buy more PCs so that the rental pool could be expanded and the cost of rental to foundation course students reduced to £50.

This demonstrates the importance for any innovator of preparing the ground well, and ensuring that there is strong support from powerful people because, in a public forum, and a truly democratic debate, the outcome is never certain. Chapman and Naughton had not expected Senate to make the decision they did, and some time later Chapman drew up a humorous list of criteria for getting an innovation through the University. The first two criteria were '1. Do not tell the Vice Chancellor what you are intending' and '2. Do not ever get into the position of having Senate discuss your proposals' (Chapman, from unpublished personal papers).

In another institution where the ethos might be to defend traditional forms of academic work it would be very difficult to have the vision of a computer on every student's desk accepted, and even in the OU it is not now accepted by all disciplines. However, in an institution such as the OU which views itself, and is viewed externally, as innovative, the arguments against an innovation need to be at least as powerful as the arguments for. One of the interesting aspects of the Home Computing Policy was that it was an idea that spread upwards from academic staff who argued it through formal and informal channels in such a way that ownership of the idea became diffused throughout the institution. If the policy had come from the top down, perhaps from an external authority, as many educational innovations do (for example the UK National Curriculum in schools), the outcome may have been entirely different.

# 9
# *Issues for the Future*

## Personal Computing in the Open University from 1988:
## An Overview

The 1980s were a period of rapid expansion in information technology (IT) developments. In education such developments were patchy: some institutions (e.g. some American universities) invested a great deal of resources in introducing IT and setting up the infrastructure to support it, whereas other institutions saw only piecemeal developments, if any. Even where projects were started to introduce IT, little evaluation has been carried out so that it is difficult to assess how well the developments are progressing once the initial phase of the project is over. It is within this context that the Open University (OU) Home Computing Policy was introduced. Other UK innovations in introducing widespread access to IT have been on a relatively small scale: the OU exercise involves 17,000 students a year as well as many more on postgraduate courses. Another important feature of the OU innovation is that access is in the students' homes. It is features like these which make it rather different from other innovations and lead it to be described as 'probably the most significant and sustained IT innovation to be undertaken in any British tertiary institution in the 80s' (Open University, 1992, p. 24). Although conservative in terms of the specification adopted, the policy was risky in terms of the administration and structural changes required; nevertheless it has been remarkably successful. The director of the University's Academic Computing Service describes its success in terms of the way it harnessed existing technology:

> The university's achievement has not been educationally innovative, in the sense of designing a new educational workstation, but is innovative in its use of existing technology. The decision to adopt MS-DOS IBM compatibility as the standard was fundamental to the success of the project. By exploiting what was commercially available, rather than developing hardware and software especially tailored to meet educational needs, the University has not got itself locked into a technical solution that has limited scope within the wider community.
>
> (Berry and Burrows, 1990, p. 949)

In the preceding chapters we have seen that some of the assumptions underlying the original policy have not been borne out – for example, it was originally expected that the growth of personal computers would be rapid. Indeed, as late as 1990, Berry and Burrows (*ibid.*, emphasis added) commented that

With its present programme it has demonstrated that it has the technical ability and the administrative and operational systems in place to support a community of 13,000 students with workstations. This system can be built upon and extended to the total student community *when home based facilities become generally available.*

The draft report of a sub-group of the University's Academic Computing Committee on the future of personal computing from 1996 notes that

It was implicitly assumed (though rarely articulated) by those involved in formulating the policy that the personal computer would follow the same path as the video recorder – i.e. that it would become so common as a household item that the university could take ownership of (or at least ready access to) one more or less for granted.

(Open University, 1992, p. 20)

Clearly this has not been the case, but this assumption – that home access to a personal computer (PC) could soon be largely assumed (as it often is, but unofficially, with video-recorders) was one of the factors which led the University to restrict itself initially to a four-year policy. However, the assumption that the use of computers in education generally and in higher education in particular would be an expectation of every student entering those institutions is more grounded in reality. The assumptions of cost decrease have not been borne out either, and the report on post-1996 computing makes the more realistic assumption that 'the cost of computing power will continue to decrease, but this will be offset to some extent by continual enhancement of what the market regards as the base-level PC specification' (Open University, 1992, p. 4).

## Considerations for Introducing PCs into Distance Education

What have we learned between 1988 and 1992 at the OU which can inform us about the most important considerations for introducing PCs into distance education? This section looks at this question by raising issues that any distance-education institution thinking of embarking on such a venture should consider.

### *Machine Specification*

Will students be required to have a microcomputer to a required specification? Deciding to do this (as the OU did) has a number of disadvantages. Trying to gauge the market in advance is very tricky. Manufacturers rise and fall. Students who have a computer but not the 'right' one, have to get hold of another. It limits the software to what's available on that machine or type of machine. However, at least two of the major types of PCs (Macintoshes and MS-DOS machines) are now producing software that will also run on the other machine. It seems likely, then, that the market is settling down (to the MS-DOS specification?), and that most software will run under this.

Hardware and software will suffer from dating. However, one main advantage is that both writing structured material and supporting students at a detailed level is much easier. In the case of writing course material, students can be supported in a detailed way, if desired, as discussed in Chapter 6, including providing them with screen photographs. It is also easier to support students when things go wrong if the type of machine is known and the exact software they are using is specified. In one sense this is analogous to the detailed study of a particular literary text: if the course entails a detailed analysis, then students need not only to have the same text but also the same edition, so that everyone is working on identical material. Unlike studying a book, some students are likely to have difficulties learning to use computer applications, and advice on this and what to do if they've got stuck is only possible when the behaviour of the application program can be reproduced in detail. It is also possible to produce in-house software without having to worry about producing a number of different versions.

If students are being asked simply to have access to a machine which perhaps can run standard software (such as tools), it won't be possible to tailor course material so closely to the student's situation. This has certain advantages: for example, students can use the software they already have, with which they're familiar, or which they can easily get hold of.

## Access

Different groups of students do not have equal access to PCs, as we have seen. Some groups have better access overall, and the machines they do have are more powerful. In the case of the OU, on one foundation course, only 15 per cent of all students owned a suitable machine. Fewer than 10 per cent have a modem. There is no reason to suppose that such findings are constrained to the OU. Other institutions need to be aware that, as a resource, the PC will be distributed unevenly, as are other resources, and that this has implications in terms of students' access to courses, and to distance education generally.

## Communications

Communications equipment was not a requirement for most OU students, but will probably be a requirement from 1996, and we predict that computer conferencing and networking will play an increasing role in distance education. This is discussed in detail later in the chapter.

## Workload and the Organisation of Practical Work

In an institution like the OU, which uses many kinds of media but is nevertheless largely text based, the introduction of the home computer increases students' workload: it is a new medium to deal with, and the software packages students use will take time to learn. Most course teams try to integrate the use of a PC into the course – partly for educational reasons and partly to make good use of what they appreciate is an expensive resource for students. However, as was pointed out in Chapter 2, when talking about organising practical work, some students dislike moving from one type of medium to another to study different aspects of the course. Experience with different kinds of media, including computers, indicates that students often apply cost-benefit judgements about whether it is worth their while breaking off from their current activity and orienting themselves towards a new activity and a new medium. If insufficient use is made of a package throughout the course, the danger is that the learning curve is not compensated for by the use made of the skill later.

One recent development which could alleviate the work organisation problem is the introduction of and increased use of the portable PC, the 'laptop'. The portability of such a machine means that, in theory, students can once again work wherever it suits them, including train journeys, etc. In practice, if there are several different course items to negotiate, it may still be too difficult to manage.

## Help and Support for Students

Many students at the OU have required help in addition to the (not inconsiderable) amount provided.

## Support for Tutorial Staff

At the OU, informal feedback and limited evaluation suggest that many tutors incur extra expense as well as significant extra work when tutoring a home-computing course, particularly during its first year.

These issues may not be universally applicable. Apart from the particular nature of the institution in question, one factor which will have a large impact on how easily new technologies can be incorporated into distance education is the type of distance-education institution in question. The next section considers different models of distance education and the possibilities of introducing new technologies into them.

## Training for Course Designers

Computer use will not be successful if it is simply 'added on' to other media in a multimedia course. It must be structured into the first outline ideas of the course designers and then it will generate new production needs that must be taken into account. The following guidelines were drawn up by Chapman (1989), for OU course designers and developers based on his own experience of integrating computer use on the foundation course in technology. They are applicable to any course designer, even when designing a face-to-face course:

1. Sort out the precise educational objectives for the computing component of the course.
2. Devise a strategy for meeting the objectives in terms of student activities and detailed relationships with other course materials.
3. Derive a specification for the course software. Include a survey of existing software – both commercial and what has been produced by [your own student computing service] for other courses.

4. Write the academic case for [including student-based computers on your course] and obtain all the necessary permissions.
5. AS SOON AS APPROVAL IS GIVEN THEN COMMISSION OR PURCHASE THE SOFTWARE.
6. Develop the computing activities in parallel with the rest of the course. Under no circumstances try to bolt a computing bit onto something already written.
7. Involve [your computer programmers] in course team meetings and course development. They are your biggest asset.
8. Test the software and associated activities in as many ways as you can, for as long as you can.
9. Use the test results to identify where students may have problems and take steps to anticipate, correct, absorb.
10. Teach your tutors how to use the computer and the software.
11. DO NOT MAKE LAST MINUTE CHANGES.
12. Pray often.

## What is the Best Model for the Use of PCs in Distance Education?

Throughout the book, the nature of distance teaching itself has been considered in various contexts. In dealing with the issues involved in providing equal opportunities, Chapter 5 considered the paradox that technology for the OU can be a liberating force in opening up the production process and the resulting products to scrutiny and debate, but this very process, because of its highly structured nature and the time taken to produce materials, may be inflexible in meeting individual students' learning needs. Other paradoxes also exist in considering the role of PCs in distance education: again in relation to equal opportunities there is a concern that the increased and widespread use of PCs exacerbates patterns of inequalities that already exist (this is not just a concern for higher education or distance education, of course). Education may easily become technologically driven. However, Chapter 5 also considered the possibility that the introduction of PCs could help to 'open up' the industrial model of distance education the OU adopts. There seems to be some evidence of this both for particular groups of students (e.g. students with disabilities), and in using the potential of computer-mediated communications (CMC) to reduce isolation and counter the over-individualised model of learning. The increasing use of computer technology in higher education has also influenced the debate about the models adopted for distance education, and this section looks at this debate and examines some of the suggested options.

Pelton (1990), in looking at the possibilities of applying new technologies to distance education, uses the term 'tele-education' to refer generally to the application of new technologies to education. Although he never makes his model of distance education explicit, this is a model of teaching using mainly telecommunications systems whereby much of the teaching is through video. One common way of applying this model is where an institution serves both a face-to-face community of students and also has a distance-education function. Lectures given face-to-face are also relayed to the students at a distance. A variant on this approach is to produce video materials especially for distance teaching.

Pelton views tele-education as having the potential for solving many educational problems, for example reaching students in rural areas. He is particularly concerned (*ibid*. p. 266) with applying two new technologies – satellite communications and fibre-optic cable: 'Satellites are still best for broadcast distributions and for rural and remote access, while fibre optics are well suited to linking centres of learning, university systems, etc. Fibre optic educational networks are well suited to be 'piggy-backed' on top of public telecommunications networks at a modest cost.'

But he also mentions other means of distributing tele-education materials, such as computer-assisted instruction (CAI). Other applications of new technologies which he finds particularly inspiring are the intelligent interactive videodisc, artificially intelligent educational toys and tele-robotic controls and remote computer networking. However, although no doubt all of these developments have potential, we have already seen the problems of realising that potential in at least two of these. Interactive videodiscs (let alone intelligent interactive videodiscs) are still prohibitively expensive for use in distance education: experiments with their possible use in OU courses were discussed in Chapter 8. Artificial intelligence (AI) has been viewed as having the potential to make computer-assisted learning (CAL) more flexible and adaptive to students' needs, yet the fact is that there are very few 'intelligent' programs in educational use. But perhaps what is most worrying about this view of the role of new technology in education is its technological determinism:

> The above . . . examples . . . reflect how dynamic and innovative the field of tele-education really is. The key point to observe here is that the various electronic and photonic techniques are tending to merge in new and creative ways. Satellite communications are connecting to fibre optics and terrestrial radio service in order to provide data, radio and video services.
>
> Educators of the twenty-first century will have all these tools and more to rely upon in designing good and responsive programs for every need group.
>
> (*Ibid*. p. 267)

Perhaps Pelton discusses the educational possibilities and implications elsewhere, but here new technology is viewed mainly in terms of offering new ways of delivering courses. Tele-education sits alongside face-to-face teaching:

> Tele-education can seldom, if ever, attempt to be the total offering. As many enriching and educating elements as possible should be made available in the form of books, exercise materials, teachers, aides, field trips, etc. In other words, the key concepts are educational enhancement and off-loading the duties of classroom teachers.
>
> (*Ibid*. p. 268)

Pelton does not reflect on what distance education should be, what it can offer, and how new technologies might be able to help in problem areas and how they could even re-conceptualise it. In an issue of *Research in Distance Education* where Pelton's article was reproduced, Bates (1991) has written a response to Pelton. He expresses (p. 10) his main concern with Pelton's view of technology in distance education as wanting 'educators – rather than technological idealists – to be in the driving seat'. Bates draws on Nipper's (1989) classification of the three 'generations' of distance education. In this classification, the OU is an example of second-generation distance teaching: the industrial model. The third generation of distance education is based on the use of electronic information technologies, but uses such technologies to provide more two-way communication, 'resulting in a much more even access to *communication between student and teacher (and also between students)*. Typical technologies are computer conferencing or networking and audio- and video-conferencing (including audio-graphics)' (Bates, 1991, p. 11).

Bates points out that Pelton's definition of 'tele-education' also includes electronic technologies of a primarily one-way nature, such as broadcast satellites. Bates (*ibid.*) believes that it is very difficult for distance-teaching institutions based on the industrial model to be innovative:

> their whole organisation, and especially their management and decision-making process, is built around the requirements of the mass production of 'one-way' teaching materials. Consequently, innovation is extremely difficult, and the newer technologies, when introduced, tend not to be used to replace existing technologies such as print, but merely to supplement them, thus adding to costs, and more seriously, increasing student workload.

There is a second reason that it is problematic:

> the same conditions that lead to successful use of the newer interactive technologies in business and commerce will also apply to educational institutions wishing to use these technologies. The 'information society' is based on and requires fast, flexible and devolved decision-making and management, and thus radically different organisational structures and methods of working from those found not only in conventional education systems but also in the large, autonomous distance teaching universities.
>
> (*Ibid.*)

Bates also questions whether the classroom method of a lecturer delivering information is a good enough teaching model, and points out that it is most successful where students are already highly motivated, highly skilled and practised in learning, and understand the key concepts in a subject area – for example in professional and postgraduate education. He argues for a different form of tele-education: 'it is the more interactive technologies such as audio- and computer-conferencing that appear to have most promise for distance education, rather than the delivery of tele-lectures to large numbers via satellite' (*ibid.* p. 14).

Lewis (1991) also sees the future in technologies that offer interaction. He identifies four models used in the delivery of IT-supported learning in higher education. These are not models of distance education, but they have implications for both distance education and open learning. The first is the classical *campus model*, where students are present on campus for their lectures, seminars, laboratories, etc. Examples were given in Chapter 1 of a number of such campuses in the USA which have introduced IT. As we saw, the introduction of IT in this situation provides an additional resource which is available on campus usually via a campus network. Interestingly, the OU's current plans for the future are partly based on such an 'electronic campus' model, although, of course, in our case our students are not on campus. The second model identified by Lewis is the *Open University* model which he characterises as delivering courses mainly through self-study paper materials and making little general use of computer technologies. Lewis mentions IT versions of the OU model: proposals for international open universities in Europe and in particular satellite-based projects. The third model is the *open-learning* model. This, according to Lewis, is one which is not dependent on fully defined and delivered courses leading to qualifications. An important aspect is that software development and thus the associated high cost of development is not an issue. He gives as an example the EuroPACE project, which

is supported (and supports) major European high-tech companies by making available advanced seminars in science and technology. Programmes are transmitted by satellite, and followed up by computer conferences involving the programme's presenter. The communities of learners are very specialized, and for this latter reason, share a common culture which to some extent transcends the problems of a national language and culture mentioned earlier as a stumbling block to international collaboration in the use of learning technologies.

(Lewis, 1991, p. 3)

Lewis's final model is based on the open-learning model and is the *ITOL* model, a model for IT-based open learning, a model which he sees as an alternative to the other three. The ITOL model supports professional development: 'Learners could take part in professional development activities without having to leave their work place. All that the learner needs is a desk-top computer and modem linked to the public telephone system: this gives them access to the on-line professional education system' (*ibid.* p. 4).

He later defines the educational philosophy underpinning ITOL as one where the learner can define his or her own learning and professional development needs. ITOL then becomes a way of meeting those learner-defined needs. Lewis sees this model as one which can overcome some of the inflexibility that is inherent in many distance-teaching systems, and which, as we have already seen, has been the subject of some criticism: in particular the problem of meeting individual learners' needs. In calling this model IT-based *open* learning as opposed to distance learning, Lewis is emphasising those aspects of open learning which are claimed to distinguish it from distance teaching. He outlines a model for ITOL that

allows any individual to communicate with a tutor or tutors (most likely university based people, but not exclusively), with other learners and with a series or collection of both university and non-university based resources.

In addition, learners may have available to them a counsellor from outside the university system, most likely someone from inside their own organization. Finally there is a university based resource manager with whom learners can also communicate.

(*Ibid.* p. 7)

Some time has been spent looking at these four models and, in particular, the open-learning models as it is important to explore possibilities which may overcome the disadvantages identified in the OU's approach with its heavy dependence on text and long lead time for courses. However, when the assumptions of the modified ITOL are examined, it is much less attractive and indeed less feasible as a model for higher education than it might at first seem. The first assumption is that the learner is a person at a professional level of employment. This in itself runs counter to the OU's equal opportunities policy and to the aims of most open-learning educators by addressing itself to a small select group. Gardner (1991, p. 7) has criticised this assumption as being based on a false view of higher education: 'It [ITOL] explicitly attributes to higher education a vocational education and training function, which many would suggest should more properly reside with other areas of non-advanced further education, or indeed wholly outwith the state education system.'

A related assumption made by Lewis is that learners will have access to a desktop computer and modem, and can work from their workplace. Certainly using a computer at work was not satisfactory for many OU students, but as this group is only engaged in professional updating, this might not be such a problem. The model also assumes that learners are able to determine their own learning needs, and are competent to structure the resources they have access to and can direct their own learning. Perhaps most importantly of all, it assumes that they can learn to use the technology which will provide them with any support they may need, without having access to that support when learning to use the technology in the first place! Possibly the target group Lewis mentions would have few problems in determining and structuring their learning: if they could do so, and the resources were adequate, they would benefit from the flexibility such a system could provide. Other advantages of such an approach include a much more communicative approach to learning via computer conferencing; the ability to tailor the course to individual needs through negotiation with tutors; and the potential for continual updating. However, it is over-optimistic to expect students to learn to use computers in this way without experiencing any difficulties. The studies discussed in Chapter 6 indicated that even experienced computer users experience difficulties in learning to use new systems. In the ITOL system, it is not at all clear where the support to do this kind of learning would come from. The biggest problem with the model as outlined by Lewis, however, is that it is only applicable to a selected population and, because of access issues, this is currently true for all models of distance education which require students to have continual access to a PC and possibly communications facilities in addition.

Although the ITOL model is not suitable for general use in higher education, there are features which can be and are likely to be used more within other models of distance education.

## Next Steps: 1996 Onwards

A sub-group of the University's Academic Computing Committee was given a brief to make recommendations on the future of personal computing at the OU from 1996. One of the reasons for developing a new policy from 1996 is the continuing increase of use of PCs in the higher education sector; also by this time, the rental pool will be depleted.

In their draft discussion document it is recommended that the University build a policy-making and administrative structure capable of supporting further IT developments; that the idea of an 'electronic campus' should be actively explored and the idea of collaborating with other universities to produce CAL should be vigorously pursued. A particular computing specification is again recommended, based on the PC MS-DOS. It is assumed that students will be responsible for providing access and, based on this assumption, that the University needs to make getting a computer worth while, by using it on a substantial number of courses, by it being able to be used for a number of activities (including administration and/or sending assignments) and by the OU producing (or buying in) other software that can be used. The report argues that the University should provide as much assistance as it can to enable students to acquire equipment, but financial assistance should be carefully targeted so as to focus the resources available. It is also recommended that a major campaign for external funding should be launched.

It seems likely that the use of computers as general-purpose tools for students (see Chapter 1) will continue to grow. Indeed, students now entering higher education will expect to use computers in this way in a variety of areas, and will expect to have access to computers so that they can do this, and employers increasingly expect students to have had such experience. In a paper reflecting on the first three years of the policy, Berry and Burrows (1990) refer to a suggestion by the Department of Trade and Industry (DTI) Select Committee in a report on IT (1988) that the best solution to IT skills shortage was increased in-service training. They comment that the government's response (1989)

indicated that it considered all those in education and training must play their part in meeting the requirements of industry, commerce and the public sector for a suitably skilled workforce. The government agreed with the Select Committee that demographic trends would increase the need for employers to undertake a massive training effort over the years ahead, directed primarily at people they already employ. To meet this demand, education and training providers need to use open, distance and flexible learning systems. No institution is better placed to assist than the Open University.

(Berry and Burrows, 1990, p. 950)

We can assume, then, that the use of PCs in higher education will be commonplace. However, we can expect the tools to continue to become more sophisticated, and we can also expect that some software (and hardware) which is currently not widely used will be used increasingly. One such example is hypermedia.

## Hypermedia: Designing for Individual Differences

Chapter 2 outlined the possibility of having distance-learning materials in the form of hypertext. In an early definition of hypertext, Nelson (1974, p. 85) wrote that

By 'hypertext' I mean non-sequential writing.

Ordinary writing is sequential for two reasons. First it grew out of speech and speech-making, which have to be sequential; and second, because books are not convenient to read except in a sequence.

But *the structure of ideas* is not sequential. They tie together every whichway. And when we write, we are always trying to tie things together in non-sequential ways. . . .

However, in my view, a new day is dawning. Computer storage and screen display mean that we no longer *have* to have things in sequence; totally arbitrary structures are possible, and I think after we've tried them enough people will see how desirable they are.

Nearly twenty years later, the day has come. Now the more general term *hypermedia* includes not only non-sequential texts, but the possibility of integrating that text with graphics, and other forms of data, such as sounds, animations and video clips, and in some software, a programming language for creating and manipulating hypermedia documents. In common with other new technology developments, hypertext has the potential of overcoming some of the problems inherent in the traditional OU model of distance education by allowing learners to determine their own learning structure and sequence. But at the same time, it introduces other, new, difficulties: 'On the plus side, allowing learners to decide the pace and sequencing of navigation offers them opportunities to accommodate their individual differences and not only learn course content but even . . . to learn how to learn. On the minus side, it introduces the problem of cognitive overload' (Zhao, 1991, p. 1).

In its double-edged nature, it is not unlike other developments. As we saw in Chapter 6, learning to use new computer applications requires effort, and is often fraught with difficulties on the way. Nevertheless, hypertext learning systems have become increasingly popular, and our prediction is that they will become as widely used as information-retrieval systems are now. For this reason alone, the potential of hypermedia in distance education is considerable. Hypermedia is also increasingly a subject of research and a tool for research. For example, the Apple application Hypercard can be used as a programming language to produce prototype interactive learning programs which have good graphics capabilities. Used in this way it is a development tool, as the prototype program can be evaluated and changed until it is 'right'. This application, unlike most of the ways of using computers described in Chapter 1, is ideally suited to collaborative learning.

But what about such applications in distance education? One research project at the OU has been investigating the use of hypertext to overcome some of the problems faced by visually impaired students (Taylor, 1991), and this was discussed in Chapter 5. It is possible that hypermedia could also ameliorate some of the problems discussed in Chapter 6, of retrieving information – for example, how a learner finds out which commands are used to do what within a particular applications package by providing a way of organising such information that is easy to search through.

## CD-ROM: The Real Alternative to Print?

So far, the experience of using desktop publishing within the University has not provided the significant benefits of either cost reductions or time reduction that were hoped for, so why should print be used at all? A CD-ROM can contain the equivalent of 250,000 pages of A4 text and, when used with a PC, can function as a powerful storage device. By 1992 the University had not produced CD-ROMs for use by students. The University's Educational Software Group (1991) were developing systems for internal staff use and jointly for use with outside agencies. These include the Educational Counselling and Credit Transfer Information System (ECCTIS), which provides information about all further education courses in the UK, and had previously been available online from a mainframe; the National Educational Resources and Information Service (NERIS), which is a database of curriculum resources for teachers; and the bibliographic database of the International Centre for Distance Education (ICDE) which is located at the OU. Perhaps an example of potential student use is a disk that is being produced which contains materials from the arts foundation course which includes a number of the set texts that students must read for the course as well as some public bibliographic databases.

The use of CD-ROM could have a significant impact on the use of PCs and enable them to be used as a domestic leisure machine. For example, it will be possible to buy the whole of the *Encyclopaedia Brittanica* on perhaps two CD-ROMs instead of paying perhaps £1,000 for a hard copy. Equally, it could revolutionise distance education. In the OU, for example, a course team could send students, on a CD-ROM, not only materials specially written for that course but also copies of other books. The University would only need to pay copyright. By doing this the course could refer to other optional materials which would be available for those who wanted to take up additional references. Learning could thus be more flexible to students' needs and desires.

## Collaborative Learning: A Way of Reducing the Distance?

However, we need to consider the use of PCs in distance education within the context of changes happening in education as a whole and in distance education in particular. In the first two chapters of the book, we discussed how there has been a change in prominence from a behaviourist view of learning to a constructivist view, particularly in schools, which have been influenced by the work of Piaget, and how this in turn is being increasingly challenged by a more social view of learning. The number of research and development projects in the area of collaborative learning with computers suggests that this is an area in which the use of PCs will expand in the future. New possibilities for educational software are continually being researched but the difficulty, of course, is to predict which will turn into marketable products. One project at the OU is investigating computer-supported collaborative learning in physics (Whitelock *et al.*, 1991). The general aim of this project is to develop computer software which supports collaborative learning between pairs of students solving physics problems. In another OU project, Laurillard (1991b) has investigated learning through collaborative computer simulations. One of the factors she identifies as facilitating students' productive reasoning is a direct manipulation interface, one of the central factors in another very recent OU development (Alexander, 1992) which is discussed below. This social view of learning is increasingly being found in adult learning too: the use of CMC by Jutland University which was discussed in Chapter 1 illustrates this approach. The OU, although emphasising the benefits of tutorials and self-help groups, has in reality a very individualistic model of learning. However, as we saw in Chapter 2, the use of PCs, and in particular CMC, offers the potential to attend to the social aspect of distance learning, which the OU has hitherto found difficult to support.

At the OU, Gary Alexander (1992) is working on designing human interfaces to promote collaborative learning. These will be applied in a pilot course on renewable energy. Alexander, like others, believes that collaborative learning offers many advantages over individual learning. He defines it as a 'structured learning experience designed so that the learner interacts with a group of peers' (p. 2).

In Chapter 1, we referred to the problem, faced by Jutland Open University, of integrating CMC into courses: where conferencing was not integrated, use was minimal; where it was integrated students used it but felt it took up too much time. In Alexander's project, collaboration is an essential part of the course activities, and the course is designed around a set of collaborative projects. The intention is that students should form themselves into 'collaborative learning groups' for each project and that each student will contribute to a section of a group report produced by the student's group. Tutors will be available to help with the projects. The course materials themselves will be less structured than is usual in OU courses, and will consist of a range of resources, including texts and computer-based material, which will cover the subject area. An important feature of this particular CMC system is the user interface, designed to emphasise people and not messages. In order to do this, images of faces will be used to show who has joined the conference since the user last connected, and to help users follow the contributions of particular individuals.

Alexander comments that although computer interface designs have changed considerably during the last ten years, this is not evident in the interfaces used by most CMC systems, which, in order to allow access by a wide range of equipment, often still use 'command line' interfaces requiring the user to know the specific set of commands and syntax required. As he points out, this can put quite a load on the novice user. Alexander's plan is to use a graphic-style user interface, which should have many of the benefits of the now common 'WIMP' style interface, which is used with much PC software. (WIMP stands for window/icon/mouse/pointer. The screen is divided into windows, each of which can be scrolled backwards and forwards; icons are used to represent objects and interaction is achieved through using a mouse or other pointing device as well as the keyboard.) The metaphor used in this design is that of the collaborative work group, and this is conveyed through the concept of 'telepresence': the illusion of the presence of other people. Four different views of the structure of the conference system will be available on screen to the user:

1. A personal view, giving information about each of the participants.
2. An overview of the conference system ('The Electronic University').
3. An overview of each conference.
4. A message view.

In order to illustrate what some of these views will look like to the user, and what the user can do, two of the views are described further. The personal view is shown in Figure 9.1.

This includes a face icon and a personalised monogram which appear in the left-hand corner. These are used elsewhere in the interface to provide instant recognition. The message view is crucial to the use of CMC as a collaborative learning tool, and a draft of this view is shown in Figure 9.2.

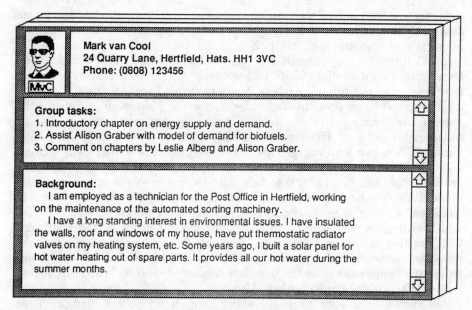

Figure 9.1  The personal view (from Alexander, 1992, p. 8)

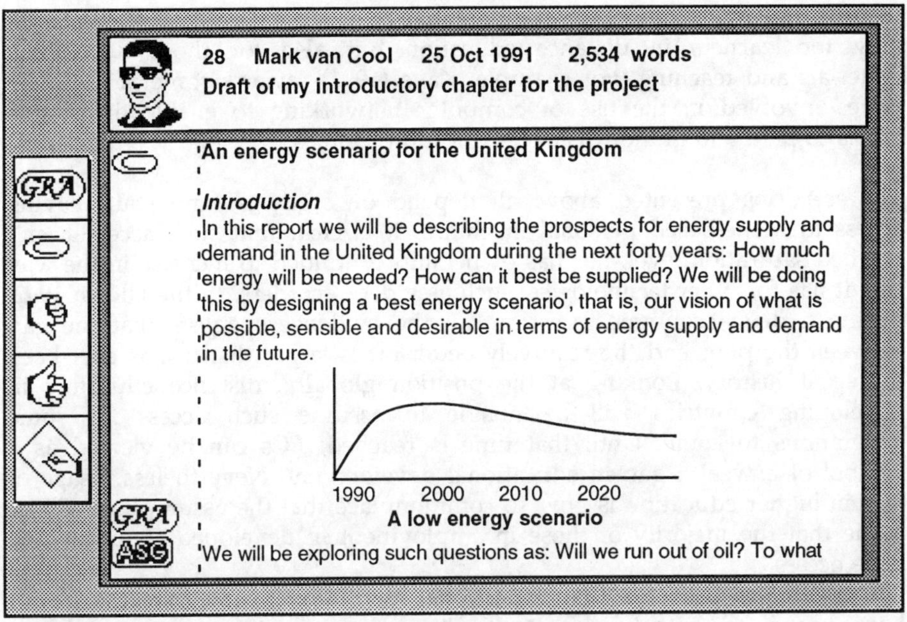
28 Mark van Cool 25 Oct 1991 2,534 words
Draft of my introductory chapter for the project
GRA
An energy scenario for the United Kingdom
Introduction
In this report we will be describing the prospects for energy supply and demand in the United Kingdom during the next forty years: How much energy will be needed? How can it best be supplied? We will be doing this by designing a 'best energy scenario', that is, our vision of what is possible, sensible and desirable in terms of energy supply and demand in the future.
1990 2000 2010 2020
A low energy scenario
GRA
ASG
We will be exploring such questions as: Will we run out of oil? To what

Figure 9.2 The message view (from Alexander, 1992)

Alexander (1992, p. 10) describes this view as follows:

> The metaphor presented is that of a document with a margin to which comments and other materials can be attached. By using this metaphor for messages, the CMC system will be integrated with other tools for creating documents and linking them to notes, references and other materials. . . .
>
> The message view presents a scrollable document . . . The presence of a comment will be indicated by the personal monogram of the sender . . . The monogram acts as a button: the comment will appear in a pop-up window, as though it were clipped to the document.
>
> The palette of icons on the left of the message offers the user a choice of ways of commenting on the main message.
>
> The 'thumbs-up' and 'thumbs-down' icons will be used to indicate basic agreement or disagreement, and will form the basis of a simple polling system. For example, someone might ask a question of the whole group, ('Are we all agreed on this plan?') to which members will reply using the thumb icon.

Alexander's project has been described in some detail as it is a good illustration of how two ideas which are currently seen as very important may be adopted in distance education: collaborative learning and making courses less structured and didactic and more flexible to learners' needs. His work on the human interface is explicitly educationally innovative in a way that the current Home Computing Policy is not because it is about designing new tools for use as part of the PC system rather than adapting conventional ones. This, then, could be one future route for distance education. In fact there is a growing interest in the potential of collaborative environments not only for learners in distance education but also for those developing materials and teaching. For example, Kaye (1991) reviews some of the main issues involved in the use of computer networking to enable distributed teams to plan and author distance-education courses.

The scenarios presented above all depend on students (and staff) having access to home-based personal machines. It is clear that such access hasn't reached saturation level, nor has ownership continued to increase in the way that it has for other technologies, such as video-recorders. In the UK, in 1992, during a deep economic recession, all the evidence suggests that the gap between the poor and the relatively better off is larger than it has ever been in recent history. Looking at the position globally, distance educators in developing countries will be unable to assume such access for some generations to come. Until that time is reached, PCs can be viewed as a symbol of a wealth gap in educational development. Nevertheless, usage of PCs in higher education is now so commonplace that the assumption will be made that the majority of those in employment in developed countries will have access.

The OU has been the first educational institution to integrate the use of home-based PCs into key courses in its undergraduate programme. As an innovation this has gone beyond a 'test bed' phase and is being disseminated throughout the institution with more courses and more students being involved every year. Many other institutions will find a similar policy an obvious way forward in some content areas.

# References

Adams, R. S. with Chen, D. (1981) *The Process of Educational Innovation*, Kogan Page/UNESCO Press, Paris and London.

Alexander, G. (1990) The Hyperview Project – progress report June 1990 (unpublished report available from the Centre for Electronic Education, Faculty of Technology, Open University, Walton Hall, Milton Keynes MK7 6AA).

Alexander, G. (1992) Designing human interfaces to promote collaborative learning, in A. Kaye (ed.) *Collaborative Learning Through Computer Conferencing: The Najaden Papers*, NATO Advanced Science Institute Series, Computer and Systems Sciences Subseries, Springer-Verlag, New York, NY.

Allman, P. (1982) New perspectives on the adult: an argument for lifelong education, *International Journal of Lifelong Education*, Vol. 1, no. 1, pp. 41–51.

Arms, W. Y., Hornig, J. F., Huggis, E. R., Jernstedt, T. G. and Roos, T. B. (1980) Minicomputers in undergraduate education, in R. Lewis and E. D. Tagg (eds.), op. cit.

Ashby, A. (1991) *Equal Opportunities – Statistical Digest Commentary*, Report No. 51, Student Research Centre, Institute of Educational Technology, Open University, Milton Keynes.

Ashby, A. and Tompkins, K. (1990) *Internal Digest of Open University Statistics 1985–1989*, Report No. 37, Student Research Centre, Institute of Educational Technology, Open University, Milton Keynes.

Bacsich, P. (1984) A viewdata system, in A. W. Bates (ed.) *The Role of Technology in Distance Education*, Croom Helm, London.

Baines, S. (1991) Personal computing, gender and distance education (paper given at the International Federation of Information Processors (IFIP) Conference, Helsinki, June).

Banks, M. E. and Ackerman, R. J. (1990) Ethnic and computer employment status, *Social Science Computer Review*, Vol. 8, no. 1, pp. 75–82.

Bates, A. W. (1980) Applying new technology to distance education: a case study from the Open University of difficulties in innovation (unpublished paper available from IET, Open University, Walton Hall, Milton Keynes MK7 6AA).

Bates, A. W. (1983) Adult learning from educational television: the Open University experience, in M. J. A. Howe (ed.) *Learning from Television: Psychological and Educational Research*, Academic Press, London.

Bates, A. W. (1986) Creating a technologically innovative climate: the British Open University experience (paper given at OECD workshop on promoting a technologically innovative environment, Paris, December).

Bates, A. W. (1991) Third generation distance education: the challenge of new technology, *Research in Distance Education*, Vol. 3, no. 2, pp. 10–15.

Berry, S. L. and Burrows, D. J. A. (1990) Computers in education: a distance learning model, in A. McDougall and C. Dowling (eds.) *Computers in Education*, Elsevier, Amsterdam.

Bob West (1989) The UDACE/RAS/RO4 report. Developing access: a case study of the Open University, with special reference to the West Midlands Region (unpublished report, Open University, Milton Keynes).

Bolton, J. P., Every, I. M. and Ross, S. M. (1990) The water videodisc: a problem solving environment, *Computers and Education*, Vol. 15, nos. 1–3, pp. 165–72.

Bork, A. (1980) Educational Technology Center at the University of California, in R. Lewis and E. D. Tagg (eds.), op. cit.

Boyd-Barrett, O. (1990) Schools computing policy as state-directed innovation, in O. Boyd-Barrett and E. Scanlon (eds.) *Computers and Learning*, Addison-Wesley, Wokingham.

Bramer, M. (1980) Using computers in distance education: the first ten years of the British Open University, *Computers and Education*, Vol. 4, pp. 293–301.

Brindley, L. J. (ed.) (1989a) *The Electronic Campus: An Information Strategy*, British Library, Boston Spa.

Brindley, L. J. (1989b) Launching pads, *The Times Higher Education Supplement*, 31 March.

Brown, R. C. W. (1989) 'Brushstrokes in flight': a strategic overview of trends in technology in higher education, in L. J. Brindley (ed.) *The Electronic Campus: An Information Strategy*, British Library, Boston Spa.

Bruner, J. S. (1967) *Toward a Theory of Instruction*, Harvard University Press, Cambridge, Mass.

Burgess, T. (1972) The Open University, *New Society*, pp. 176–8, 27 April.

Burrows, D. J. (1989) The Open University's Home Computing Policy, in T. O'Shea and G. Kirkup (eds.) *Home Computing in Practice 1988–1989, Possibilities for 1992*, Report No. 83, Centre for Information Technology in Education, Institute of Educational Technology, Open University, Milton Keynes.

Butcher, P. G. (1986) Computing aspects of interactive video, *Computers and Education*, Vol. 10, no. 1, pp. 1–10.

Butcher, P. G. and Greenberg, J. M. (1992) Educational computing at the Open University: the second decade, *Education and Computing*, Vol. 8, pp. 201–15.

Carroll, J. (1990) *The Nurnberg Funnel: Designing Minimalist Instruction for Practical Computing Skill*, MIT Press, London.

Carroll, J. M., Smith-Kerker, P. L., Ford, J. R. and Mazur-Rimetz, S. A. (1988) The minimal manual, *Human–Computer Interaction*, Vol. 3, pp. 123–53.

Centre for Educational Research and Innovation (CERI) (1989) *Information Technologies in Education. The Quest for Quality Software*, OECD, Paris.

Chapman, J. (1989) The T102 experience, in T. O'Shea and G. Kirkup (eds.) *Home Computing in Practice 1988–1991 and Possibilities for 1992*, Report No. 83, Centre for Information Technology in Education, Institute of Educational Technology, The Open University, Milton Keynes.

Chapman, J. (1990) *Can Computers Assist Learning?* Unit 1 of EH232, *Computers and Learning*, Open University Press, Milton Keynes.

Cohen, M. D., March, J. G. and Olson, L. P. (1972) A garbage can model of organizational choice, *Administrative Science Quarterly*, Vol. 17, no. 1, pp. 1–25.

Computer Board for Universities and Research Councils (1983) *Report of a Working Party on Computer Facilities for Teaching in Universities*, London.

Culley, L. (1986) *Gender Differences and Computing in Secondary Schools*, Department of Education, Loughborough University of Technology.

Culley, L. (1988) Girls, boys and computers, *Educational Studies*, Vol. 14, no. 1, pp. 3–8.

Dale, E. and Kirkup, G. (1991) *T202: Set Up, Start Up and Blocks 1 and 2. Report on Student Survey July 1990*, Report No. 132, Centre for Information Technology in Education, Institute of Educational Technology, Open University, Milton Keynes.

Davies, A. (1989) Tutoring DT200, in G. Kirkup and T. O'Shea (eds.) *Home Computing in Practice 1988–1991 and Possibilities for 1992*, Report No. 83, Centre for Information Technology in Education, Institute of Educational Technology, Open University, Milton Keynes.

Deci, E. (1975) *Intrinsic Motivation*, Plenum Press, New York, NY.

Department of Education and Science (1989) Survey of information technology in schools, *Statistical Bulletin 10/89*, HMSO, London.

Donaldson, M. (1978) *Children's Minds*, Fontana, London.

Du Boulay, B., O'Shea, T. and Monk, J. (1981) The glass box inside the black box: presenting computing concepts to novices, *International Journal of Man-Machine Studies*, Vol. 14, pp. 237–49.

Dyer, G. (1991) Empowerment and reduction of isolation of housebound disabled students: a computer-mediated communications project at the UK Open University, *Electronic Networking*, Vol. 1, no. 2, pp. 23–8.

Educational Software Group (1991) Applications in educational computing (unpublished report available from the Open University Academic Computing Service, Open University, Walton Hall, Milton Keynes MK7 6AA).

Edwards, M. G. (1979) Experience of teaching the subject of computers in education to teachers (paper presented at CAL '79, Symposium on Computer Assisted Learning, Exeter, 4–6 April).

Entwistle, N. (1984) Contrasting perspectives on learning, in F. Marton, D. Hounsell and N. Entwistle (eds.) *The Experience of Learning*, Scottish Academic Press, Edinburgh.

Evans, T. and Nation, D. (1989) Dialogue in practice, research and theory in distance education, *Open Learning*, Vol. 4, no. 2, pp. 37–42.

Every, I. (1987) MERLIN: a system for combining telephone tutorials with computer assisted learning, in A. Jones, E. Scanlon and T. O'Shea (eds.), op. cit.

Fife-Schaw, C., Breakwell, G., Lee, T. and Spencer, J. (1986) Patterns of teenage computer usage, *Journal of Computer Assisted Learning*, Vol. 2, pp. 152–61.

Fletcher, B. (1985) Group and individual learning of junior school children on a microcomputer-based task, *Educational Review*, Vol. 38, pp. 251–61.

Forester, T. (1988) The myth of the electronic cottage, *Futures*, pp. 227–40, June.

Foster, J. (1988) Justifications in computers in education, *The Times Educational Supplement*, p. 61, 18 November.

Gardner, N. (1988) Integrating computers into the university curriculum: the experience of the UK Computers in Teaching Initiative, *Computers in Education*, Vol. 12, no. 1, pp. 27–32.

Gardner, N. (1989) The electronic campus, the first decade, *Higher Education Quarterly*, Vol. 43, no. 4, pp. 333–50.

Gardner, N. (1991) Evaluating information technology in higher education: models and approaches, *The CTISS File*, no. 11, pp. 7–9.

Gardner, N. and Darby, J. (1990) Using computers in university teaching: a perspective on key issues, *Computers in Education*, Vol. 15, nos. 1–3, pp. 27–32.

Gardner, N. and Slater, J. B. (1990) *Computers in Teaching Initiative: Detailed Descriptions*, CTISS.

Gershuny, J. (1978) *After Industrial Society? The Emerging Self-Service Economy*, Macmillan, London.

Gibbs, G., Morgan, A. and Taylor, E. (1984) The world of the learner, in F. Marton, D. Hounsell and N. Entwistle (eds.) *The Experience of Learning*, Scottish Academic Press, Edinburgh.

Gilligan, C. (1982) *In a Different Voice: Psychological Theory and Women's Development*, Harvard University Press, Cambridge, Mass.

Golding, P. and Murdoch, G. (1986) Unequal information: access and exclusion in the new communications market place, in M. Ferguson (ed.) *New Information Technologies and the Public Interest*, Sage, London.

Goodyear, M. (1976) *A Study of Student Motivation at the Open University* (report commissioned by the Institute of Educational Technology), Open University/Market Behaviour, London.

Gray, A. (1988) Armchair heroes, *Marxism Today*, p. 47, October.

Grundin, H. (1983) *Audio-Visual Media in the Open University: Results of a Survey of 93 Courses*, Papers on Broadcasting No. 224, Institute of Educational Technology, Open University, Milton Keynes.

Grundin, H. (1985) *Report on the 1984 AV Media Survey*, Papers on Broadcasting No. 261, Institute of Educational Technology, Open University, Milton Keynes.

Gunter, B. and McLaughlin, C. (1992) *Television: The Public's View*, Independent Television Commission Research Monograph, John Libbey, London.

Haddon, L. (1988) The home computer: the making of a consumer electronic, *Science as Culture*, no. 2, pp. 7–51.

Harris, D. (1987) *Openness and Closure in Distance Education*, Falmer Press, Lewes.

Harris, D. (1988) The micro-politics of openness, *Open Learning*, Vol. 3, no. 2, pp. 13–16.

Hartley, D. (1988) Project Granta: a central strategy for decentralised action (unpublished paper presented at the Inter-University Committee on Computing Biennial Management Conference, Loughborough, 28–30 March).

Hesburgh, T. M. (1971) The nature of the challenge: traditional organization and attitude of universities toward contemporary realities, in S. D. Kertesz (ed.) *The Task of Universities in a Changing World*, University of Notre Dame Press, Notre Dame, Ind.

Jackson, A., Fletcher, B. and Nesser, D. (1986) A survey of microcomputer provision in primary schools, *Journal of Computer Assisted Learning*, Vol. 2, pp. 45–55.

Jonassen, D. H. (1986) Hypertext principles for text and courseware design, *Educational Psychologist*, Vol. 21, no. 4, pp. 269–92.

Jones, A. C. (1990) *Empirical Studies of Novices Learning Programming*, CITE PhD Thesis No. 10, Centre for Information Technology in Education, Institute of Educational Technology, Open University, Milton Keynes.

Jones, A. C. (1991) *Conceptual Models of Programming Environments: How Learners Use the Glass Box*, CALRG Technical Report No. 107, Centre for Information Technology in Education, Institute of Educational Technology, Open University, Milton Keynes.

Jones, A. C. and O'Shea, T. (1982) Barriers to the use of computer assisted learning, *British Journal of Educational Technology*, Vol. 13, no. 3, pp. 207–17.

Jones, A., Scanlon, E. and O'Shea, T. (eds.) (1987) *The Computer Revolution in Education*, Harvester, Brighton.

Jones, A. and Singer, R. (1990) *Report on the Use of Home Computing on M353*, Report No. 110, Centre for Information Technology in Education, Institute of Educational Technology, Open University, Milton Keynes.

Jones, A. and Singer, R. (1992) *Why Students Don't Take Home Computing Courses*, Report No. 163, Centre for Information Technology in Education, Institute of Educational Technology, Open University, Milton Keynes.

Kaye, A. (1989) Computer-mediated communication and distance education, in R. Mason and A. Kaye (eds.), op. cit.

Kaye, A. (1991) *Computer Networking for Development of Distance Education Courses*, Report No. 1146, Centre for Information Technology in Education, Institute of Educational Technology, Open University, Milton Keynes.

Kaye, A., Mason, R. and Harasim, L. (1989) *Computer Conferencing in the Academic Environment*, Report No. 91, Centre for Information Technology in Education, Institute of Educational Technology, Open University, Milton Keynes.

Kirkup, G. (1989a) Equal opportunities and computing at the Open University, *Open Learning*, Vol. 4, no. 1, pp. 3–8.

Kirkup, G. (1989b) *T102 Set Up, Start Up and Block One. Report on February Survey 1989*, Report No. 80, Centre for Information Technology in Education, Institute of Educational Technology, Open University, Milton Keynes.

Kirkup, G. (1992) The social construction of computers: hammers or harpsichords?, in G. Kirkup and L. S. Keller (eds.) *Inventing Women: Science, Technology and Gender*, Polity Press, Cambridge.

Kirkup, G., Carter, R., Keller, L. S., Lewis, J., Saxton, C. and Sutton, D. (1991) Home based computing for women students, in G. Lovegrove and B. Segal (eds.) *Women into Computing: Selected Papers 1988–90*, Springer-Verlag, London.

Kirkup, G. and Dale, E. (1990) *T102 Tutors' Use of the Home Computing Facility 1989*, Report No. 107, Centre for Information Technology in Education, Institute of Educational Technology, Open University, Milton Keynes.

Kirkwood, A. (1988) Computers in distance education; student access and issues of openness, *Open Learning*, Vol. 3, no. 3, pp. 18–22.

Kirkwood, A. (1990) *Access to Microcomputing Equipment for Study Purposes – Undergraduate Students in 1988*, Report No. 33, Student Research Centre, Institute of Educational Technology, Open University, Milton Keynes.

Kirkwood, A. and Dale, E. (1989) *DT200 End of Year Report 1988*, Report No. 77, Centre for Information Technology in Education, Institute of Educational Technology, Open University, Milton Keynes.

Kirkwood, A. and Kirkup, G. (1989) *Computing on DT200, M205 & M371 – Report of the Initial Survey of Spring 1988*, Report No. 65 (mimeo), Centre for Information Technology in Education, Institute of Educational Technology, Open University, Milton Keynes.

Kirkwood, A. and Kirkup, G. (1991) Access to computing for home-based students, *Studies in Higher Education*, Vol. 16, no. 3, pp. 199–208.

Knowles, M. (1970) *The Modern Practice of Adult Education: Andragogy versus Pedagogy*, Association Press/Follett, Chicago, Ill.

Latham, S., Moore, W., Ritchie, G., Rothwell, B. and Wilde, L. (1990) Mitchell College/IBM distance learning project, *Research in Distance Education*, pp. 7–14, January.

Laurillard, D. (1979) The process of student learning, *Higher Education*, Vol. 8, no. 4, pp. 395–409.

Laurillard, D. (1985) The teddy bear's disc, *Media in Education and Development*, pp. 37–41, March.

Laurillard, D. (1987a) Computers and the emancipation of students: giving control to the learner, *Instructional Science*, Vol. 16, no. 1, pp. 3–18.

Laurillard, D. (1987b) The problems and possibilities of interactive video, in A. Jones, E. Scanlon and T. O'Shea (eds.), op. cit.

Laurillard, D. (1989) *CAL and Numeracy*, Technical Report No. 68, Centre for Information Technology in Education, Institute of Educational Technology, Open University, Milton Keynes.

Laurillard, D. (1991a) *How Computers Assist Learning*, Unit 3 of EH232, *Computers and Learning*, Open University Press, Milton Keynes.

Laurillard, D. (1991b) *Learning through Collaborative Computer Simulations*, Report No. 148, Centre for Information Technology in Education, Institute of Educational Technology, Open University, Milton Keynes.

Lerman, S. (1984) Project Athena at MIT, *EDUCOM Bulletin*, Vol. 19, no. 4, pp. 5–7.

Lewis, C. and Mack, R. (1982) *The Role of Abduction in Learning to Use a Computer System*, IBM Watson Research Center, Report RC9433 No. 41620, Yorktown Heights, NY.

Lewis, R. (1991) Computers in higher education teaching and learning: some aspects of research and development, *The CTISS File*, no. 11, pp. 3–6.

Lewis, R. and Tagg, E. D. (1980) (eds.) *Computer Assisted Learning: Scope, Progress and Limits*, North Holland, Amsterdam.

Lewis, R. and Want, D. (1980) Educational Computing at Chelsea (1969–1979), in R. Lewis and E. D. Tagg (eds.) *Computer Assisted Learning: Scope, Progress and Limits*, North Holland, Amsterdam.

Light, P. (1990) *Two Heads are Better than One: Learning Together Using the Computer*, Unit 6 of EH232, *Computers and Learning*, Open University Press, Milton Keynes.

Light, P., Foot, T., Colburn, C. and McClelland, I. (1987) Collaborative interactions at the microcomputer keyboard, *Educational Psychology*, pp. 13–21.

Liverpool Polytechnic, SEGES/Liverpool Business School (1991) Proposals for BA business information management and BA business studies by distance learning (unpublished report, Liverpool, March).

Lorensten, A. (1989) Presentation and Analysis of 'Project Computer-Aided Distance Teaching', PICNIC News no. 4E, Department of Language and Intercultural Studies, Aalborg University.

Loxton, C. (1989) The Help Desk (academic computing service report, unpublished paper available from the author, Open University, Walton Hall, Milton Keynes MK7 6AA).

Mack, R., Lewis, C. and Carroll, J. (1982) *Learning to Use Word Processors: Problems and Prospects*, IBM Watson Research Center, Report C9712, No. 42886, Yorktown Heights, NY.

Manpower Services Commission (1984) *A New Training Initiative*, Sheffield.

Marton, F. and Säljö, R. (1976) On qualitative differences in learning – II outcome as a function of the learner's conception of the task, *British Journal of Educational Psychology*, Vol. 46, no. 2, pp. 115–27.

Marton, F. and Säljö, R. (1984) Approaches to learning, in F. Marton, D. Hounsell and N. Entwistle (eds.) *The Experience of Learning*, Scottish Academic Press, Edinburgh.

Marullo, G. and Laurillard, D. (1990) *An Adaptive Tutoring Program for Second Language Learning*, Report No. 130, Centre for Information Technology in Education, Institute of Education Technology, Open University, Milton Keynes.

Mason, R. (1989) An evaluation of CoSy on an Open University course, in R. Mason and A. R. Kaye (eds.), op. cit.

Mason, R. (1991) Analysing computer conferencing interactions, *Computers in Adult Education and Training*, Vol. 2, no. 3, pp. 161–73.

Mason, R., Jennings, L. and Evans, R. (1984) A day at Xanadu: family life in tomorrow's computerized home, *The Futurist*, pp. 17–24, February.

Mason, R. and Kaye, A. (1989) *Mindweave: Communication, Computers and Distance Education*, Pergamon Press, Oxford.

Mayer, R. (1975) Different problem-solving contingencies established in learning programming with and without a meaningful model, *Journal of Educational Psychology*, Vol. 67, pp. 725–34.

McConnell, D. (1984) Cyclops: shared-screen teleconferencing, in A. W. Bates (ed.) *The Role of Technology in Distance Education*, Croom Helm, London.

McIntosh, N. E. (1975) Open admission – an open or revolving door?, *Universities Quarterly*, Vol. 29, no. 2, pp. 171–81.

McIntosh, N. E., with Calder, J. A. and Swift, B. (1976) *A Degree of Difference*, Society for Research in Higher Education, Guildford.

Mercer, N. (1990) Unit 7 of *Computers and Communication in the Classroom*, EH232, *Computers and Learning*, Open University Press, Milton Keynes.

Meverech, Z., Silber, O. and Fine, D. (1987) *Peer Interaction and Logic Programming: A Study of the Acquisition of Micro-Prolog*, Information Technology and Education Programme, Occasional Paper ITE/17/87, Economic and Social Research Council, London.

Miles, I. (1988a) *Home Informatics*, Pinter Publishers, London.

Miles, I. (1988b) The electronic cottage: myth or near-myth?, *Futures*, pp. 355–66, August.

Mohamamedali, M., Messer, D. and Fletcher, B. (1987) Factors affecting micro-computer use and programming ability of secondary school children, *Journal of Computer Assisted Learning*, Vol. 3, pp. 224–39.

Moore, M. (1983) The individual adult learner, in M. Tight (ed.) *Adult Learning and Education*, Croom Helm, London.

Morgan, A. (1989) *Home Computing Evaluation Project: Students' Experiences of Study – M205*, Report No. 28, Student Research Centre, Institute of Educational Technology, Open University, Milton Keynes.

Morgan, A., Gibbs, G. and Taylor, E. (1981) *What do Open University Students Initially Understand about Learning?* Study Methods Group Report No. 8, Institute of Educational Technology, Open University, Milton Keynes.

Morgan, A., Taylor, E. and Gibbs, G. (1982) Variations in students' approaches to studying, *British Journal of Educational Technology*, Vol. 13, no. 2, pp. 107–13.

Morley, D. (1986) *Family Television: Cultural Power and Domestic Leisure*, Comedia, London.

Morley, D. and Silverstone, R. (1990) Domestic communication – technologies and meanings, *Media, Culture and Society*, Vol. 12, no. 1, pp. 31–55.

Nelson, T. (1974) *Dream Machines/Computer Lib: New Freedoms through Computer Screens – a Minority Report*, Theodore Nelson.

Nipper, S. (1989) Third generation distance learning and computer conferencing, in R. Mason and A. Kaye (eds.), op. cit.

Northedge, A. (1990) *The Good Study Guide*, Open University Press, Milton Keynes.

Office of Population Censuses and Surveys (1991) *General Household Survey 1990*, Government Statistical Office, London.

Open University (1979) *Microcomputers for Managers: A Short Pack*, Open University Press, Milton Keynes.

Open University (1984) *Inside Microcomputers: A Short Pack*, Open University Press, Milton Keynes.

Open University (1985) *Learning about Microelectronics: A Short Pack*, Open University Press, Milton Keynes.

Open University (1990) Equal opportunities. The report of the Equal Opportunities Team (unpublished University document, April).

Open University (1991a) Equal opportunities statistical digest (internal document, August).

Open University (1991b) *Guide to the BA Degree Programme*, Open University Press, Milton Keynes.

Open University (1992) Personal computing for students in the Open University: a strategy for 1996 onwards (unpublished internal report of Academic Computing Committee Working Group).

Open University Educational Software Group (1991) *Applications in Educational Computing*, Academic Computing Service Report, Open University, Milton Keynes.

O'Shea, T. (1984) The Open University 'Micros in Schools' project, in F. B. Lovis and E. D. Tagg (eds.) *Informatics and Teacher Training*, North Holland, Amsterdam.

O'Shea, T. and Self, J. (1983) *Learning and Teaching with Computers*, Harvester, Brighton.

Papert, S. (1980) *Mindstorms*, Harvester, Brighton.

Pelton, J. N. (1990) Technology and education: friend or foe, in *Distance Education: Development and Access*, Proceedings of the 1990 Conference of the International Council for Distance Education, Caracas, Venezuela.

Perry, W. G. (1970) *Forms of Intellectual and Ethical Development in the College Years: A Scheme*, Holt, Rinehart & Winston, New York, NY.

Perry, W. and Rumble, G. (1987) *A Short Guide to Distance Education*, International Extension College, Cambridge.

Ramsden, P. (1979) Student learning and perceptions of the academic environment, *Higher Education*, Vol. 8, no. 4, pp. 411–27.

Rowntree, D. (1985) *Who Needs a Home Computer?*, Methuen, London.

Säljö, R. (1979) *Learning in the Learner's Perspective I: Some Common-Sense Conceptions*, Report No. 76, Institute of Education, University of Göteborg.

Saxton, C. (1989) *To Compute or not to Compute?* Report No. 84, Centre for Information Technology in Education, Institute of Educational Technology, Open University, Milton Keynes.

Scanlon, E., Jones, A., O'Shea, T., Murphy, P., Whitelegg, E. and Vincent, T. (1982) Computer assisted learning, *Institutional Research Review*, no. 1, Open University, pp. 59–79.

Self, J. (1985) *Microcomputers in Education: A Critical Appraisal of Educational Software*, Harvester, Brighton.

Seymour, D. T. (1988) *Developing Academic Programs: The Climate for Innovation*, ASHE-ERIC Higher Education Report No. 3, ERIC-ASHE, Washington, DC.

Sharples, M. (1987) The design of a user friendly system, in A. Jones, E. Scanlon and T. O'Shea (eds.), op. cit.

Shipp, K. and Sutton, D. (1991) An analysis of attempts to remember that some students are female, in G. Lovegrove and B. Segal (eds.) *Women into Computing: Selected Papers 1988–90*, Springer-Verlag, London.

Silverstone, R. (1991) *Beneath the Bottom Line: Households and Information and Communication Technologies in an Age of the Consumer*, PICT Policy Research Paper No. 17, Economic and Social Research Council, Oxford.

Startup, R. and Brady, P. (1989) Widening student access to computer facilities, *Evaluation and Research in Education*, Vol. 3, no. 1, pp. 25–35.

Swarbrick, A. (1986) Women in technology: a feminist model of learner support in the Open University, *International Council for Distance Education Bulletin*, Vol. 12, pp. 62–8.

Swift, B. (1992) Public awareness and image of the Open University – 1992 (unpublished paper available from the Student Research Centre, Institute of Educational Technology, Open University, Walton Hall, Milton Keynes MK7 6AA).

Taylor, E. and Morgan, A. (1984) *Students' Open University Careers*, Study Methods Group, Report No. 14, Institute of Educational Technology, Open University, Milton Keynes.

Taylor, M. E. (1991) *Talking Hypertext: An Alternative to Print for Visually Impaired Students*, Report No. 157, Centre for Information Technology in Education, Institute of Educational Technology, Open University, Milton Keynes.

Taylor, M. E. (1992) *Enabling Hardware and Software for Open University Students with Disabilities Taking Undergraduate Courses*, unnumbered report, Centre for Information Technology in Education, Institute of Educational Technology, Open University, Milton Keynes.

Taylor, M. E., Vincent, A. T. and Child, D. A. (1992) *Alternatives to Print for Visually Impaired Students Feasibility Project*, Report No. 156, Centre for Information Technology in Education, Institute of Educational Technology, Open University, Milton Keynes.

Thorpe, M. (1989) *The Tutor Perspective on Computer Mediated Communication in DT200, An Introduction to Information Technology*, Report No. 76, Centre for Information Technology in Education, Institute of Educational Technology, Open University, Milton Keynes.

Toffler, A. (1980) *The Third Wave*, Pan, London.

Trade and Industry Committee (1988) *First Report: Information Technology*, Volume 1, November, HMSO, London.

Tucker, M. S. (1984) Computers on campus: working papers, *Current Issues in Higher Education*, Vol. 2, pp. 1–38.

Turkle, S. and Papert, S. (1990) Epistemological pluralism: styles and voices within the computer culture, *Signs: Journal of Women in Culture and Society*, Vol. 16, no. 1, pp. 128–57.

Turnbull, J. (1987) Undergraduate teaching in the Information Technology Institute, *The CTISS File*, no. 3, April.

University Funding Council (1990) *Annual Report*, London.

University Grants Committee (1988) *UCCA 25th Report 1986/87*, Cheltenham.

Unwin, A., Harding, L. and Buckley, B. (1990) Project MACINTOSH (paper presented at the Conference on Numerical Mathematics and Algebraic Computing, Belfield, 15–17 May).

Vincent, T. (1989) Students with disabilities: future developments involving information technology, in T. O'Shea and G. Kirkup (eds.) *Home Computing in Practice 1988–1991 and Possibilities for 1992*, Report No. 83, Centre for Information Technology in Education, Institute of Educational Technology, Open University, Milton Keynes.

Vincent, T. (1991) *Case Study B: Meeting Individual Needs: Some Experiments Involving Students with Special Educational Needs*, in EH232, *Computers and Learning*, Open University Press, Milton Keynes.

Vygotsky, L. S. (1978) *Mind in Society: The Development of Higher Psychological Processes*, Harvard University Press, Cambridge, Mass.

Watkins, D. (1983) Depth of processing and the quality of learning outcomes, *Instructional Science*, Vol. 12, no. 1, pp. 49–58.

West, B. (1989) The UDACE/RAS/RO4 Report. Developing Access: A Case Study of the Open University, with special reference to the West Midlands Region. Open University Unpublished Report.

Whitelock, D., Taylor, J., O'Shea, T., Scanlon, E., Sellman, R., Clark, P. and O'Malley, C. (1991), Report No. 139, Centre for Information Technology in Education, Institute of Educational Technology, Open University, Milton Keynes.

Whitelock, D., Taylor, J., O'Shea, T., Scanlon, E., Sellman, R., Clark, P. and O'Malley, C. (1991), *Investigating computer supported collaborative learning about collisions with a change of reference*, Report no. 139, Centre for Information Technology in Education, Institute of Educational Technology, Open University, Milton Keynes.

Woodley, A. (1980) How open is open?, *Higher Education Review*, Vol. 13, no. 1, pp. 3–18.

Woodley, A. (1991) Access to what? A study of mature graduate outcomes, *Higher Education Quarterly*, Vol. 45, no. 1, pp. 91–108.

Woolfe, R. (1977) Education, inequality and the role of the Open University, *Adult Education*, Vol. 50, no. 2, pp. 77–83.

Woolfe, R. and Murgatroyd, S. (1979) The Open University and the negotiation of knowledge, *Higher Education Review*, Spring pp. 9–16.

Young, R. (1981) The machine inside the machine: users' models of pocket calculators, *International Journal of Man-Machine Studies*, Vol. 15, no. 1, pp. 51–85.

Zhao, Z. (1991) *The Effects of Visible Link-Types on Learning in the Hypertext Environment: An Empirical Study*, Report No. 155, Centre for Information Technology in Education, Institute of Educational Technology, Open University, Milton Keynes.

Weir, D. (1976) *The CRACT LAMPOR Report: Developing a case study in the Crest University*, with special reference to the WEA. Milton Keynes: Open University Unpublished Report.

Winbush, D. (1980) *...Gender...*, ...London: Consultative Council on...

Open University Report, No. 1, Centre for Information Technology in Education, Institute of Educational Technology, Open University, Milton Keynes.

Warburton, D., et al. (1980) ... *The Sheldon, I. Sheffield, G. Coles, R. and ... Chard, G. (1980)* ...interview with computer-supported collaborative group about ... *Information Technology in Education*, ..., London: PGT alternative Technology. Open University, Milton Keynes.

McCasney, A. (1978) New types of support in the Information Age. Vol. 18, no. 1, pp. 12-18.

Woodley, A. (1981) Access to what: A study of adult's graduate studies ... *Higher Education Quarterly*, Vol. 35, No. 4, pp. 39-50.

Woods, R. (1981) Open and distance learning and the role of the Open University, *Adult Education*, Vol. 53, no. 2, pp. 79-83.

Woods, P. and Murgatroyd, S. (1982) The Open University and the population of ... education, Milton Keynes, SRHE.

Young, M. (1976) ...machine made ... machine made... made of popular education, ...international journal of ... continuing studies, ..., pp. 5-13.

Zoetman, E. (ROBOT), Miller, W. (1980) ... *The Open University in its Regional Environment*, Capital Annual Report No. 1, Centre for Information Technology in Education, Institute of Educational Technology, Open University Milton Keynes.

# Index